EVERY MAN'S STORY OF
THE OLD TESTAMENT

PILGRIMS JOURNEYING.

Frontispiece.

EVERY MAN'S STORY
OF
THE OLD TESTAMENT

BY
ALEXANDER NAIRNE, D.D.
Regius Professor of Divinity in the University of Cambridge

WITH SIXTY-TWO ILLUSTRATIONS
AND FIVE MAPS

WIPF & STOCK · Eugene, Oregon

Wipf and Stock Publishers
199 W 8th Ave, Suite 3
Eugene, OR 97401

Every Man's Story of the Old Testament
By Nairne, Alexander
Softcover ISBN-13: 978-1-7252-9653-4
Hardcover ISBN-13: 978-1-7252-9654-1
eBook ISBN-13: 978-1-7252-9655-8
Publication date 1/5/2021
Previously published by A. R. Mowbray & Co. Ltd., 1923

This edition is a scanned facsimile
of the original edition published in 1923.

PREFACE

THIS book is written with all possible simplicity. It tells the story of Israel and of Israel's writings: the two run naturally together. That story expands and deepens as it flows on, and perhaps the account of it here given changes style in like proportion. But simplicity and brevity have been aimed at throughout. In the Epilogue something a little more elaborate has been attempted.

In the List of Illustrations acknowledgement is made to those who have kindly allowed the use of material. It will be evident that some of them are adapted from the life of modern Arabs to a Biblical purpose. I have to thank the Publishers for their large share in choosing and arranging the illustrations, for providing the index, and for other friendly and valuable help in the completion of the book.

A. N.

THE CLOISTERS,
   WINDSOR CASTLE.
     September 6, 1922.

CONTENTS

CHAP			PAGE
1 CAMELS AND TENTS	The Patriarchs		1
2 CHURCH AND BOOK			7
3 REDEMPTION FROM EGYPT	Moses		14
4 ELOHIM AND JAHVEH			21
5 JOSHUA			26
6 THE CHAMPIONS OF THE TRIBES	Judges		33
7 SAMUEL THE PROPHET			42
8 THE DIVINE RIGHT OF KINGS	David		52
9 SOLOMON'S TEMPLE			61
10 TO YOUR TENTS O ISRAEL	The Northern Kingdom		71
11 JAHVEH OUR GOD, JAHVEH ONE	Elijah		80
12 MIRACLE			90
13 PREPARE TO MEET THY GOD	Amos		96
14 THE LOVING-KINDNESS OF JAHVEH	Hosea		105
15 THE HOLY ONE OF ISRAEL	Isaiah		111
16 BETHLEHEM EPHRATAH	Micah		132
17 THE JUST SHALL LIVE BY HIS FAITH	Habakkuk		137
18 REFORMATION	Josiah		143
19 IN THEIR HEART I WILL WRITE IT	Jeremiah		152
20 THE VISION OF THE SCRIBE	Ezekiel		162
21 COMFORT YE	Isaiah 40		174
22 THE FIRST CHURCHMEN	Ezra and Nehemiah		182
23 THE LAST PROPHETS	Haggai Zechariah Malachi		193
24 THE MANIFOLD WISDOM OF GOD	The Jewish Church after the exile		201

CHAP.			PAGE
25	DISCREET AND LEARNED MINISTERS OF GOD'S WORD	*Making the Bible*	207
26	THE TWO-EDGED SWORD OF THE SAINTS	*The Maccabees*	213
27	THE KINGDOM OF HEAVEN	*Daniel*	221
28	ESTHER		229
29	THE SPIRIT OF MAN IS THE LAMP OF THE LORD	*Proverbs and Job*	236
30	VANITY OF VANITIES	*Ecclesiastes*	243
31	ALEXANDRIA	*The Septuagint*	249
32	SIRACH AND SOLOMON	*Ecclesiasticus and Wisdom*	256
33	THRONED ON THE PRAISES OF ISRAEL	*The Psalter*	269
34	THE SERVANT OF THE LORD	*Isaiah 53*	281
	EPILOGUE		288
	TABLE OF DATES		307
	INDEX		312

LIST OF ILLUSTRATIONS

	PAGE
PILGRIMS JOURNEYING (by permission of Messrs Lehnert & Landrock, through the *Cambridge Magazine*)	*Frontispiece*
PILGRIMS ADORING (by permission of Messrs Lehnert & Landrock, through the *Cambridge Magazine*)	3
CHARLES DOUGHTY (by permission of Mr Jonathan Cape, London)	5
TABLET INSCRIBED WITH A PART OF THE BABYLONIAN ACCOUNT OF THE CREATION (by permission of the British Museum)	7
CREATION THE FIRST DAY (after the painting by Sir Edward Burne-Jones Photograph by Frederick Hollyer)	8
CREATION THE FIFTH DAY (after the painting by Sir Edward Burne-Jones Photograph by Frederick Hollyer)	9
PAGE FROM A THIRTEENTH-CENTURY MANUSCRIPT OF THE HEBREW BIBLE (in the Advocates' Library, Edinburgh, by permission of Prof A R S Kennedy, D D)	11
ASSYRIAN SEAL illustrating the Temptation (from *The Bible and the Monuments*, by permission of Eyre & Spottiswoode, London)	13
RAMESES II the Pharaoh of the Oppression From his Statue at Turin (from *Egypt and Israel*, by permission of Prof Flinders Petrie)	15
MERNEPTAH II the Pharaoh of the Exodus From his Statue at Cairo (from *Egypt and Israel*, by permission of Prof Flinders Petrie)	17
MOUNT SINAI AND THE PLAIN OF ASSEMBLY (from a photograph by the Underwood Press)	18
WALLS OF JERICHO (from Handcock's *The Latest Light of Bible Lands*, by permission of the S P C K, London)	29
AN ARAB	36
"THE YOUNG SAMUEL" (by permission of Messrs Lehnert & Landrock, through the *Cambridge Magazine*)	43

LIST OF ILLUSTRATIONS

	PAGE
PHILISTINES (from *Egypt and Israel*, by permission of Prof Flinders Petrie)	44
A PHILISTINE (from *History of Civilization in Palestine*, by permission of the Royal Asiatic Society)	47
ABSALOM'S TOMB (from *Earthly Footsteps of the Man of Galilee*, by Bishop Vincent, Dr Lee, and R E M Bain)	53
"FOUNTAIN OF DRAGONS" (from *Earthly Footsteps of the Man of Galilee*, by Bishop Vincent, Dr Lee, and R E M Bain)	56
WATER CARRIER (from *Earthly Footsteps of the Man of Galilee*, by Bishop Vincent, Dr Lee, and R F M Bain)	59
KING DAVID (from *Fifty Pictures of Gothic Altars*, by permission of the Alcuin Club and A R Mowbray & Co Ltd)	62
JERUSALEM (from a photograph by the Photochrom Co)	67
BABYLONIAN MAP OF THE WORLD (from a photograph by permission of the British Museum)	74
HILLS AND FIELDS OF JUDEA (from a photograph by the Underwood Press)	76
GERIZIM AND HILLS OF SAMARIA FROM MOUNT EBAL (from a photograph by the Underwood Press)	78
MOUNT CARMEL AND THE BROOK KISHON (from a photograph by the Underwood Press)	81
"LA ILAHA ILLALLAH—JAHVEH HE IS GOD" (by permission of Messrs Lehnert & Landrock, through the *Cambridge Magazine*)	84
ESDRAELON AND MOUNT CARMEL (from a photograph by the Underwood Press)	87
"BY THE STILL WATERS" IN THE PLAIN OF JEZREEL (from a photograph by the Underwood Press)	97
THE SUBMISSION OF JEHU (from a photograph by permission of the British Museum)	99
EVACUATION OF A CITY AND THE COUNTING OF THE SPOIL (from a photograph by permission of the British Museum)	103
CAPTURE OF A CITY BY THE ASSYRIANS (from a photograph by permission of the British Museum)	106
ASSYRIAN BULL (from a photograph by permission of the British Museum)	109

LIST OF ILLUSTRATIONS

	PAGE
ASSYRIAN WARRIORS (from a photograph by permission of the British Museum)	112
ASSYRIAN ARCHERS ATTACKING A FORTIFIED CITY (from a photograph by permission of the British Museum)	114
SENNACHERIB (from a photograph by Mansell & Co)	118
BAKED CLAY CYLINDER OF SENNACHERIB, KING OF ASSYRIA (from a photograph by permission of the British Museum)	121
SEA OF GALILEE (from a photograph by the Underwood Press)	130
MOUND OF MEGIDDO FROM THE SOUTH-EAST (from a photograph by the Underwood Press)	147
JERUSALEM, SHOWING THE GIHON CATTLE MARKET (from a photograph by the Underwood Press)	170
SACRIFICES NEAR THE GATES OF JERUSALEM (from a photograph by the Underwood Press)	171
BAKED CLAY CYLINDER INSCRIBED WITH AN ACCOUNT OF THE CAPTURE OF BABYLON BY CYRUS, KING OF PERSIA, 538 B C (from a photograph by permission of the British Museum)	175
"EZRA" (by permission of Messrs Lehnert & Landrock, through the *Cambridge Magazine*)	185
"NEHEMIAH" (by permission of Messrs Lehnert & Landrock, through the *Cambridge Magazine*)	188
DARIUS (from Handcock's *The Latest Light of Bible Lands*, by permission of the S P C K , London	194
SEAL OF DARIUS (from a photograph by permission of the British Museum)	197
PLOUGHING IN THE VALLEY OF AJALON (from a photograph by the Underwood Press)	209
HELIODORUS AND THE HEAVENLY RIDER (from a photograph of Raphael's picture, by Anderson, Rome)	219
"WHEN THE ALMIGHTY WAS YET WITH ME" (from Blake's *Designs for the Book of Job*)	239
PAGE OF AN ELEVENTH-CENTURY MS OF THE SEPTUAGINT (by permission of the Editors of the *Cambridge Septuagint*)	251
SYNAGOGUE IN JERUSALEM, SHOWING HOLY PLACE AND READER'S PLATFORM (from a photograph by the Underwood Press)	257

xii   LIST OF ILLUSTRATIONS

	PAGE
A SYNAGOGUE (from a photograph by permission of Cassell & Co)	259
HEBREW SYNAGOGUE ROLL Fourteenth Century (From *Our Bible and the Ancient MSS*, by permission of Sir Frederick Kenyon) - - - - - -	262
SAMARITAN PENTATEUCH ROLL (from *Our Bible and the Ancient MSS*, by permission of Sir Frederick Kenyon) - -	265
PAGE FROM A MODERN HEBREW PSALTER (from a photograph by permission of Bodley's Librarian, Oxford) - -	271
ROBERT LOWTH (from the original painting in the Hall of New College, Oxford, by permission of the Warden of New College) - - - - -	274
HARPER AND CHOIR, 3000 B C (from *The Bible and the Monuments*, by permission of Messrs Eyre & Spottiswoode) -	277
SEA OF GALILEE (from a photograph by the Underwood Press) -	284
ARTHUR PENRHYN STANLEY (from a photograph by permission of Mr Augustus Rischgitz) - - - -	289
WILLIAM ROBERTSON SMITH (from portrait by permission of the Master of Christ's College, Cambridge) - -	290
SAMUEL ROLLES DRIVER (from a photograph by permission of Elliott & Fry) - - - - -	291
THOMAS KELLY CHEYNE (from a photograph by permission of Elliott & Fry) - - - - - -	293
ANDREW BRUCE DAVIDSON (from a portrait supplied by Messrs T & T Clark, Edinburgh) - - - -	305

MAPS

SKETCH MAPS BY THE AUTHOR - - -	- 27, 72
THE ANCIENT WORLD - - ⎫	
ASIA MINOR, ASSYRIA, BABYLONIA, ETC ⎬ - -	- at end.
THE KINGDOMS OF JUDAH AND ISRAEL ⎭	

Every Man's Story of the Old Testament

CHAPTER 1

CAMELS AND TENTS

GENESIS is the loveliest of all books except the Gospels. Like the Gospels it is the dawn of day. Let there be light, and there was light, and the evening and the morning were the first day. Thus the Hymn of Creation with which it opens, flooding earth with the solemnity and exuberance of God. Then think of the Lord God walking in the garden in the cool of the evening; of Jacob dreaming at Bethel, courting Rachel so gravely at the well; of Joseph and his brethren: these are the patriarchs, the children's first friends, all dwelling in tents in the land of promise as dwelt their father Abraham.

So says the writer of the Epistle to the Hebrews, as usual striking the key-note of the story. Abraham came journeying like a nomad from the east. There the Bible with its tale agrees with the ethnologist with his inquiries into prehistoric movements of nations. But for the historian of Israel the stress falls on "nomad." The tents and camels, the sojourning as though no mere earthly country could be home, gives character to all the faith and fortune of Israel henceforward. I am a stranger and a sojourner among you, said Abraham to the sons of Heth when he bought a grave for Sarah. We are strangers and sojourners as all our fathers were, says David in Chronicles, and the Psalmist when he muses on the mystery of life and death. Others may be glad when corn and wine and oil increase but the people of God use another measure for their happiness. Genesis and the sermon on the mount, patriarchs prophets psalmists, the Lord Jesus and His apostles, all move onwards from camp to camp, "mansion" to mansion in the Father's house of life eternal, laying up treasure in the secret home, sojourners nomads not citizens of stable civilizations, for ever "seeking a country."

Camels and tents, shepherds not farmers nor empire builders, that is the first point. But the second is that these pilgrims loved the scene of pilgrimage divinely well. Even here, they say, we are sojourners "with God." They were good philosophers it seems: they dreamed not of another world: their heaven was not far away, but within the actual life they lived, within not beyond. With God, that was home, that was the life of the "called." The presence of God is the genius of the story. When Abraham moved from Ur of the Chaldees we read first the bald statement that he and his father and his family did move: it is the migration of a tribe, an ethnologist's fact. Then the fact is described again from within, from the heavenly view. This time we read that the LORD bade him go, and forth he went, guided by the unseen guide, not knowing whither, a pilgrim "with God." Here too, in the double narrative, there is a scientific interest. It is one of the clues by

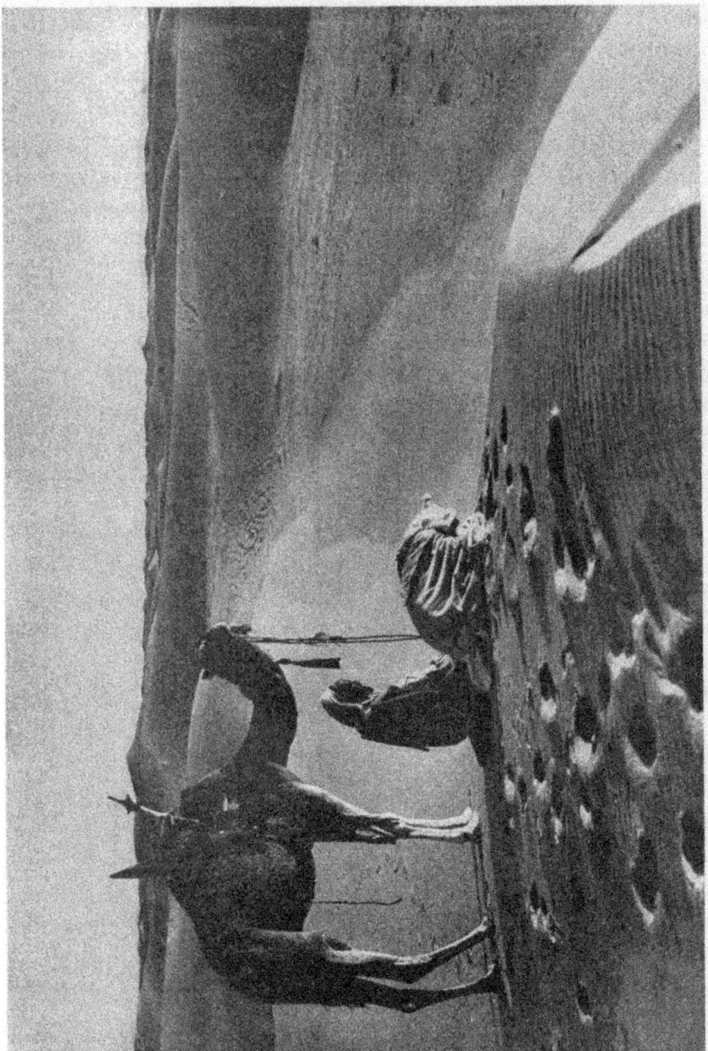

PILGRIMS ADORING.

which the sources and composition of these "Mosaic" books are tracked. But when the historian has found and used such clues and has thereby got firm hold of the main outline of events, and is freed from fanciful interpretations of plain tales, then as a real historian of Israel's fortunes faith and place among mankind, he seizes on this consciousness of the presence of God as characteristic of all that is to follow. Things will have depth. Many trivialities will after all be not trivial. The folklore of the Old Testament will be divinely touched. There will be a significance not allegorical in the sacrifice of Isaac. Jacob will wrestle with the angel at Peniel in other wise than men had told the legend round camp fires. Babylonian mythology will reappear with artistic purification and create clean heart new spirit and consciousness of God in all the kindred of the pilgrims.

Folklore, mythology : but is there any real history ? Are these patriarchs persons or personifications ? They certainly live as persons in the affection of unsophisticated readers. Yet do they all ? Abraham Isaac Jacob, yes. But what of Abraham's second wife Keturah and her children ? These are surely names which stand for clans or tribes. Ishmael again and Esau : there are one or two incidents in the account of each where they stand right vividly as persons before us, but in each case they get this vividness from relationship with father or brother. Read the story again and see how little we know about Ishmael and Esau, how left to themselves the two men shade off into tribes. So it is with most of the twelve sons of Jacob : they fade into the twelve tribes of Israel. Only in the main line of the chosen family is the distinctness of personal history and character preserved. Esau is more attractive than Jacob for one moment or for two. But we know no more of Esau : the mean youth Jacob is tried and schooled, converted, drawn to God ; we study his whole development and its bearing on all that follows.

Nor need we be ashamed of the trite argument about the dark touches in these lives of the patriarchs. There is an ideal beauty about their portraits, but it is the true ideal which neither artist nor historian produces except by including adverse facts : mere fancy evaporates. A student of Genesis ought to know Charles Doughty's *Wanderings in Arabia*.[1] Mr. Doughty is an idealist whose eyes are open to the realism of Arab life. His book is rich in detail. Genesis is broadly sketched : there is little historic detail : the picturesque touches are legitimate art : the historical economy and frankness win confidence. At least we may conclude that Genesis reports ancient tradition about the real forefathers of the Children of Israel, that the author

CHARLES DOUGHTY.

[1] Cambridge University Press, 2 vols., 1888.
Abridged edition, Duckworth.
New edition of whole, with preface by Lawrence, Medici Press, 1921.

refrains from altering or decking out the simple lines of tradition; his simplicity may be trusted; when we meddle further with it, we spoil it; we may not treat his tales as elaborated history, nor may we fill up his outline with our secondary imaginations.

And this must be added. Outline is not the aptest metaphor. There is more colour than outline. These tales are poetic, and they are diversified by pieces of actual poetry, songs from the primitive world, made to music before men wrote prose. Such a piece is Jacob's Blessing in Genesis 49. Here you have tribes—not personified but lyricized: you do not stay to ask that scientific question, Tribes or persons? And such a fire of poetry burns throughout Genesis, indeed through the larger part of the Old Testament. It must be allowed for: it does not permit us to be too matter-of-fact in our enjoyment. But it is intensely sincere, it stirs the innermost conscience. It is rich but austere, contrasting with the bizarre embroideries of Egypt and Babylonia. It is more like the genius of Arabia—camels and tents, not luxury and exuberance.

CHAPTER 2

CHURCH AND BOOK

WE have talked in a free and easy way of tales and history, of traditions and authors. What do such terms mean? Whence and how have these records come to us? Genesis, Exodus, etc., are part of the Bible of the Jewish Church. A Bible is a set of documents edited for convenient use, and the Old Testament is the Bible which the Jewish Church edited for instruction and worship after the exile. Jew, short for Judean, is the name by which this people were known in their later days. The nomads of the wilderness were called in those earliest times (as nomad

BAKED CLAY TABLET INSCRIBED WITH A PART OF THE BABYLONIAN ACCOUNT OF THE CREATION.

CREATION: THE FIRST DAY.

Arabs call themselves now) *beni Yisrael*, sons of Israel. These nomad tribes gathered in Canaan into a nation under a king. The kingdom split into two parts; the nation of Israel in the north, the clan of Judah in the south. Northern Israel fell before the Assyrians and ceased to exist. The Judeans under their kings of the house of David henceforth represented the nation. They too fell, before the Chaldeans, and were carried into exile at Babylon. When Cyrus took Babylon the exiles returned, and a new community with a new temple and a matured faith and settled law was established round Jerusalem. The kingdom was gone, but so too was the lawlessness and pagan superstition against which the prophets had striven so long in vain. The kingdom of Israel and Judah had become the Jewish Church.

Before the exile history had been making. Those were times of action: reading and writing were rare accomplishments. Isaiah (like Habakkuk) wrote some great placards which he might run who read, but he moved the people by oratory not by writing. Jeremiah dictated to his friend Baruch a professional scribe prophecies already delivered in speech. Ezekiel seems to have written his own book, and after Ezekiel in exilic and post-exilic days the scribe and "rabbi" became prominent. Reading and writing were now a general habit. Worship demanded a Bible. The early histories poems prophecies were collected selected edited. The Hebrew Bible was the result of this process. It is divided into three parts which were formed and accepted as canonical one after the other. The first was the Torah or Law which we call the Pentateuch: this comes effectively into Israel's history (however ancient its material may be) from the time of Ezra. The second was the Nebiim or Prophets, which includes the prophetic histories Joshua Judges Samuel Kings, and all those

CREATION: THE FIFTH DAY.

books which we call the Prophets, with the important exception of Daniel. Daniel belongs to the third division the Writings, in which are gathered all the rest of the books of our English Bible, except the Apocrypha: these apocrypha are mainly Greek books which have come to us from that earliest translation of the Hebrew Bible, the so-called Version of the seventy elders, the Septuagint; for the Jews of Alexandria, the Church of the Septuagint, added these books of their own. The three divisions of the Hebrew Bible are alluded to in the last chapter of the Gospel according to S. Luke; and since the terms Writings and Psalms are there used interchangeably, it would appear that this last part of the canon was not settled by the time of our Lord. A list of books quoted in the New Testament would agree with that, and what we know of Jewish history from other sources leads us to suppose that the final settlement was made after the rebellion of Barcochba, the last effort of the Jews against the Roman Empire, at about 150 A.D.

Modern criticism of the Old Testament has already won half its battle when we turn from our English version to the Hebrew Bible. Not only does the original order of the books give a rough outline of their chronological relations, so that for example we may expect to find Ruth and Chronicles far later than Judges and Kings; but the titles of authorship disappear. "The first book of Moses, called Genesis," is simply "In the beginning" according to the Hebrew Bible. Our Exodus is but "These are the names": and so with the rest of Torah. The Septuagint, which (through the Latin Vulgate) our English version follows, placed "The Lamentations of Jeremiah" immediately after

PAGE FROM A THIRTEENTH-CENTURY MANUSCRIPT OF THE HEBREW BIBLE.

Jeremiah : but in the Hebrew Bible that poem is far away among the Writings and is entitled 'How' or 'Ah,' from its opening word.

Thus hints are afforded about dates ; much is late which we fancied early, less is prescribed about authorships than our borrowed prejudice allowed. We are free to start from what the books tell us about themselves ; how Moses wrote down certain things, but not the whole Pentateuch ; how Deuteronomy is an account of Moses' exhortation, not his very words written out by himself. And we are free again to draw reasonable conclusions from a survey of the whole of the Old Testament ; that the Law entered Israel's life in three stages, the short code of Exodus 20–24 during the early settlement in Canaan, Deuteronomy by the reformation of Josiah, Leviticus with Ezra ; how the historical narrative corresponds : an early prophetic history, interesting, imaginative in style ; a later deuteronomic or sermonizing kind ; last a legal, generally dry antiquarian kind. These three styles have too their counterpart in the great prophets. The early prophetic story resembles Isaiah, the deuteronomic sermon Jeremiah, the legal matter Ezekiel. And that is worth notice because it prevents our underrating any part. The legal matter for instance is akin not only to the rubrics of Leviticus but to the theology of Ezekiel, and to this legal or priestly section belongs the glorious Hymn of Creation with which Genesis opens. Read that opening chapter ; mark its solemnity, ritual phrase, reverence as in presence of God who passeth understanding, inhabiteth eternity : then go on to the next chapter and read of the garden of Eden, the LORD God walking and talking with Adam and Eve and

ASSYRIAN SEAL.
To illustrate the Temptation.

the serpent, cross-examining, sentencing; but finally caring for them still, clothing His foolish exiled children, in the suffering they have incurred still forgiving, restoring them to happiness of another sort, still in the divine presence. That is what Milton dwelt upon in the most beautiful concluding pages of *Paradise Lost*:

> Yet doubt not but in Vallie and in Plaine
> God is as here, and will be found alike
> Present, and of his presence many a signe
> Still following thee, still compassing thee round
> With goodness and paternal Love, his Face
> Express, and of his steps the track Divine.

All this however seems far away from the Camels and Tents. We have in these two chapters put beginning and end over against each other. But all is continuous. The serious enthusiastic nomad faith informs the whole of the Jewish book. Criticism discovers differences variety development: criticism shows how God works by natural means. But conscience, refreshed by criticism, restores the unity and through the natural means recognizes God. Criticism sets the divine free in the historian: conscience lifts the events into the divine. From beginning to end the gist of the Bible is, Man a pilgrim and sojourner with holy loving God.

CHAPTER 3

REDEMPTION FROM EGYPT

TENTS and camels, yes: but to the prophets and priests who built up Israel's faith, it was not so much Abraham and the patriarchs that mattered, but Moses and his nomads in the wilderness. The redemption from Egypt was the call of the nation; the Red Sea was the type of salvation: " When Israel was a child, then I loved him, and called my son out of Egypt "; " Thus saith the Lord, which maketh a way in the sea, and a path in the mighty waters; which bringeth forth the chariot and the horse, the army and the power; they lie down together, they shall not rise; they are extinct, they are quenched as flax . . . Remember ye not the former things neither consider the things of old. Behold I will do a new thing; now it shall spring forth; shall ye not know it? I will even make a way in the wilderness and rivers in the desert. . . . Remember these things, O Jacob; and Israel, for thou art My servant: O Israel thou shalt not be forgotten of Me. I have blotted out, as a thick cloud, thy transgressions, and, as a cloud, thy sins: return unto Me; for I have redeemed thee;" " When Israel went forth out of Egypt, the house of Jacob from a people of strange language; Judah became His sanctuary, Israel His dominion."

So prophets and psalmists apply the deliverance at the Red Sea to the interpretation of later history, of Assyrian invasions, of exile and return, as the continuous working of God's will. And the early historians had already shaped their narrative on that great line. In the Song of Moses, Exodus 15, comes the very word which was to be dominant in the second part of the book of Isaiah: "Thou in Thy mercy hast led the people which Thou hast redeemed": thence, from that "Comfort ye" prophecy, it will be taken up by S. Paul, and through S. Paul will engrave its character on all Christian theology.

RAMESES II.
The Pharaoh of the Oppression.

These early historians who formed from ancient song legend and tradition the prophetic narrative of the patriarchs in Genesis, have continued their narrative in Exodus, forming from like materials a history of Moses. His birth and rescue from the Nile resembles the legendary story of a certain king of Babylon, a real person emerging from the shades of far-off ages. Moses brought up as an Egyptian prince, learning at court the wisdom of Egypt, the habit of command, the legislation of the ancient East: then exiled to the desert, where, like his nomad ancestors, he communes with God, and receives the revelation of Jahveh, Israel's own God, Israel's and presently the world's true God: then returning to Egypt to contend with Pharaoh and deliver his oppressed fellow countrymen from bondage, to command them and to give them laws, and to bind them to faith and obedience to Jahveh:—there are the three "forty years," the three stages, the large governing curves of his career. As with the patriarchs, so with Moses; the large lines are credible, no criticism rubs them out. But details are added: can we be so easily satisfied with these? What are we to make of the ten plagues and all the miracles that accompany the journeying tribes?

Once break loose from the titles in the English version, and the narrow view of sacredness with which the Septuagint and later Jewish prejudice cramped enjoyment of the Bible, and we shall gladly recognize that legend and history do mingle in these ancient records. The old historians delighted in the variety, and the doctors of the Jewish Church who selected from the old historians and made the Bible, had a genial care for the little children who would read it. And children still find happiness—the truest theology—in the bulrushes and the astonishing serpent-rods and plagues. Matured in prosaic curriculum we scruple at such things. But even we might take them differently if we would read right on. The stream of narrative, the drama, the manifesting will sweeps on: sublime and trivial, credible and offending, grave and gay, all the mingle-mangle, like real life, moves on dimly; but as it moves the meaning gathers and the crisis advances. Take this or that one of the first nine plagues by itself and it may seem excrescent. But read the whole story at a sitting and see how all falls into place, how by all manner of means the historian holds our interest, intensifies our expectation, till we hold our breath at the solemn death of the firstborn; the preparation, ritual and religious, for departure; the pursuit, panic, halt, removal of the pillar of cloud, passage of Israel, pressing on of Egypt, Jahveh looking out from the cloud in the morning watch, and with His terrible face discomfiting the foes; their utter overthrow, and Israel safe, delivered, redeemed.

Having read in that fashion you hardly care to calculate how far the narrative allows the event to have been mediated through natural causes: how "Red Sea" is but septuagintal adaptation of Hebrew "Sea of reeds"; how no great "sea" was crossed, but a piece of desert water which might be shifted in a storm; how the movement of the pillar of cloud was the looming up of the thunderstorm; how all the theophanies in Old Testament are sacramental tempests. In like manner when we come to Sinai and the giving of the Law we read in Exodus that cloud thunder and lightning were the accompaniment, but S. Paul says these were angels, and no Israelite would have asked the difference—"He maketh

MERNEPTAH II.
The Pharaoh of the Exodus.

winds His angels and His ministers the flaming fire." To-day we ask another set of questions: whether Leviticus in all its length and breadth was given at Sinai

MOUNT SINAI AND THE PLAIN OF ASSEMBLY.

or was a much later development of some primitive simpler law. All analogy would make it development, and as we go on with subsequent history we shall see pretty clearly how the development came about. Meanwhile consider for a moment the opening verses of the Sinaitic legislation, the Ten Commandments. According to the rigour of the narrative the ten commandments first given perished with the stones on which they were engraven, other stones and quite another set of commandments were preserved. Plainly the rigour of the narrative is not to be insisted upon. Like Israel, we accept the excellent commandments without curious inquiry when and how God gave them, not to Israel only but to our Lord Jesus Christ and through Him to mankind. And yet again, the reader who reads right on is impatient with such delaying curiosity. He has come with adventurous Israel to Sinai. He hears, in Exodus 19, Jahveh speak to Moses, arrange the terrific scene, bid him tell the people what their divine Redeemer has done for them—" how I bare them on eagles' wings "—and then follows Law and Commandments.

And in that sequence lies the broad theology of all divine law. "I am Jahveh thy God, Who brought thee out of the land of Egypt, out of the house of bondage : Thou shalt have none other gods but Me." " Brethren, we are debtors." God's way : He gives all freely ; and then we are debtors. All starts from Him : " We love, because He first loved us " ; " Lord have patience, and I will pay Thee all." That is the theme of Deuteronomy, the book of the love of God, of heart-religion, the S. John of the Torah :

> "And now, Israel, what doth the LORD thy God require of thee, but to fear the LORD thy God, to walk in all His ways, and to love Him, and to serve the LORD thy God with all thy heart and with all thy soul, to keep the commandments of the LORD, and His statutes, which I command thee this day for thy good ? Behold, unto the LORD thy God belongeth the heaven, and the heaven of heavens, the earth with all that therein is. Only the LORD thy God had a delight in thy fathers to love them, and He chose their seed after them, even you above all peoples, as it is this day. . .   Love ye therefore the stranger : for ye were strangers in the land of Egypt. Thou shalt

fear the Lord thy God, Him shalt thou serve; and to Him shalt thou cleave. He is thy praise, and He is thy God, that hath done for thee these great and terrible things, which thine eyes have seen. Thy fathers went down to Egypt with threescore and ten persons; and now the Lord thy God hath made thee as the stars of heaven for multitude. Therefore thou shalt love the Lord thy God, and keep His charge, and His statutes, and His judgements, and His commandments, alway"

CHAPTER 4

ELOHIM AND JAHVEH

MANY names are used of God in Old Testament and each has its deep import. "The hour of controversy has passed, said the Mohamedan to the Christian, Tell me your beautiful names for God and I will tell you mine." Two of these names are constantly employed, Elohim and Jahveh. In the English Bible Elohim is rendered God. For Jahveh a title is substituted, The LORD: whenever LORD is thus printed in capital letters, the ineffable Name, as this has been termed, will be found in the Hebrew. This has come about through the ineffability. In rabbinic days the Jews ceased to pronounce this name; they substituted Adonai, Lord, in reading. The Septuagint translated what was read, not what was written, by Kyrios; the Latin followed with Dominus, the English with The LORD. In " pointed " Hebrew Bibles the vowel points of Adonai were attached to the consonants (left unaltered) of Jahveh: hence was derived the sonorous but quite fanciful Jehovah, no distinction being made between the short *e* and the short *a*. Sometimes, often in Ezekiel, the Hebrew has a real Adonai followed by Jahveh. Then Adonai Elohim was read instead of the written Adonai Jahveh, and this is represented by The Lord GOD, with GOD in capitals. In Genesis 2 and 3 The LORD God is different, and represents Jahveh Elohim in the Hebrew, a combination which does not occur elsewhere.

This elementary information is here set down to explain and justify the usage of this Every Man's History. The LORD will be used generally, with capitals, as in R.V. But it will often be necessary to write the real name so as to bring out the feeling of a Person, the divine yet national, august yet antique and sometimes rudely antique King, Redeemer, Warrior of Israel. Then we will say Jahveh. The alternative would be Jehovah. That has grand associations in English literature: but those very associations are distracting, and Jehovah is not a real word at all. Jahveh has its modern associations. It has been popularized by critical discussions and so loses reverential awe. Let us try to forget that, and when we say Jahveh let us try to feel as an Israelite felt when he listened to the prophets, or as an apostolic Christian felt when he bowed the head before the name of Jesus.

But first let us consider the name Elohim. This is a plural word generally signifying a singular, namely the one God whom Israel worshipped and who at last was worshipped as the one and only God in heaven and earth. Now and then Elohim is in Old Testament an actual plural: thus of the gods of Jezebel, of human judges and great men in Psalms or Samuel. And every now and then there is a reminiscence of an older, perhaps more pagan use, Elohim meaning spirits, spiritual powers, the divine splendours of earth and heaven. Thus in the prologue to Job "sons of God" is really "the sons of the elohim" "the company of heaven," according to a Hebrew idiom in which "sons of" signifies "belonging to the class, company, guild of," as "sons of the prophets," "sons of Korah" for the Korahite choir of psalmists. So again in Psalm 8 "Thou madest man little lower than Elohim" meant no doubt to the Jewish churchman much the same as "in the image of God." But the phrase may go back to an earlier piety, and the Septuagint rendering "angels" is perhaps not far from right.

The name Elohim suggests what we call natural religion, both in the profundity and in the limitations of that term. According to the "priestly writer" from whom the Torah received its final contents and form, the name Jahveh was not revealed to Israel before the Exodus. "I am that I am" is "Ehveh," the first person of the Hebrew verb of which "Jahveh" is the third. Jahveh seems to be "He who is": hence Matthew Arnold's equivalent, The Eternal, an equivalent which has much force in many passages, throughout the "Comfort ye" prophecy for instance, but which oftener fails because The Eternal is too abstract, not personal enough. This theory of the priestly writer about Jahveh and the Exodus may well be good history. The Mosaic Law at Sinai was just that, the inauguration of Israel's service to Jahveh the LORD of their national faith and life. But the priestly writer was not an exact critic, and he allows many a story to stand in its old form, telling of the patriarchal worship of Jahveh. Quite at the beginning of Genesis we read, "And to Seth, to him also there was born a son; and he called his name Enosh: then began men to call upon the name of the LORD" (4. 26).

No mere likelihood of modern seeming induces us to suppose that the Jewish Church did arrange their Torah for worship and for instruction. The idea once grasped any attentive reader will perceive how much it explains in the narrative and laws. And it is evident that the priestly writer or writers to whom this editing was entrusted had a historical document at least as early as the earliest prophets from which to draw. Closer attention will show that this early history was not in one document but two. A rough clue for distinguishing these two sources from which narratives have been derived is afforded by the varying names of God, Elohim or Jahveh. Other indications make it probable that the Jahveh history was composed in Judah, the Elohim in northern Israel. Northern Israel came sooner than Judah into contact with the wider world around, lived larger, thought more actively ; and in northern Israel conscience was awakened by Elijah and the first prophets, by their vigorous contention for the true faith. Perhaps that was why the historian of the north preferred the name Elohim. Jahveh was too national too naive a designation. Already a kind of reverence made him shrink from the freedom with which the Jahvists represented their clear-cut and almost child-like imagination of the divine. Anyhow this difference appears. In the Jahveh history God shows Himself visibly, acts and speaks with human gesture force directness. In the Elohim history God is unseen mysterious, known by dream and scarce by symbol ; He speaks to the inner heart of man. Read of Moses and the Burning Bush. Mark how the whole passage falls into paragraphs, more or less precisely separated by the changing name. Then mark how the two sets of paragraphs make two versions, each all but complete still in spite of having been fused into one ; and how Elohim speaks with solemnity but there is no visible sign ;

how Jahveh is revealed in the burning bush and speaks with an almost passionate rhetoric that carries the listener away.

Jahveh always does that. There is a pathos a sympathy a purity of religion around Elohim of which we recognize the grandeur. But there is a sacramental imagination that glows about Jahveh, and which (many at least would feel it so) conveys an even richer more penetrative truth. This is art, sacrament, half more than whole ; that is philosophy, thinking truth out.

CHAPTER 5

JOSHUA

THE Torah is a medley controlled and harmonized by serene faith and mastertural art. Hence it is both serious and delightful. Scraps of primitive poetry, legends consecrated to theology, law in successive stages, poetic philosophic and prosaic history, sermons and rubrics, geographic and antiquarian notes: now a sketch of nomad life in the wilderness, the journeying clan with the hallowed tent to lead them, a sketch drawn by an ancient artist with his eye upon the subject: now an elaborate picture of an architectural tabernacle, the central shrine of a ritualistic nation, as the romantic past appeared to one who looked back upon it, across a stretch of centuries, from the doors of the second temple. A certain book, or library, of modern history was once described as a "breathless statement of facts." That is not how the Jewish Church wrote history. But we would not lose the tabernacle and the detailed Levitical scenery from the Torah. It is ideal in a valuable sense. In the Torah as in no other book the soul of a nation broods on things to come, on the Israel that is to be, and then on a wider people of God who shall come home at last out of the whole world. On goes the story through Exodus and then through Numbers. At last, just before the invaders camp in view of Canaan, Balaam is brought in, a prophet of Jahveh from outside the chosen people, and proclaims more than the triumph

JOSHUA

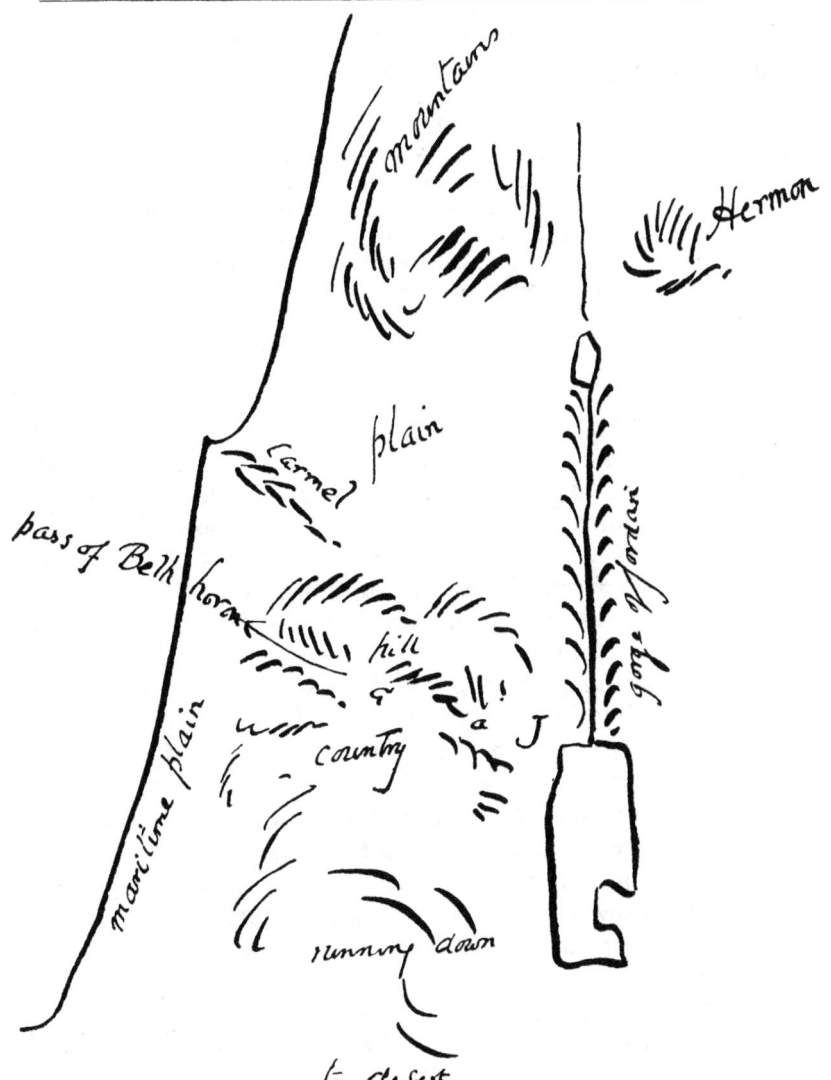

For the use of this Map cf. p. 72.

of that people, in a vision which ranges beyond the horizon of the Old Testament:

> Balaam the son of Beor saith,
> The man who is in very truth a seer[1] saith :
> He saith, which heareth the words of God,
> And knoweth the knowledge of the Most High,
> Which seeth the vision of the Almighty,
> Falling down, and having his eyes open :
> I see Him but not now :
> I behold Him but not nigh.
>
> *Numbers* 24.

As in Isaiah,—"the king in his beauty, a land of far horizons"—so here the prophet is really possessed. He returns in the next line to particulars of his own place and time, but he has had involuntarily a glimpse of more than he understands ; " les dispositions sont prises là-haute." It is lost labour to read Old Testament unless we are prepared for these sublime irrationalities now and then : the Spirit of the desert and the mountains breathes therein.

Something like that said Sir George Adam Smith in *The Historical Geography of the Holy Land*.[2] Before starting upon Joshua the second chapter at least of that exhilarating book should be read, the chapter on the physical features of the land. Read it, and think it over with the eye of the mind. Then—most important—draw from memory a very simple map for yourself in bold lines to show mountains river passes plains. Then you will easily follow the spirited account in chapters 2–11 of Joshua's campaign.

First he sent spies to discover the lie of the land, the temper and resources of the inhabitants. Then he

---

[1] So Septuagint.   [2] Hodder & Stoughton, 1st ed. 1894.

crossed the Jordan with some ceremony, established a base at Gilgal, and made ready to attack the first obstacle, the strong and walled city of Jericho. Again he held religious ceremonies. These, our author tells us in his admirable manner, were commanded by Jahveh. So was the whole campaign, so Joshua performed all his military service. To our duller modern imagination it is of interest to compare the histories of other eastern invaders, who heartened armies, which (like Israel in the long wandering) had lost *moral*, by sacred ceremonial. Thus inspired Joshua's army, at the culminating moment of enthusiasm, delivered the assault and took Jericho at a rush.

WALLS OF JERICHO.

The next obstacle was Ai, a smaller city, but commanding the entrance of the pass into the mountain country. The first attempt on Ai failed. Yet the failure was not without utility. It was discovered to be due to the disobedience of a soldier who had taken booty for his private aggrandisement. That would never do. The task of the Israelites was hard. They were a small number to conquer a whole country and that a difficult highland country: many of the Israelites themselves had judged the adventure to be impossible. With absolute self-sacrificing enthusiasm, the enthusiasm of a *herem*, a divine war, it would not be impossible, but that was the only way. So Achan died for his fault, forgiven by his captain and his brethren yet paying full penalty, a willing victim to purify the army and ensure success. Success came at the next attempt, and Joshua had the entrance into the mountains open.

Then came the men of Gibeon, with a story and trick to gain alliance in spite of the ruthless *herem*. Joshua was not with his officers when the Gibeonites came. Returning he acquiesced, with certain conditions, in the alliance which he could not have allowed himself. Glad indeed he must have been to do so, for Gibeon was the fortress which dominated the interior of the pass; this alliance gave him the key to the position. But the neighbours of Gibeon were as indignant as Joshua was glad, and laid siege to the traitorous city. Joshua was too active for them. He set out at once from his base, marched through the night, and fell upon the besiegers in the darkness. He drove them off, and drove them westwards along the pass. A storm burst on them as they fled. At Beth-horon, where the hills run down into the maritime plain in a rough descent, panic and storm together promised utter rout. Morning began to dawn. Joshua looked eastwards and saw the sun rising over Gibeon while in a break of the clouds the moon still showed over the vale of Ajalon. Then, as the ancient song though not the later marvel-loving prose described it, he cried, Be silent sun—O for another hour of storm and darkness; and his cry was heeded. The storm continued and the destruction of the enemy was complete. They were—such seems the allusion of a psalmist (*Ps.* 35)—" as chaff before the wind, and the angel of Jahveh driving them on"; their way was " darkness and slippery places, and the angel of Jahveh pursuing them."

Joshua now held the pass, though not the mountains themselves. Up and down this pass Saul would later spend his arduous reign warring against the Philistines. Those Philistines at last drove Saul out of his native highlands and bringing their chariots and horsemen to bear upon the rude infantry of Israel, defeated and killed him. That same plan was now formed against Joshua. The kings of the north, where the plain lies beneath the great northern mountains, gathered their cavalry in readiness for the prey when he had been hunted out. Once again Joshua was too active for them. He marched without delay and marched swiftly. He fell upon the camp by the waters of Merom, scattered the confederate army and prevented its recovery and retaliation by houghing all the horses.

This ended the campaign. The next chapter introduces what Dean Stanley called The Doomsday Book of Israel, the roll of lands and possessors which was made in later years when the Israelites actually enjoyed possession of the whole country. This is not precisely said to have been achieved so soon. To a moderately careless reader it seems implied. When the Jewish

Church put their Bible together the editor of this book does not seem to have been scrupulous about such niceties one way or another. At any rate he leaves it plain in other passages that the final mastery was as long a business as any soldier who has fought in highland country would expect it to be. The passes and the plains were seized and held by Joshua through a few bold strokes of strategy. About seven years of guerilla warfare went on after that in the mountains. "Thy enemies shall come cringing to thee, and thou shalt tread upon their high places" is the regular phrase of a Hebrew poet for total supremacy, and at last even that was won.

CHAPTER 6

THE CHAMPIONS OF THE TRIBES

THE book of Judges opens with detached notes, as economical in diction as the notes a historian sends to-day to a historical journal : and perhaps as important for accurate history. They show that what we gathered from Joshua as a whole is right ; the complete conquest of Canaan took a long time. Maybe they show more. The invasion was perhaps achieved by more than one invading host. Joshua did not lead a whole nation but only one set of tribes. Other Israelite tribes at various points and various times made their way, and when at last all were settled in the land years had still to run before Israel achieved national unity. The question is discussed in very scholarly fashion by Dr. Burney in *The Book of Judges with Introduction and Notes*,[1] a commentary of the first rank as readable as it is thorough. It may conduce to the happiness of "every man" if a reference to some of Dr. Burney's topics leads him to this admirable book. He shows of course how and of what material the book of Judges was built up. He describes the general characteristics of the period of the Judges. Most interesting are the "additional notes" or brief essays on Some divine names, on The early development of the worship of Jahveh, on The language and poetic form of the song of Deborah, on The use of writing among the Israelites at the time of

[1] Rivingtons, 1918.

the Judges, on Human sacrifice among the Israelites, on The origin of the Levites, on The mythical elements in the story of Samson, and on the problem already noticed of the settlement of the tribes in Canaan. And the volume is illustrated by that rare boon, excellent maps, pleasing to the eye, tempting the amateur to imitation.

Judges opens, then, with these valuable notes of history. In the second chapter we have the author writing his reflections on the whole period, showing Israel's unsteadiness in faith, now serving Jahveh, now falling away to sheer paganism; with the remnants of the native people dwelling among them; themselves not yet a united nation and open to mischievous influences from these neighbours. He generalizes without much care for strict chronology, but deduces the principle that pure faith goes with bold patriotism, and apostasy brings defeat and subjection to enemies: for besides the tribes of Canaan in their midst there were strong hostile people, Moab Ammon and the Philistines, ready to enslave them from beyond the border. Again and again these people did enslave them. Yet again and again Israel returned to cry to their own Lord, Jahveh, for help. And Jahveh again and again heard and heeded. The book of Judges is one mode of the continuous music of Holy Scripture, namely the unwearied forgiveness of God:

> He being full of compassion forgiveth iniquity and destroyeth not. Yea, many a time and oft turneth He His wrath away, and doth not suffer His whole displeasure to arise.
>
> So He remembered that they were but flesh; even a wind that passeth away, and cometh not again.

Heeding and forgiving Jahveh raised up, now in

one tribe now in another, a champion, a deliverer, or judges as these champions are called in this book. By their strong hand and His holy Spirit within them, He delivered His people, and again they fell away and yet again He saved them.

The author wrote this chapter in his own accustomed language and style. We might compare S. Luke in his Gospel and the Acts. From various quarters S. Luke drew his information, and he preserved the words and accent of what he read and listened to while he wrote it out "in order," with a skilful touch, now more now less, of literary art. But once and twice he put in something simply his own, the few verses of preface to the Gospel for instance ; and then he used the educated style which was natural to him. So the author of Judges has listened to the stories of countrymen, the traditions of the tribes, the tales of the champions of his Christendom ; or has read documents, rudely written for the most part, yet with a native vigour of their own : he has reduced these to order preserving sometimes a good deal of their primitive simplicity, sometimes using them as opportunities for composing a grand or a pathetic version of the romantic tale ; sometimes content to huddle up the facts in note-book style that he may get on the quicker to the next arresting narrative. And he has brought all this variety together into one onward moving series, with an idea, a hope, a historical foresight informing its progress. The will of God rides on in majesty, gathering and moulding the nation that is to be out of the scarce-connected masses of the tribes. And once or twice and notably in this second chapter the author puts in reflections that are simply his own, just in his own accustomed style. That style is the sermonizing, deuteronomic. But let us not infer too much from that. Who wrote Deuteronomy and when, Moses or one of the early prophets, or some reformer in the time of Josiah, or some pupil of Jeremiah's, long after the reformation in Josiah's reign which Deuteronomy seems to either prepare for or to put on record:—these are complicated questions of criticism which would be tedious for the sensible "every man." What is plain to any constant reader of the Bible is the deuteronomic style, sermonizing, somewhat or abundantly rhetorical, a style in which a writer attempts to say fully what he means, in which a writer is always able to be didactic, nor less able to use a very charming piety, the religion of the heart. At what date this style began to be written, how long it was in fashion, whether or no it went on side by side with other styles, how far

An Arab.

it was influenced by the book of Deuteronomy itself;—
these are questions which would need a clever person to
answer, which a wise person will not willingly attempt to
answer. It is fine to have a historical mind, and to be
precise about dates, but it is often impossible for a
student of Old Testament to be so fine.

After which piece of private deuteronomizing let us
continue our review of the book of Judges. Chapter 3
tells of Cushan-rishathaim, which sounds like a nick-
name, Blackamoor of double-dyed wickedness; and of
Ehud and Eglon, a story racy from the soil. Then,
in 4 and 5 we come to Deborah and Barak, the defeat
of Sisera at the ancient river Kishon, and the death
of Sisera at the hand of Jael. All this is celebrated
gloriously in the song of Deborah. There is little doubt
that this poem is very old. " Then sang Deborah and
Barak" perhaps these very words made for them by
a minstrel of those days. He tells how Jahveh came
from His home in the southern desert, where Moses
first and afterwards Moses with the people had met and
consecrated themselves to Him. Jahveh came shaking
the earth with His horrific tread, manifesting His presence
in the tempest, to take command of the army of Israel.
The tribes are summoned to rally to the help of Jahveh
and His righteous cause. Some hang back and are
cursed, some jeopard their lives in the battle and are
made famous for ever. We hear their war cries—
" After thee Benjamin "—and see their array: this is
the inauguration of the movement towards national
unity which was at last achieved in the reign of David.
The enemy is broken and scattered, Sisera flies, and in
his flight takes refuge with Jael whose husband was
of a tribe friendly to Sisera. But he was absent then,

and the woman, alone, with daring treachery—or should it be rather called independent zeal for Jahveh and the oppressed against the tyrant?—slew the warrior.

It is interesting to notice how such ancient poems were used by later writers. A psalmist drew upon this song to compose another sacred poem (*Ps.* 68) in which the defeat of Sisera was still the motive but theology was the elaboration. A chronicler, or perhaps unwritten popular speech, turned the poem (ch. 5) into prose (ch. 4), and the historian of Judges took the poem and the prose, wrought them by one touch—"Then sang Deborah and Barak"—into a continuous whole, and set it in his narrative. And one sees how such handling gradually blurs truth to fact. Here is a remarkable instance. The poem describes Sisera asking for rest and refreshment. Jael brought a bowl of milk arming herself at the same time with a bludgeon. Sisera took the bowl in both hands and bent forward to drink. While he was thus defenceless Jael smote him on the forehead, and

> At her feet he bowed, he fell, he lay:
> At her feet he bowed, he fell:
> Where he bowed, there he fell down dead.

That describes very well what happened. But it would not describe a man being transfixed by a nail driven into his forehead with a hammer while he lay asleep, as the prose has it. There is a simile in the poetry: Jael smote Sisera as you smite the tent-pin with the hammer. The form of the simile was determined by the regular form of Hebrew poetry, in which a statement is doubled by parallelism; hence both hammer and tent-pin. And there is that vividness of poetry which seems obscure to the scrupulous imagination of prosers.

And so the second picture was drawn of Sisera entering the tent, lying on the bed, and being killed while asleep.

Chapters 6, 7, 8 follow with the history of Gideon the Abiezrite, a great judge deliverer and reformer. The author of Judges here seems to draw from tribal tradition, the style and matter of which he partly raises to a more literary dignity. But he preserves carefully what he considered so important in the naive original, the angel, the dream, the marvellous. For all that witnessed to the salvation coming from Jahveh and not through the strength or wisdom of men : Jahveh would save by few not by many, by a dream and lights and pitchers rather than by an army with swords. And for Jahveh Gideon contended, a fierce Puritan, against his own countrymen and family, and won a name thereby in religion, Jerubbaal. If national unity was to be achieved it would be centred upon the pure faith in Jahveh, the one righteous God of Israel.

The story of Gideon has a sequel in the story of his family after his death, and especially of Abimelech. This our author repeats pretty well in its primitive simplicity, artfully catching our attention by the contrast, and giving us a holiday from theological reflection while we simply enjoy this fresh verisimilitude of the intrigue the folly and the violence. With further nicety of art he inserts a series of brief notes about judges of whom he has no wonderful deeds to record ; and so passes to another act in his drama, a story he intends to handle in quite a different manner from any he has used heretofore. Jephthah, with the stain upon his birth and the royalty of his manners, urbane diplomatist, the Spirit of Jahveh upon him when he takes the field victoriously : his daughter, chivalrous as himself, the sweetest lady in the Old Testament : the reticence and mystery, as though all were seen in shadows, almost as though events were mingled with some nature-myth of autumn and spring, a midsummer evening's dream tender and melancholy : no doubt parts of this had been often told in various manner, and this historian has felt the whole ; the idea has descended upon his meditations as from another world (which is inspiration), and he has rivalled the epic of Deborah with his idyll.

A few more brief notes, yet vivified by picturesque touches—the forty sons and thirty sons' sons riding on their threescore and ten ass colts—lead on to the delightful tale of Samson. Samson is Shimshon from Shemesh the sun : the places have sun names, the halo of the hero's hair, the fiery foxes are sun-like : is this a sun myth as ingenious people have conjectured ? Hardly ; unless from some far-off origin some such mythology has impinged upon another tradition, as might be for instance in psalm 19. When our historian wrote and for many generations before him no one guessed that they were telling nature myths when they told of their strong man. They told merry tales of him, and for all the sadness of the conclusion the historian has kept the gaiety. There is little show of piety in the rude narration he has adopted. Yet the zeal and trust, the deeds without words for Jahveh's cause, the vow so scrupulously kept till at last the breaking of it brings disaster, the power of the Spirit which waxes and wanes with the faithfulness of the vow, and finally the sacrifice of Samson's own life in overwhelming vengeance on the enemies of Jahveh :—well, this is edifying in an unsophisticated way ; it was edifying to people who called God Jahveh in a primitive unreflecting faith.

But the faith of the Old Testament was more than that ; the faith of the author of Judges was more than that. For him Samson stands as type of an old state of things which should not last. Samson leads on to the grim narratives of Micah and his Levite, of the violence of the sons of Dan, of the other Levite and the beastly vice of men, of the Benjamite war which ensued. Throughout these latter pages the refrain is repeated, There was no king in those days : every man did that which was right in his own eyes. Presently Samuel Saul and David are to appear. Israel is to be gathered into one nation under a king. Order freedom, and would that it might be also true religion, shall be then. The book of Judges is but the prelude to the history of Israel.

CHAPTER 7

SAMUEL THE PROPHET

JOSHUA Judges and Samuel are clearly books about these persons not books written by them. Who wrote the books we can but infer from the matter and manner of the contents, and our inferences pass largely into guesses. If we read the commentary Dr. Burney has given us on Judges we see that he will not let imagination play on a single author of the whole, as we have done in our last chapter. Dr. Burney is more concerned with the gradual process through which the completed book was constructed out of a series of documents brought by various writers nearer and nearer to a final shape, a connected whole. These two views do not quite exclude one another, and the " author " fancy is perhaps legitimate in spite of patient critical science, greatly though every honest mind must respect that science. Now, in approaching Samuel, we will again keep both kinds of view in mind, yet be somewhat bold in postulating an " author " who uses a variety of material as a historian uses material, setting it in order and inspiring it with an idea.

We will imagine our author as writing some considerable time after the events he records yet not a very long time after : certainly before the fall of the monarchy with Zedekiah, almost certainly before the reformation of Josiah : if there are a few things in the book which seem to indicate a later date it is easy to suppose that these would come in when it was revised for inclusion in the Bible of the post-exilic Jewish Church.

We may imagine this author with a little library about him and from Samuel itself we can discover four of the volumes he had therein, which he used for the writing of Samuel, and from which he has preserved four concluding summaries at 1 Samuel 7. 15-17, 14. 47-52, 2 Samuel 8. 15-18, 20. 23-26. These might be the last pages of a history of Samuel, a history of Saul, and two histories of David in the first and latter parts of his reign. When we read our Samuel through we recognize traces of those former histories from which we can tell pretty well what kind of treatment their authors had already given to the subject. Open the book at 1 Samuel 8 and read in that chapter how the elders of Israel came to Samuel as to their leader and master, the judge of all Israel: how they asked for a king, how

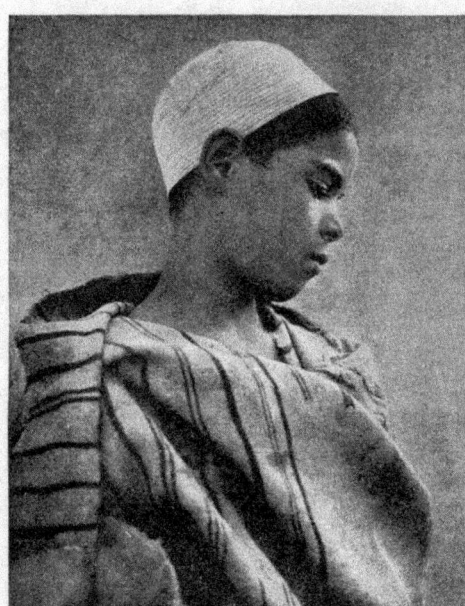
"THE YOUNG SAMUEL."

Samuel was displeased, yet obeying the word which the LORD spoke to him, he refused not, but warned the people that the king would be a doubtful boon. He describes the king they will get in the very language in which Moses in Deuteronomy 17. 14 ff. describes the kind of king who must not be in Israel, while he declares that a king they are indeed to have. Now go

PHILISTINES.

on to chapter 9. A fresh bit of narrative starts with a fresh style: you seem to have turned from a sermon in Deuteronomy to a piece of lively story telling about an Ehud or a Samson. The young squire Saul with his servant giving up the search for the lost beasts would go home. The servant tells him that in the city they have come near dwells a seer who can tell fortunes, and proposes they should make trial of his skill before returning, and offers his master a piece of money for the fee. So these two youths go to the city, ask the maidens they fall in with about the seer, and go up to meet him as he comes to sacrifice and hold a village feast. They find Samuel, for Samuel is this—not great judge of Israel, but country parson as it were—and he brings them to the feast. And now we remark how dignified and authoritative Samuel shows himself. The servant drops into the servant's place without a word. Saul is honoured, but is commanded to be ready for his high destiny. All is to be according to the word of the LORD, which tremendous word this country prophet authoritatively declares. We remark too how all is joyful, hopeful: The LORD has chosen His king, all will be well now. So Saul is anointed and sent home to wait till occasion points to the LORD's will for his next move: on the way he is assured by signs, and the Spirit of the LORD comes upon him. He waits as bidden. Then one evening he is called to the rescue of Jabesh Gilead, quickly gathers an army and performs the task. Triumphantly returning he is acknowledged as king.

In these two passages we have variant accounts of Samuel, of Saul, and of the inauguration of the kingdom. In one (8) Samuel is the great judge of Israel: the LORD, whose minister he is, may alone be Israel's king: only because of the obstinate desire of the people is permission given from the LORD through the reluctant Samuel to appoint an earthly king: the king who shall be appointed is condemned beforehand as unworthy of his office. In the other (9–11) Samuel is the seer of an obscure country town who inspired with enthusiasm anoints Saul as the king whom the LORD has chosen for great deeds. And the two passages are distinguished by contrasted language and style.

As the narrative proceeds this variety persists, but it is less and less easy to separate one kind from the other.

The author has not been making extracts from his books, but constructing his own continuous history from these and perhaps other sources which he handles freely : sometimes the continuity is blurred ; was Saul really anointed twice ? how did David first become known to Saul ?

Now consider Samuel as a whole and picture the situation of Israel in this period. When it began there was a notable sanctuary at Shiloh, a centre of worship for at least a large tract of country. But the sanctuary was not well ordered : some discontent was felt with the ascendancy of its priesthood. Into that priestly family the child Samuel entered : there he was educated in the ancient faith. Shiloh and its priesthood were presently ruined. The Philistines conquered and dominated Israel. The historian describes the condition of his people. It makes us think of the condition of Italy under the Austrians in the early part of the last century. Indeed it will help us to understand the book of Samuel if we think of the *risorgimento* of Italy. For in Israel as in Italy they settled down : slavery became to many tolerable. Samuel seems to have taught, kept religion alive, kept order, acquiescing in political dependence, cherishing an inner ideal of the people of God with Jahveh as their true sovereign, careless of outward prosperity ; the ideal of the camels and tents of their forefathers. But all did not share this contentment. There was a young Israel who grew into a definite party, who dreamed of national freedom through national unity, and believed that unity could be created by a king. If Samuel stood for the quiet of the "Church," these were perhaps more "secular" : yet a pious woman like Hannah might be with them, if we may trust that Magnificat of hers (1 *Sam.* 2); for it closes with an

A PHILISTINE.

exultant anticipation of the LORD's Anointed, which (in Hebrew Messiah, in Greek Christ) is the designation of Israel's kings in the Old Testament. This young

Israel presently found their hero Saul, and made him king; Samuel agreeing much as the Pope agreed with Garibaldi. And Saul did free Israel. When he was defeated and slain in his last battle he had not failed: after one more battle we hear of no further trouble from the Philistines: David succeeded to a kingdom which he was able at once to make independent, and soon dominant over the old enemies.

Can we not fancy two histories of this *risorgimento*, one in which Samuel and the old religious ideal is the theme; in which Samuel is the great good priestly judge and Saul the godless rebellious king who failed in his office: another of which Saul is the hero who fought for freedom, and won it even at the cost of his own life and his sons'?

These would be the two early books which correspond with our two first summaries. The third summary belongs to a history of David's adventures, and attainment of full possession of the throne, which he soon made secure and glorious. The fourth summary belongs to a second history of David, of the later years of his reign, the troubles within his family, Absalom's rebellion, its suppression and David's restoration. There remain the last chapters to account for. These are an appendix which, if we may sit so free to generally accepted criticism as to suppose that this too comes from the pen of the historian of the whole, may help us to form an opinion of his method in dealing with his material generally.

The books he had were biassed, the two on Samuel and Saul strongly so, those on David also in some measure. The course of events, even the facts, were sometimes in contradiction of one another. He had to form a judgement and construct a story. This he did, not piecing extracts together, yet altering the language of his authorities as little as need be : a good memory and a firm impression would lead him to reproduce a good deal unconsciously. In the later history of David especially in Absalom's rebellion he had a vivid, perhaps contemporary narrative and no disturbing rival narrative, and here he seems to have repeated the original with little change : his instinct as artist would recommend this procedure, and our enjoyment is certainly the keener for it. In the earlier part adjustment was often difficult. We catch the drift without much sense of difficulty as we read right on. Now and then we are pulled up. We cannot see, for instance, when and how David first came to Saul ; as a boy who had slain Goliath with a sling and stone, or as a young man already skilled in arms as well as music. In a modern printed book the author would state the problem, how there is a flat contradiction in his authorities ; and he would very likely add an excursus with full discussion. The ancient author, lacking the conveniences of print and paper, trusted to the wit of his readers, and just put both accounts of the event together, and went on. Yet something he did in modern style. In an appendix he collected documents and traditions which would not fit into the narrative, or about which he had doubts, a few perhaps which came to hand after he had finished the narrative. Among these is a note which bears on this question of David's first coming to Saul. If the story of Goliath had been left out, all might have run on smoothly. But fancy a book of Samuel without the story of David and Goliath. Nevertheless that story was not so perfectly attested as might be wished, and in the appendix is a note (2 *Sam.* 21. 19) of a tradition belonging to another family of Benjamin, that their ancestor Elhanan was the person who slew Goliath.

But far more important than these ordinary problems of a writer's craft was the problem of Samuel, his office and his relation to God and the people and the movement for monarchy. Was he the famous judge or an obscure priest? Was he for or against the monarchy? Was he prejudiced or did he really know and follow the will of God? The eminence of the author as a sacred historian, his inspiration, appears in his masterly treatment of that problem. He solves it by an idea, the idea of a prophet which shall henceforth prevail: Samuel was the prophet of the LORD, and as such all becomes clear enough. The common idea of a prophet in those days may be gathered from the description of Saul among the prophets in chapter 10, or of the irreverent way in which Saul's servant proposed to ask their fortunes of Samuel. Prophets told fortunes or danced and whirled in ecstasy like dervishes. Serious people would think better than that, but to that the popular mind, even among the prophets themselves, had fallen. Our author says a prophet is one whose ear Jahveh uncovers (9. 15 R.V. margin). As a man lifts the linen veil on the head of his friend and whispers the secret in his ear, so does Jahveh to his prophet: the prophet shares the innermost mind of Jahveh. If Samuel enjoyed such a divine dignity it mattered little whether he were famous and authoritative by his earthly office or not: great judge or country priest? that question may be left undecided. Again, if Samuel were prejudiced against the monarchy, then came round to it; if he foretold a troublesome king, yet received Saul with enthusiasm; is not that just what the prophet of Jahveh might rightly do? The prophet was directed from day to day; he did not choose his own path, trust his own judgement, ask to see the distant scene. As each need arose, as duty followed duty, Jahveh uncovered his ear, gave bidding, and was obeyed. "Hath Jahveh as great delight in burnt offerings and sacrifices, as in obeying the voice of Jahveh?" said Samuel afterwards to Saul. Obedience in trustful union with God's will, that is the essence of prophecy. Prophecy is nearly the same as inspiration, and there is more of this obedience, this noble Calvinism, throughout the Bible than we are quite glad to admit: "I bid you notice how often in the Gospels our Lord said, I must," was always part of the confirmation addresses of Bishop Festing of St. Albans.

CHAPTER 8

THE DIVINE RIGHT OF KINGS

THE prophet of the LORD looks not anxiously into the future, yet visions of the LORD's purpose for the future are given him. When Saul found Samuel such a vision came to Samuel. And yet it was not fulfilled. Rather it was disappointed and then fulfilled in a manner the prophet had not foreseen. Thus prophecy reaches its heights in the great line of prophets. They have a vision of the LORD's holy reign, and it seems near. It is delayed and the glorious language in which it was foretold is only satisfied in the Gospel of the New Testament. Here is inspiration again, working mightily, but not as our definitions would have it work.

Saul became king, was rejected, and the king that was required appeared in his successor David.

Here our historian had another and more difficult problem set him. We may suppose that his authorities gave him two portraits of Saul. One presented him as the hero of young Israel, the warrior who united the nation, created an army, fought the Philistines and gained freedom for Israel: a noble gentleman, austere in morality, never a taint of luxury about him, enduring hardship as a soldier should, and at last dying honourably on the field of battle, not victorious indeed in that battle, yet leaving the harvest of his constant toil to be easily carried by the rival who ousted his family from their rightful throne. Perhaps we may even surmise that Saul was depicted as a thinker in advance of his times, who disliked all that savoured of superstition and idolatry in the traditional religion, but disapproved also of cruel wars of utter destruction — of women children and cattle — even if the enemy were Amalekite sinners; a free thinker and a rebel against God in the eyes of Samuel, a clear thinking follower of the really divine will as others judged.

All this is fanciful. Yes, there is always a deal of fancy in the reconstruction of imaginary documents. Yet read Dr. A. B. Davidson's sermon on Saul's reprobation;[1] then read 1 Samuel again; and perhaps it may not seem extravagantly fanciful. As for the other document in which Samuel is the good judge of Israel, the people much to be blamed for desiring a king, Saul disobedient to the command of the LORD, and rightly rejected from continuance; not much fancy is postulated here, this is the general argument of 1 Samuel as we read it now.

ABSALOM'S TOMB.

And yet are we satisfied with such a reading? Would the author be satisfied by being so read? Does he not

[1] *Called to be Saints.* T. & T. Clark, 1903.

show that he too admires Saul and reveres him in his downfall? Are his sympathies all with Samuel against Saul? No, they are not. And yet again he acquiesces in the popular judgement on the whole. He does mean us to decide that Saul was rightly rejected, and that David was the king after the LORD's heart.

There is our real stumbling-block, David not Samuel. David's sin was not even a great sin; it was a mean sin. Adulterous treachery, base attempts to hide it, cold-blooded calculated murder of his faithful servant by other hands than his own: all this disgusts us. And his winning ways, his popularity, there is an ambiguity about the superficial charm: he makes us think of "that vile politician Bolingbroke." What is the formal disobedience of Saul on a point of ritual, or in that sparing of Agag and the cattle, what is that disobedience compared with these grave sins, this unpleasing suppleness of David? Why should Samuel and the historian and God prefer David to Saul?

Let us try to answer. First, David himself would sadly agree to most of what has just been said. In that eighteenth psalm which is included in the appendix to Samuel and is therefore more decidedly connected with David himself than any other psalm, he—the David of this psalm—says to God "Thy gentleness hath made me great." He looks back on his successful reign and takes no credit to himself. His deserving has been nought, God's mercy has been all. And secondly springing out of that lowly temper, we find him submitting serenely to God's will in Absalom's rebellion and all the peril and shame that came to him therein. It is true that the words which touch us all so deeply, "O Absalom my son, my son," are less beautiful when we read them in the context of Joab's rude but faithful rebuke: You care more for Absalom than for the fidelity and lives of all your servants who have died for you to-day: and now if you do not go down and show yourself to the people it will be worse for you than ever it was before. And David did what this rough soldier, so dogged in his loyalty, bade him do, and Joab saved him a second time that day, and David never forgave him. It is true that something of the old "politician" comes out here again. But it is more noticeably true that David's character deepens and improves as his life goes on: it deepens within the transforming influence of his trust in God, his love for God. He was a sinner and a mean one, but he loved God, knew penitence, and grew great; for great he was on a large view of his career: the gentleness of God did make him great.

That love of God, that trust and communion, was (so far as we can see from the written history) quite outside the ken of Saul. The author intends to leave that impression upon us, and he gathers up the whole impression into an explanation and solution of the problem in 2 Samuel 7. David, at rest from all his enemies, purposes to build a house for the Lord. Nathan the prophet approves, but presently learns the will of the Lord more perfectly, and tells David this may not be. He has no message about David being a man who has shed blood, such as the grosser imagination of a later school conceived in Chronicles. The Lord's word in Kings is ardent towards His loved servant. There were other and truer reasons for delay. Meanwhile let David be happy in the assurance that the Lord has built for him a secure house not made with hands. Jahveh will establish David's line as His own kings for ever. "I will be his father and he shall be My son: if he commit iniquity, I will chasten him with the rod of men, and with the stripes of the children of men; but My mercy shall not depart from him, as I took it from Saul, whom I put away before thee. And thine

"THE FOUNTAIN OF DRAGONS."
(Nehemiah 2. 13.)

house and thy kingdom shall be made sure for ever before thee: thy throne shall be established for ever."

There is the divine right of kings. The true king is the son of God, not in the formal sense of Babylonian or Egyptian reverence, but in the Bible sense: All cometh from the Father, and no one knoweth what it is to be a son but the father, or what to be a father except the son, and to whomsoever the son willeth to reveal it (see Luke 10. 22). Such a divine right

David with all his weakness could understand, and Saul with all his excellence could never enter into.

Nevertheless the promise, you will say, was not fulfilled. Samuel's vision, the LORD's promise, alike ended in disappointment. For ever made sure? No: the kingdom of David was divided, then one half after the other fell, and now David has no throne.

No throne of this world, it is true. But did the promise mean that? Nathan thought so, David thought so, but the Old Testament, the Bible of the deep-faithed Jewish Church speaks with a larger voice than a David's or a Nathan's. As the prophetic message proceeds from Nathan's lips a divine abstraction is felt. Times and persons lose their outlines. The idea of sovereignty looms before us: the divine right not of king this or king that, but of all true kingship from earth to heaven, from time to eternity: the seed of David is not physical descent but moral heirship. For the problem of David's preferment over Saul the solution found by the historian in David's mystical sense of the divine, is after all not much more than a makeshift. The better solution would be that the problem ought never to be set. The later life of David is real history: we know a good deal about it. Of his youthful years we know little. Saul scarce enters history at all. He is a grand dim figure of heroic days, a

> gray king, whose name, a ghost,
> Streams like a cloud, man-shaped, from mountain peak,
> And cleaves to cairn and cromlech.

We lack matter, as we have no moral right, to call the successful man and the tragic hero to a bar of judgement. But think of Saul as hero or victim of that vast abstract mode of the working of God's will which we call tragedy, and we may learn something therefrom.

Tragedy portraits the terrible ruin of a noble character. Contemplating ruin we pass no moral judgement. We see a great person conquered by circumstance. We do not say his defeat is caused by sin : we might say, by fault ; there has been something faulty in his act or inactivity, and from that faultiness all the sorrow has arisen. But we do not say this. Tragedy is too magnificent to allow us to talk thus. We leave all that to God who alone transcends tragedy. Offences must needs come : woe unto him through whom they come. Woe, and must needs : our Lord loved Judas to the last, and spoke no bitter, but some very tragic words of him.[1]

That "must needs" lies at the heart of tragedy. There is an impersonal force at work, a dread power we cannot understand. An evil spirit ? From the LORD ? Is it God ? Is it only a shadow ? Is tragedy just this, that a great soul is jangled till it makes a shadow into an irresistible reality ?

Tragedy reaches its height when it happens to one in great place, one who is not just an ordinary person, but has an abstract universal element about him, a king, a giant of old time, who grows into the history of the race, who stands solitary yet each man feels a secret kinship with the type. Saul is especially tragic as a king whose reign scarce emerges from the dark ages of Israel.

Divinely chosen to free Israel, to make Israel a nation, Saul started grandly. Then came the quarrel with Samuel. Samuel called it disobedience. We like Saul may respond, That is the question. But that was

[1] cf. GIOVANNI PAPINI, *Storia di Cristo*, Firenze, 1921, pp. 412 ff.

DAVID

not the important question. The important question was, how Saul should take this check. He took it gallantly in so far that in spite of disgrace he stuck to his duty. Yet not quite gallantly. He brooded. The evil spirit would come over him from time to time. Then David was brought to cheer him, and Saul loved David. And then again fate went against him. David provoked his jealousy, and Saul by degrees became David's enemy. Jonathan seemed to side with David, and the enmity grew passionate. Success in arms began to fail Saul. He betook himself to Endor, and whether or no he yielded at the last to the superstition he had hitherto discountenanced,

WATER CARRIER.

he did go to his last battle as oppressed by irreversible fate. There is tragedy : the tragic hero creates fate out of circumstance.

From Saul to David is from the half mythical to history : it is also the passage from abstract grandeur to simplicity. The check which came to David had no ambiguity : it was a plain and horrid sin. And having sinned he turned to God his Father and got free. So, it would seem, he always did. He had that kind of affectionate child-like trust in God. If Saul created fate out of circumstance David might seem to have created God. But the difference cuts deeper. There is no such thing as fate : to raise circumstance to fate is a parody of creation. God is : and to find God is to use circumstance as grace :

> With the kindly Thou wilt show Thyself kind
> With the crooked Thou wilt show Thyself subtle.[1]

The Gospel, which began when true religion began, abolishes the shadow, fate. That is what our Lord did when He cast out devils. When we lose Gospel simplicity then fate the old serpent of the nations revives, and tragedy ensues.

[1] Ps 18 26, 27 in *The Book of Common Prayer, an edition containing Proposals and Suggestions compiled by John Neale Dalton, M.A , F.S.A., Canon of Windsor.* Cambridge, at the University Press, 1920. cf. p 140.

CHAPTER 9

SOLOMON'S TEMPLE

AFTER all we have ended with the very beautiful simplicity of David ; he had a piety which well became the office of the LORD's Anointed, Jahveh's Christ. When ye pray, say Our Father which art in heaven : David could do that. And after all he did his duty well as king. He ruled righteously, and stablished the kingdom, and Israel under him became a nation with better morals and truer religion than the neighbouring peoples. We may indulge in modern scruples about him : his own countrymen loved him and thought highly of him. And as time went on they raised him to an ideal eminence. He became the type of kingship, which in the Old Testament is the type of Christhood. For we must remember that Christ is just the Greek for Anointed ; that in the Old Testament kings and priests and prophets, sometimes even a foreign deliverer like Cyrus, often the whole people as the chosen people of God, are designated the LORD's Anointed, Jahveh's Christ : that the epistle to the Hebrews opens reasonably by declaring that our Lord Jesus inherited His name Christ from these Christs of whom the Old Testament, the history of His ancestors, is full : and that this epistle adds, quite reasonably too, the privilege of divine sonship to such Christhood.

David grew into a type, and above all a religious

type. He was royal but he was the royal psalmist. The fancy that he wrote all the psalms is late and prosaic. The Psalter as the mind of David, the picture of all that David typically represents of love and trust

KING DAVID.
(From an English fifteenth-century *Horae*.)

towards God, this was the devotional happiness of the Jewish Church. "David" was to the Jewish churchman what "Christ" is to us. And as to us "Christ" means more than "Jesus," including an idea in a person, yet the idea is not fanciful but continuous with the person, so it was to the Jews with David. David was a historical person. He made and ruled a great kingdom. The historian in Samuel records his penitence and trust in God, in his appendix he includes two psalms which illustrate his poetic and religious temper; the Psalter and the model of kingship are the continuation of these earlier beliefs about him.

David became "pleasant in the psalms of Israel," and at last "the sweet psalmist of Israel" himself. A like transformation happened to Solomon his son. He prayed for wisdom to rule well, and that wisdom was granted him. Then very picturesquely the historian of Kings describes a more spacious wisdom that was ascribed to him : " God gave Solomon wisdom and understanding exceeding much, and largeness of heart, even as the sand that is on the sea shore. And Solomon's wisdom excelled the wisdom of all the children of the east, and all the wisdom of Egypt. For he was wiser than all men ; than Ethan the Ezrahite, and Heman, and Calcol, and Darda, the sons of Mahol : and his fame was in all the nations round about. And he spake three thousand proverbs : and his songs were a thousand and five. And he spake of trees, from the cedar that is in Lebanon even unto the hyssop that springeth out of the wall : he spake also of beasts, and of fowl, and of creeping things, and of fishes. And there came of all peoples to hear the wisdom of Solomon, from all kings of the earth, which had heard of his wisdom." Then he became the type of that "wisdom" of the Hebrews which represented a different type of piety from the devotional ardour of the psalms. And wise men wrote books in the name of Solomon : proverbs too were collected and grouped round his name. For a while this literary device was understood as it was practised : in the book of Proverbs various collections are added, with their distinctive titles, to the Solomonic set. But at last prose killed imagination, and Solomon the type of wisdom was dogmatized into the actual writer of all the wisdom books which the Jewish Church had set in order for her children's instruction and delight: a spirit was sharpened into a pen.

Still, here too, all was continuous, and perhaps the difference between the wise piety of Solomon and the old-fashioned simplicity of David was one reason why Solomon built the temple which David had dreamed of building but left unbuilded. No doubt there were other reasons, all of which are gathered up in the sufficiency of the divine command; for it is the peculiar dignity of the Old Testament to sum up all in God, and leave secondary causes for the ingenuity of historical criticism to inquire after: that bold rapture of the inspired writers kept them from ever being dull. Solomon was rich and powerful, he advanced the kingdom of his father to the pomp of an empire: other empires had their famous temples, their gods were the wonder of the world, Jahveh should be at least as famous. Perhaps too the inconveniences of "high places" and a priesthood interpenetrating country life in its length and breadth were already felt. Here indeed Solomon's "wisdom" begins to show itself. Like Saul he rose superior to superstition; teraphim and the half pagan observances of the high places, the harvest homes of the farms, were mischievous in his eyes. Other scruples about novelty in worship would not daunt him. A temple which should be both the king's chapel and a rallying point of national faith, could be brought under discipline and might do much to improve the patriotism of the empire.

And Solomon knew himself to be wise enough to carry out the innovation without serious offence.

There would be offence to many of the purest hearts in Israel. David and Nathan had known that, and the word of Jahveh which came to Nathan was a word of direction in a decision about which they were still doubtful: David was to wait. The patriarchal tradition from nomad days was that all the wide heaven was God's dwelling-place: there were theophanies in the storm when God manifested a special presence riding upon the cherubim of the winds, sending the seraphim of the lightning before Him, His voices or thunders issuing from the dark pavilion where He kept His own still invisible state. From this rudely spiritual conception it was an advance, not without loss, when God revealed Himself as Israel's exclusive sovereign, Jahveh, with a particular home on earth among the mountains of the desert. There He gave His law; thence He came in time of need to put Himself at the head of the host of Israel, as when Deborah and Barak fought against Sisera. Now Jerusalem was to be His home; even the mystery of the far-off desert would be lost. Now a temple was to be built for His habitation, no moving unsubstantial tent which might be thought of as an altar might, a symbol of a gracious temporary visitation: "In every place where I record My name, I will come unto thee and I will bless thee." Now the "house" is to be walled and settled, a city-dweller's house to confine Elohim the Spirit who fills all heaven and earth. In David's reign that could not be endured.

Solomon built the house, exceeding magnifical. He finished it, and then he called all the people together for its dedication. There was a solemn service with sacrifice and feasting. King Solomon pontificated. Israel was still living under the simple code of Exodus 20; the Levitical proprieties of the Chronicles have no place in the early prophetical history of Kings. And Solomon recited the prayer of consecration, part prayer, part sermon, as it well might be in the deuteronomic style of the author of Kings, who nevertheless may well be trusted to have preserved the gist of the actual oration.

Solomon took as a kind of text a verse from an ancient hymn: it was enshrined the Septuagint tells us in the sacred collection of such hymns, the book of Jashar.[1]

> Then spake Solomon, The LORD hath said that He would dwell in the thick darkness. I have surely built Thee an house of habitation, a place for Thee to dwell in for ever. And the king turned his face about, and blessed all the congregation of Israel: and all the congregation of Israel stood. And he said, Blessed be the LORD . .

So the oration begins in 1 Kings 8. "Surely built" represents a Hebrew idiom "building built" which emphasizes the root idea of the verb; italics would give the effect in our printing. Solomon flatly contradicts the ancient theology; stops, turns and blesses the people. They stand, and he proceeds to explain his temerity in a further speech which runs into a long prayer. The

[1] It is only fair to admit that the Septuagint leaves no place for Solomon's audacity. The quotation from the poem comes at the end of the prayer in the Septuagint, and "portrays the glorious descent of Jahveh in the thunder-cloud from His abode in the darkness of the sky, to set His seal to the building, and to enter into possession of the new celestial abode on earth which Solomon has prepared to receive Him." See articles by F. C. Burkitt and H. St. J. Thackeray in *Journal of Theological Studies*, April 1909, July 1910

SOLOMON'S TEMPLE

JERUSALEM.

essence is: This house is but a symbol of God's presence; may God of His mercy make it an effectual symbol.

> Will God in very deed dwell on the earth? behold heaven and the heaven of heavens cannot contain Thee; how much less this house that I have builded! Yet have Thou respect unto the prayer of Thy servant, and to his supplication, O LORD my God, to hearken unto the cry and to the prayer which Thy servant prayeth before Thee this day. that Thine eyes may be open toward this house night and day, even towards the place whereof Thou hast said, My name shall be there: to hearken unto the prayer which Thy servant shall pray toward this place And hearken Thou to the supplication of Thy servant, and of Thy people Israel, when they shall pray toward this place: yea, hear Thou in heaven Thy dwelling place; and when Thou hearest, forgive

Instance after instance follows of special needs which may be satisfied by this "real presence." Each consecration of these needs closes with the same pathetic solemnity. Heaven is still Thy dwelling-place, forgive our desire for sacramental communion. The mystery is deepened by "toward." None enter the house. From the open air without the worshippers revere the unseen visitant. The ancient faith in the free, all-filling, unconfined, spiritual deity is not abated; it is more reverently affirmed than ever. At this unique temple it will be remembered better than it has been at a thousand careless country shrines. Yet there is a special sacramental "coming"; Jahveh comes to His own people, His own city, His own most holy house.

> And let these my words, wherewith I have made supplication before the LORD, be nigh unto the LORD our God day and night, that He maintain the cause of His servant, and the cause of His people Israel, as every day shall require: that all the peoples of the earth may know that the LORD, He is God; there is none else.

> Let your heart be therefore perfect with the LORD our God, to walk in His statutes, and to keep His commandments, as at this day.

The LORD did hear, did come, did forgive. The simpler primitive faith "God is Spirit" lasted, and will last for ever: through all changes that has gone on; cleansing its stream as it runs to the sea. The temple answered to a temporary need, but it answered truly, and its dedication was the first step in a long development of faith and life. When the kingdom was divided and the wanton North tried strange worships and won a conscience through the strife and suffering that sprang therefrom, Judah was maybe steadied in her more placid conservatism by having the king's chapel with its decent order. When northern Israel went under, Isaiah had the Judean temple as a rallying point of hope. In that temple Hezekiah was at last converted, and the temple was the home of Jahveh's holiness which at last the prophet could promise should never be violated by the Assyrian. When Josiah carried through his reformation the temple at Jerusalem was the centre upon which he could focus all the institutions of disciplined worship. At the same time Jeremiah began his protest against formal trust in such outward symbol: and so prepared for the new covenant written on the heart when Solomon's temple was destroyed by the Chaldeans. But—again coincidently—Ezekiel promising restoration concentrated the new order of a new world upon a restored and holier temple: from that restored temple a deeper theology of law and sacrifice was to be elaborated. The "Comfort ye" prophecy carried Jeremiah's hope forward to a very glorious ideal of purely spiritual religion. The exile ended and the new temple was built in lowlier state than Ezekiel had foretold : but the promise was given which went beyond Ezekiel's hope,

> Thus saith the LORD of hosts: Yet once, it is a little while, and I will shake the heavens, and the earth, and the sea, and the dry land ; and I will shake all nations, and the desire of all nations shall come, and I will fill this house with glory, saith the LORD of hosts. The silver is mine, and the gold is mine, saith the LORD of hosts. The latter glory of this house shall be greater than the former, saith the LORD of hosts . and in this place will I give peace, saith the LORD of hosts.

And if any one, coolly considering it, cannot allow that Haggai was looking far forward, or meaning more than a quiet evening after the storms of Israel's late trial, it is difficult to suppose that the Jewish Church did not read much more than that into the book which was chosen to conclude the whole volume of her prophets. "Behold I send My messenger—My angel 'Malachi' —and he shall prepare the way before Me : and the LORD whom ye seek shall suddenly come to His temple. . . . For I the LORD change not : therefore ye, O sons of Jacob, are not consumed."

CHAPTER 10

TO YOUR TENTS O ISRAEL

SOLOMON, the type of wisdom, was also a real and magnificent monarch. He expanded the kingdom of David to something like empire, and his imperial ambition brought trouble in its train. Saul had ruled and led in battle like the chief of a tribe, though he made his own tribe but a member of a nation. David reigned as king of a people, but as one of them: he was remembered as the shepherd-king. Solomon had a fine court, spent treasure on the country which had to be gathered from the country, enforced labour for his building, married foreign wives, lived splendid and aloof. During his reign mutterings were heard of discontent. Jeroboam made essay as a labour leader, unsuccessfully for the time but not without prophetic backing. When Solomon died and Rehoboam came to the throne, the storm burst.

The scene is vividly set forth in 1 Kings 12 : the remonstrance of Jeroboam and the congregation with its ominous decisive brevity; Rehoboam's consultation with the elder councillors of Solomon and their temperate advice; his conversation with "the young men that were grown up with him, that stood before him"; their arrogant formula and Rehoboam's word for word repetition of it to the people—" My father made your yoke heavy, but I will add to your yoke : my father chastised you with whips, but I will chastise you with

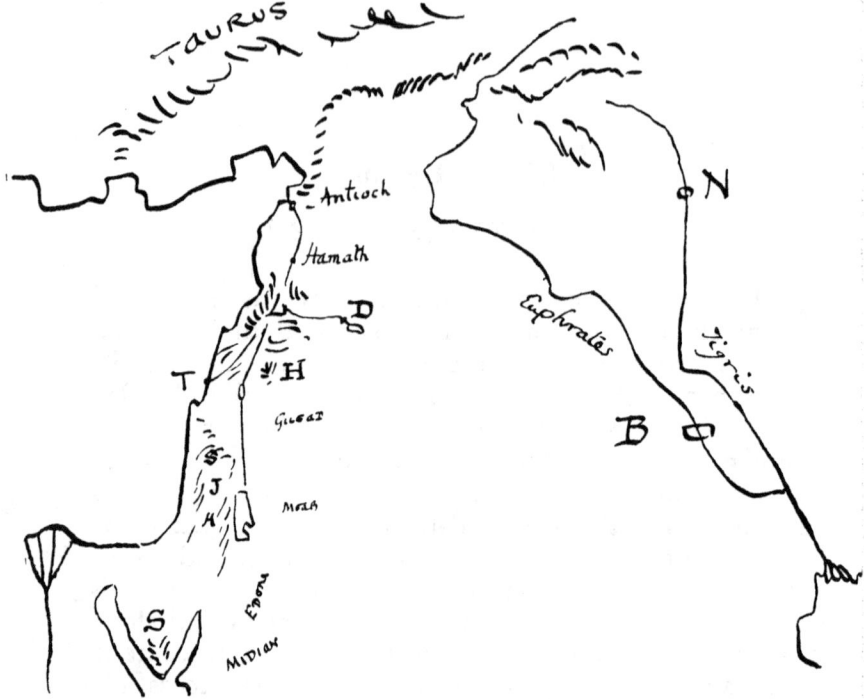

Accurate detail is not wanted but no false curves etc must be put in purposely The main run of the mountains must be shown, the rivers issuing from them, the cities on each river Thus from Lebanon three rivers, Orontes Abana Leontes issue, carrying the cities Antioch Damascus Tyre there is a fourth, the Jordan in the gorge of which no city is built but it has all Palestine for its own. Take care to get the important bends of the Tigris and Euphrates. Notice how the northernmost bulge of the Euphrates is level with Antioch, and Nineveh on the Tigris almost level with both how Tigris bends towards Euphrates just above Babylon, which is level with Samaria Notice the position of Hermon which gives the most splendid view of the whole country east west north and south A rough manuscript map is soon confused by having names written over it. Only a few names are needed for the very general purpose of this map, and as each is associated in the map-maker's mind with the features of the country round it, initials are indication enough for private memory Of course the whole thing is private A reader makes a map for himself, anyhow he likes for memorandum. A teacher makes one for his class on a blackboard with bold strokes of the chalk, the fewer the better he may do the drawing how he likes if only he makes the class see not the blackboard but the land

THE NORTHERN KINGDOM

scorpions"; and then the answer—" What portion have we in David? neither have we inheritance in the son of Jesse: to your tents, O Israel: now see to thine own house, David."

So Israel departed unto their tents, writes the historian. But as for the children of Israel which dwelt in the cities of Judah, Rehoboam reigned over them. The antithesis of tents and cities is meant to be noticed. Was this the clever appeal of Jeroboam the demagogue to a windy ideal, or do we hear the uncompromising zeal of Ahijah the Shilonite; camels and tents again, no more courts and harems and faith-denying civilization? Was the revolt a "going out" of "covenanters" with noble recklessness of temporal loss, or was it from the first a vindication of a right to general prosperity? At any rate it was the defection of a whole nation from (as it then seemed) an intruding dynasty which had only lasted three generations. Israel the nation went and set up a new king: Judah a little clan was left and Rehoboam was perforce reduced to mere chieftaincy. That reduction was in the end the surer establishment of his house and realm. But for a long while national history was made in northern Israel if not quite alone, at least in the main.

At this point, as once before, the Bible reader should draw a map for himself, marking with bold lines and curves the romantic position of these northerners. They were highlandmen for the most part with far more charm in their mountains than Judah had, wilder and higher, yet with fertile glades. Above (on the map) the garden, or Carmel, of Canaan spreads out. Corn olive and oil were there; and as the plain of Esdraelon is the only expanse of level land that side of Jordan, it is in northern

Israel's story that those exciting chariot drives all occur. North-west of the plain the line of the Carmel hills runs like a greyhound up to the cliff that looks over the western sea, and to the snow-capped mountains of the farther north, and eastward across the plain and the tropic gorge of Jordan to the steppes of Gilead, the place of flocks and herds and cavalry camps. That high ground will make a grand stage soon for the contest of *Elias contra mundum.* The map must show how northern Israel was in natural contact with the nations round about, and especially with the powerful empire of the Aramaeans or (as the Septuagint has translated their name from the Greek kings who afterwards possessed their country) Syrians. And it must stretch far away to the east and show Babylon and Nineveh, the Euphrates and the Tigris, and the long road to Egypt skirting the desert along the northern boundary of

BABYLONIAN MAP OF THE WORLD.
(Seventh or eighth century B.C.)
Showing the ocean surrounding the world, and marking the position of Babylon on the Euphrates, the mountains at the source of the river, the countries of Assyria and Bit Yakinu, and the swamps at the mouth of the Euphrates.

THE NORTHERN KINGDOM 75

mountains, passing through Syria, then through northern Israel; but leaving Judah on the east it then sinks to the maritime plain, the home of the Philistines.

In the midst of this beauty and riches and fullness of life the kingdom of the north arose. It was in the highway of the nations. The people were quick to exchange ideas. They were spirited ambitious, under some of their kings powerful; and they mixed with their neighbours in war as well as peace. From Canaanite within and foreigner beyond their boundaries they learned strange rituals and were for most of their time half pagan, with the luxury cruelty and vice of pagans. Prosperity brought feud between rich and poor. They were restless and ill to govern. There was no divine right in the northern highlands and dynasty gave place to dynasty as one captain after another slew his master and made himself king. Yet they could be touched by gallant deeds and the poetry of words. To stem the pagan tide prophets arose, sooner or of more rugged force than there were in Judah. Conscience awoke in the northern kingdom first. So, when the brief brilliant course was run and downfall imminent, they were found a better people than the uncivilized, misbelieving nations round them. They had represented Israel for two centuries, carrying the divine idea along the road of history, till it was with them as it often has been with such Christophers, as it was with Athens and with the Byzantine empire: they broke down morally and materially under the burden; the divine idea killed them while itself it passed on to higher manifestation.

This is not indeed what one would gather from the book of Chronicles. But it is what we gather from Kings and Prophets. And for the history of these two

HILLS AND FIELDS OF JUDEA.

centuries we must follow the prophets, who are actors themselves in the drama ; and Kings, which is a product of this prophetical period. Chronicles was written about 300 B.C., more than four centuries after the fall of Samaria. It was written by Jewish churchmen, living under the full Levitical law, in the shadow of the second temple, to whom Judean or Jew was the proper designation of the whole nation, while the northern kingdom

THE NORTHERN KINGDOM 77

meant little more to them than the lost tribes do to us. We can no more expect an accurate account of the times of Jeroboam or Ahab from such writers than we could expect a real history of republican Rome from the scriptorium of a mediaeval monastery. This does not mean that one book of the Bible is true, another untrue. All are true, but the truth is of various kinds. There is a truth of poetry and another truth of prose. There is a direct and an indirect truth of history. "One of the distinctive features of an old-world antiquary, says a historian of our day,[1] is that he cannot grasp what is meant by 'authority'; for him one authority is as good as another." Kings is an authority for the history of the monarchy in Israel; Chronicles is but a secondary authority for that period. It does not flatly contradict Kings, and that tempts the old-world antiquary to set about the task of squaring the narrative in Kings with the bare words of Chronicles. But by omission, shifting of emphasis, and addition, Chronicles presents a picture of the disruption of the kingdom as a miserable attempt of a party of rebels and dissenters to set themselves against the firm and rightful sovereignty of the house of David, an attempt which utterly failed and was most righteously punished. Moreover Kings (which was an "authority" to the Chronicler himself in the main) represents priesthood, worship, law at a simple early undeveloped stage. The Chronicler cannot imagine that things of that kind would have been so different from what he was accustomed to himself; so he adds (with little direct contradiction) much ritual and law to the ancient story.

[1] J. H. Round, in "The legend of Eudo Dapifer," *English Historical Review*, Jan. 1922.

GERIZIM AND HILLS OF SAMARIA: FROM MOUNT EBAL.

He did it inevitably, scarce consciously. But in this respect we must disregard his "authority." On the other hand if we would learn how "Jews" believed, worshipped, kept the law in the post-exilic church we find in Chronicles an authority which for that period is firstrate. And indeed the Jewish churchman of that period had a very noble faith and a profoundly reverent worship, and a brave pure benevolent morality. There is no disparagement of the Chronicler in thus distinguishing him from the author of Kings. His religion was not quite evangelic: there was much still waiting to be taught by our Saviour and His apostles. Yet for a devotional mind the Chronicler has manly nourishment to give. And when we also reflect on the masterful art which fitted him to impose his view of Israel's whole story upon the mind of men through age-long reading, we must very submissively respect him.

However, as Kings tells us, for two centuries northern Israel was the nation of Israel. But Judah was waiting meanwhile. In Judah the clan was still attached with cousinly affection to its royal chief. There was another manner of romance in Judah from the northern romance of history making. The house of David was faulty but beautiful, an inspiration like the Stuarts. Twice and again there was revolution and bloodshed, but each time the people of the land, the commonalty of the clan, restored the beloved family at once:

> Thus saith the LORD . . . I will not take the whole kingdom out of his hand . . for David My servant's sake, whom I chose . . and unto his son will I give one tribe, that David My servant may have a lamp alway before Me in Jerusalem, the city which I have chosen Me to put My name there.

CHAPTER 11

JAHVEH OUR GOD, JAHVEH ONE

HEAR O Israel: Jahveh our God, Jahveh one. That verse from Deuteronomy 6 is the Shema of the Jew. Shema is the opening Hebrew word of this confession of faith, as I believe, *credo*, is the opening word of our "creed." The Hebrew (like the confession modelled on it in Hebrews 13. 8) has no verb: it is a battle cry rather than a creed: there is the difference between the imaginative heart of the Old Testament and the logical head of modern western people. But we all alike hold a belief loyally. The belief of the Shema is that Jahveh is the only God for Israel: I am Jahveh thy God: thou shalt have none other god but Me. That is the meaning of the first clause. The second clause, Jahveh one, cannot be so easily defined. The Semitic heart is speaking, and will not be tied down to precise explanation. It means at least, There is none like Him: it means, He is always the same and always good; as in Exodus 34 when Jahveh passed before Moses and proclaimed—

> Jahveh, Jahveh, God full of compassion and gracious, slow to anger, and plenteous in mercy and truth; keeping mercy for thousands, forgiving iniquity and transgression and sin and that will by no means clear the guilty; visiting the iniquity of the fathers upon the children, upon the third and upon the fourth generation

Those last stern words were afterwards expanded by Ezekiel into exacter truth, and by our Lord with His

MOUNT CARMEL AND THE BROOK KISHON.

Forgive us our debts as we forgive; and the one and the same God became to later prophets the only God of all the world. Perhaps Elijah and the Israelites of his day had not yet asked the question whether or no there could be other gods for other nations. But the question whether there could be other gods in Israel was put with insistence before them, and Elijah compelled them to answer it once for all.

The Children of Israel had settled among the remnant of the Canaanites. They had taken possession of their farms and vineyards. The Canaanites were their neighbours and their servants. They worked on the land together, and kept harvest festivals together. The Canaanites had kept these festivals in honour of the Baals or divine lords of their various districts. The farmers of Israel were no theologians and saw no great harm in old customs and ceremonies; and so their devotion to Jahveh was mingled with the worship of the Baals. But there was harm in this. Even if it were not considered theologically there was harm. Paganism, the worship of the many Spirits of the Corn and the Wild, is cruel, impure, superstitious. Read Sir James Frazer's two volumes with that title in his *Golden Bough*, and you see how cruel impure and bad it is: those volumes are a fit introduction to Kings and the Prophets of Israel. And presently things got worse. Dynasties rose and fell with wrath and bloodshed in northern Israel. Zimri slew his master and Omri took the throne from Zimri. Omri held the fortress city of Samaria and left the kingdom to his son Ahab in some security, and Ahab became a powerful king. He married Jezebel a Zidonian princess who brought the worship of the Phoenician Baal into Israel. That was far more serious than the country festivals. The rites were perhaps more abominable. The queen's patronage changed irregularity into all but national apostasy. The prophets of Baal were multiplied and protected, the remnant of Jahveh's faithful were persecuted.

Then suddenly Elijah, the John Baptist of the Old Testament, appeared. "And Elijah the Tishbite who was of the sojourners of Gilead, said unto Ahab, As Jahveh, the God of Israel liveth, before whom I stand, there shall not be dew nor rain these years, but according to my word." Thus with the first verse of 1 Kings 17 the history of Elijah opens, a vivid narrative, sublime in rude simplicity, which seems to spring from the very time of the events; the writer of Kings appreciating its art and truth just repeats the words as he heard or read them.

Every one knows the story: the famine, the ravens, the meeting with Ahab, the challenge, and at last the contest on Mount Carmel. Against four hundred and fifty prophets of Baal and king Ahab and the people of Israel, Elijah stood alone. The prophets of Baal prepared sacrifices, invoked their god, leaped and cut themselves, and waited in vain for the miracle. Then at the time of the evening oblation Elijah repaired the altar of Jahveh, drenched it and his offering with water, came near and said, "O Jahveh, the God of Abraham, of Isaac, and of Israel, let it be known this day that Thou art God in Israel, and that I am Thy servant, and that I have done all these things at Thy word. Hear me, O Jahveh, hear me, that this people may know that Thou, Jahveh art God, and that Thou hast turned their heart back again. Then the fire of Jahveh fell . . . and all the people

"La Ilaha Illallah—Jahveh He is God."

fell on their faces : and they said, Jahveh He is God, Jahveh He is God."

This is one of the passages where the spirit is quite lost if the Name be dissolved into the title. It is Jahveh in whom Elijah believes so intensely nationally and fiercely. Take the prophets of Baal ; let not one of them escape. And they took them : and Elijah brought them down to the brook Kishon, and slew them there. That is zeal for Jahveh : it shocks us when we are thinking of the Nicene Lord God. And from that day forward there could be no more doubt about Jahveh and Israel. Jahveh alone is God in Israel. There is the first article of the creed which the succession of great prophets will build or rebuild for Israel. Each will add his particular article as the whole creed grows : In divers ways and by divers portions God spake to the fathers by the prophets. That day God spake by Elijah, and Elijah established that first clause of faith, Jahveh our God, Jahveh alone God in Israel.

But there remained a second article for Elijah also to establish. From Jezebel's vengeance he fled to Horeb, the desert home of Jahveh, the fount of the ancestral puritan simplicity. There Jahveh met him. And first, he was to learn that fierceness and bloodshed was after all alien to Jahveh's character. Not in wind earthquake or fire, but in that still voice onward came the LORD. In the Old Testament there are imperfections, fierce ideas of God, exercises of faith that are nigh to superstition. But these never stand still there. They are always moving forward, the less to the more perfect revelation. Use the Old Testament superstitiously, opening it anywhere and taking what you find and being content ; thus you will discover many faults. But use it diligently, reading onward through the whole, and it will appear very differently. The Old Testament is the record of a progressive revelation.

At Horeb Elijah was bidden to anoint Elisha as prophet in succession after himself and to provide for the carrying on of work which he might only begin. God prepares good works for His servants to walk in, not to finish, and Elijah had already learned that day that success is not a churchman's word. But there was one more good work for himself to do. He returned to Samaria and found that Ahab had been doing dreadful things. Naboth refusing to sell him the vineyard he coveted, Jezebel had Naboth removed by a judicial murder.

> And the word of the LORD came to Elijah the Tishbite saying, Arise, go down to meet Ahab king of Israel : behold, he is in the vineyard of Naboth, whither he is gone down to take possession of it. And thou shalt speak unto him, saying, Thus saith the LORD, Hast thou killed, and also taken possession ? Thus saith the LORD, In the place where dogs licked the blood of Naboth shall dogs lick thy blood, even thine. And Ahab said to Elijah, Hast thou found me, O mine enemy ? And he answered, I have found thee : because thou hast sold thyself to do that which is evil in the sight of the LORD. Behold I will bring evil upon thee and will utterly sweep thee away. . . . And of Jezebel also spake the LORD saying, The dogs shall eat Jezebel by the rampart of Jezreel

A bold denunciation, considering Ahab's power, and Jezebel's vindictive savagery, and Naboth's fate. A bold denunciation which would take notable effect in Israel. The farmers of Israel were no theologians and that cry from the heart of the multitude, Jahveh alone is Israel's God, might seem after all to many of them to be a great to-do about a little matter: a kindly thought for the Baals of their Canaanitish labourers

Esdraelon and Mount Carmel.
(Wooden plough in foreground.)

at harvest home had no great harm in it. But when it had come to a Baal-worshipping foreigner like Jezebel murdering freeborn Israelites because they would not part with the acres of their forefathers at the pleasure of a Jezebel's husband, that surely was very bad. And when they heard that the prophet of Jahveh had denounced Ahab and Jezebel, and declared that such crimes were abominable to Jahveh, and that Jahveh would overthrow the royal dynasty because of them; then they would reflect that no prophet of Baal would have dared so much in Baal's name, and that indeed there was no reason to suppose that Baal was extremely interested in such matters: Baal wanted a share in sacrificial feasts and was no foe to a little drunkenness in season, but Baal and righteousness had little in common.

Thus Elijah established a second article in Israel's creed: Jahveh is righteous, and demands as His true worship righteousness. And that is an article of faith which will be found in the course of a few generations to have lifted Israel far above the neighbouring people.

The first book of Kings ends almost immediately after this with the dramatic narrative of Micaiah's prophecy and the battle of Ramoth-Gilead and the death of Ahab according to Elijah's warning. But before that finale there is a curious and beautiful episode. The historian recounts in terse and burning words the guilts of Ahab. Then he tells how, when Ahab heard Elijah's condemnation, he rent his clothes, and fasted, and lay in sack-cloth, and went softly. "And the word of the LORD came to Elijah the Tishbite, saying, Seest thou how Ahab humbleth himself before Me? because he humbleth himself before Me, I will not bring the evil in his days : but in his son's days will I bring the evil upon his house." It would be a jejune criticism that saw here but the addition of some harmonizer who had noticed that Elijah's denunciation included the whole family of Ahab while the fact was that his son Ahaziah succeeded his father as king. However and by whomsoever these verses were brought in, they express an article of Israel's faith which needed no renewal by the mouth of this or that prophet. This article is constant throughout the whole Old Testament : I believe in the forgiveness of sins.

CHAPTER 12

MIRACLE

ELIJAH at Carmel brings a question before us which cannot be shirked by readers of the Old Testament, the question of miracle.

Holy Scripture certainly records miracles, and miracles are still worked which confirm the record: who has not had miraculous answers to prayer, miraculous deliverance in danger or temptation? But there are degrees, there is (so to say) propriety in miracle. The resurrection of our Lord Jesus Christ; our Lord's miracles in S. Mark and His miracles in S. John; the fire descending on Elijah's oblation and Elisha making iron swim; are miracles in different kinds, and it is less important to believe the last than the first of these. And a marvellous interference in the regular course of things is not the supreme witness of God's providence. Jeremiah thought the instinct of the stork was a pledge of the trustworthiness of God, and S. Augustine considered the regular course of seed time and harvest a greater miracle than those which astonish us by rarity.

Yet many feel otherwise, and are even fain to heighten the fitness of the natural into what seems more wonderful. Thus the people at Troas said Eutychus was killed by his fall. S. Paul said he still breathed, and took care of him, and he revived. But some readers of Acts to-day side with the people against S. Paul. Our Lord said Jairus' daughter was not dead but sleeping, when the noisy household took for granted she was dead. Are we sure our Lord did not simply mean what He said on that occasion?

In the Old Testament we sometimes perceive this heightening in process when one writer uses what an earlier writer has left him. Thus the author of Judges quotes an ancient poem in which Joshua bids the sun "keep silence." He had routed the enemy in the dark night; a storm increased their confusion; the day was breaking; he looked eastward to the rising sun as it began to pierce the gloom; and he cried for another hour of dark storm that the victory might be complete: and God gave it him. But the author of Judges, having given the verses from the poem goes on with an explanation in prose; and taking the Hebrew word for "keep silence" in another sense, tells how the sun did not go down to its setting and how the long day was thus made longer.

The interpretation of the original Hebrew sometimes misleads ourselves. The "fell down flat" of the English Bible in the chapter about Jericho makes a picture in our minds which the Hebrew writer did not intend. He uses the same Hebrew word as is used of Asahel falling in his tracks (as we might express it) when Abner killed him. In the story of Jericho it depicts a wall collapsing into itself, which is how walls generally fall. The narrative seems to describe a solemn ceremony culminating at a set moment in a terrific assault: a great breach is made in the walls with the suddenness of a veritable miracle: the city is immediately carried. This is alluded to in Hebrews 11, but nothing is written there which such a reading of the miracle would not satisfy.

It would be a miracle ; not only as the whole divinely ordered campaign of Joshua would be miraculous to the mind of S. Augustine, but as the crossing of the Red Sea was miraculous though the miracle was helped (if the phrase may be allowed) by natural means, by a tempest. Again our English version, following the ancient Greek version, misleads us with its Red Sea. We think of deep water and a geographical sea. But the Hebrew has the sea of reeds, a piece of desert water which a violent tempest might shift.

That the old Hebrew writers recognized the storm as the means God used for the deliverance of His people from the Egyptians is plain in their references to this event ; notably in Psalm 77 : and most readers will have noticed that throughout the Old Testament the tempest or thunderstorm is the acknowledged mode in which God manifests His presence. That agrees with the verse about angels in Psalm 104 which is quoted in the epistle to the Hebrews :

> Who maketh His angels winds
> His ministers a flaming fire.

The margin of R.V. is here followed, for again the ambiguity of translation complicates things. One word in Hebrew means both wind and spirit, another both angel and messenger. R.V. margin is surely right, and it does not lower the dignity of angels but enhances the miracle of nature.

The idea persists in the New Testament. Thus S. Paul speaks of the law being ordained by angels, but in Exodus we only read of the thunders and lightnings at Sinai. Thus it seems to be indifferent in the New Testament whether the advent of the

Son of Man shall be with angels or with clouds. The Bible does not draw so arbitrary a line as we do between nature and miracle. Its antithesis is moral, nature and grace; and even that antithesis trembles into unison when it is touched by the wisdom of our Saviour.

But, you may object, all this is vague. Whatever S. Augustine thought, most men mean by miracle a wonder which cannot be explained in accordance with the ordinary course of nature: you may tone down this or that, but the Old Testament on the whole asserts that such thorough miracles happened: did they? Let us have a plain answer, yes or no.

Is that plain answer possible? Would it be of any value if it could be given? Do good men think of miracle just as a wonder which cannot be explained in accordance with the ordinary course of nature? If that really were what we mean by miracle would miracle have any place at all in the faith of our Lord Jesus Christ the Lord of glory? Giovanni Papini in his life of Christ [1] describes miracle more thoughtfully. "Miracle, he writes, is, for Jesus, the confluence of two good wills; the living contact that comes through the faith of him who acts and the faith of him who is acted upon. The collaboration of two forces. An embrace, a convergence of saving certainties." The confluence of two good wills, and then an act of salvation. That is as clear at Carmel as in Galilee: why seek more precise information? The historical detail, the logical observation of the external process does not matter.

And however painfully you seek it, you will not find. Certainly not in these miracles of the Old

[1] *Storia di Cristo.* Firenze, 1921.

Testament where the attestation is so far away in time, so meagre in extent. That is the real difficulty for the literalist about the Old Testament. There is no sense in saying either, The thing is miraculous and therefore cannot have happened; or, The thing is recorded in the Bible and therefore happened just as it is recorded. An act of salvation from the confluence of two good wills may very well have happened, as such acts do still happen. "Just as it is recorded": no, the record in the Bible is far too varied, picturesque poetical, as well as precise, historical, and sometimes also prosaically leaning to the marvellous, for any such generalization. If we appeal to Caesar, to Caesar we must go. If we weigh the unspiritual evidence for unspiritual miracles, we must confess that it falls short of convincing logical minds. But there is another way. For Old Testament Papini's sentence is almost too ethereal. Often in Old Testament the miracle is not the confluence of two good wills, but the will of God triumphing, in His magnificence of goodness, over the weak or wicked wills of His children. But there it is: there is God: the whole of the Old Testament is instinct with the fullness of God. If you do not care about the miracles of the Old Testament, you will not care for the Old Testament at all: it is not worth your while to consider this problem any further. But if you revere the Old Testament as the book that breathes God everywhere, then in the miracles you will hear the fathers of the heroic childhood of the world as they tell in large grave utterances how Jahveh made known His goodness, how the I am, the Eternal, broke through the veil of use and wont, and wrought saving certainties. When the Eternal breaks through you cannot describe what happens with the plainness that you use when you describe what we call facts. Here is the faith of the poet:[1]

> faith that forward sets
> But feeds the living fire,
> Faith that never frets
> For vagueness in the form.

And Ruskin has a few paragraphs worth attention on this matter in *The Queen of the Air* I §§ 45-47. He is talking of the faith of the Greeks in their myths. He says "The Greek creed was, of course, different in its character, as our own creed is, according to the class of persons who held it. The common people's was quite literal, simple and happy. . . . The creed of the upper classes was more refined and spiritual, but quite as honest, and even more forcible in its effect on the life. . . . Then, thirdly, the faith of the poets and artists was, necessarily, less definite, being continually modified by the involuntary action of their own fancies; and by the necessity of presenting, in clear verbal or material form, things of which they had no authoritative knowledge. Their faith was, in some respects, like Dante's or Milton's: firm in general conception, but not able to vouch for every detail in the forms they gave it: but they went considerably farther, even in that minor sincerity, than subsequent poets; and strove with all their might to be as near the truth as they could." The Old Testament records instances of the first two forms of faith about miracles. The writers themselves of the Old Testament wrote with the third kind of faith about miracles.

[1] George Meredith, *The Spirit of Earth in Autumn*.

CHAPTER 13

PREPARE TO MEET THY GOD, O ISRAEL

ON 20 August 1912 Ernest Arthur Edgehill died from an accident which befell him while working with his boys in camp. He was a brilliant scholar and promised to be more than brilliant as a theologian. A young priest, an ardent churchman, with a passion for righteousness and a great heart of love for the multitude —who could but be sorry that he had to leave good work just touched and so painfully interrupted? He left the manuscript, three parts finished, of his second book, a commentary on Amos. Dr. G. A. Cooke, with affection, completed it for publication, and now it holds a place all its own among the Westminster Commentaries.[1] There was much in Amos to attract Mr. Edgehill; the austere reality of religion in righteousness, the language with its unconventional strength, its rough-hewn excellence. And it is evident that for Mr. Edgehill Amos lived and spoke a real man. That keen feeling of the reality of Amos made him the more uncompromising in his recognition of the book as being an edition of the prophet's utterances, an edition arranged by the Jewish Church of later times, with post-exilic words of consolation added to the warnings of the ancient prophet. Mr. Edgehill will not compromise

[1] *The Book of Amos with Notes by Ernest Arthur Edgehill, B.D.* Edited with an Introduction by G. A. Cooke, D.D. Methuen, 1914.

"By the still waters" in the Plain of Jezreel.

about that, but neither will he wander into critical fancies; he does not need to obelize abundantly. The reality of it all keeps him honest sane clear-sighted. The outcome of his criticism is an Appendix of The words of Amos retranslated and rearranged : a translation in masculine English vividly representing the vivid Hebrew; and such a rearrangement as makes us hear again what was once cried aloud, now here now there,

H

by the living prophet drawn by the living God from village to village of Israel.

Let this digression be forgiven. It is a grateful memory of youth laid down for Christ and the brethren. It also helps us to realize that we are now passing a milestone in our present study. Hitherto we have depended on historians writing at some lapse of time after the events. Now in the great prophets we hear the very voices of men who were making history in action.

Elisha became prophet in Elijah's room. He sent and anointed Jehu; and Jehu overthrew the dynasty of Ahab, wrought with bloodshed a reformation of religion, and established his own family upon the throne. His great grandson, Jeroboam II, extended the sway and wealth of Israel farther than it had ever gone before. Israel was glad and proud. Never were such a good people they thought: the day of the LORD is at hand, righteousness and peace among men, and Israel their glorious centre.

Amos a small farmer watched this glorifying of Israel from among his flocks and orchards over the Judean border. He also saw that things below the surface were not so well; national character had degenerated: and he saw that there was an ominous cause of the prosperity. A military nation on the Tigris, the Assyrians, had become masters of the Babylonian empire which—like Rome in a later age—was ever the wonder and the spoil of hard-fighting barbarians. These Assyrians were pushing westwards, greedy for conquest. Already they had brought many people under their yoke. The Aramaeans of Damascus, Israel's chief rivals, already felt the coming shock, and therefore were leaving Israel to expand unmolested. But Israel too would feel it soon; and then, how would Israel bear the trial? Thus the Judean farmer-politician watched and reflected. And then the word of Jahveh came to him and turned him into a prophet. Will he nill he, his message was put upon him: he must watch indifferent no longer; he must go and warn his neighbours, tell them of this Assyrian who is Jahveh's instrument of judgement, rouse them from their fools' paradise, call them to repent.

The book opens with denunciations of the nations around Israel; Aram, Philistia, Tyre, Edom, Moab. These would be heard with complacency. Then the prophet turns to Judah, coming surprisingly near home to his audience. Then he lets loose Jahveh's wrath upon themselves. He

Panel from the Black Obelisk of Shalmaneser II.
(Representing the submission of Jehu, 842 B.C.)

repeats the same refrain, but now it is, "Thus saith the LORD: For three transgressions of Israel, yea, for four, I will not turn away the punishment thereof; because they have sold the righteous for silver, and the needy for a pair of shoes: that pant after the dust of the earth on the head of the poor, and turn aside the way of the meek: and a man and his father will go unto the same maid, to profane My holy Name: and they lay themselves down beside every altar upon clothes taken in pledge, and in the house of their God they drink the wine of such as have been fined." It was no doubt a dramatic effect. But it was more. The sins of all these nations were one; frightfulness in war; the sin of a low civilization and a bad religion. To pass from them to Israel was to pass to the sins of a high civilization and a good religion: Moses and the law, Elijah at Carmel and in Naboth's vineyard, Jehu's reformation in spite of its fierceness; all this had done something; Israel was right in thinking herself Jahveh's chosen people, with a divine destiny. But high civilization and a good religion are apt for corruptions of their own, and these corruptions were spoiling Israel's destiny. Prosperity had brought the feud of rich and poor, injustice: wealth had brought luxury, drunkenness, sexual vice: religion had become ritual divorced from practice. Amos bids them look back upon their past, Jahveh's deliverances and chastisements, and how hitherto these have been in vain; the chosen people have a Lord GOD of immense goodness but history does not show them responsive. Listen to Mr. Edgehill on 2. 10 ff. "Also I brought you up out of the land of Egypt . . .":

> The deliverance from Egypt was that to which Israel's greatest teachers looked back as to the beginning of the nation and of the

national religion. Not in the courts of the temple with its unhallowed union of wickedness and worship could true religion flourish ; but on the broad fields of a nation's history where the ploughers had ploughed and made long furrows, where also God had with His own hand cast the golden grain and given the increase of it. There men can learn best to know God and His purposes.

Then Amos bids them look at the present. They long for the day of the LORD : Thy kingdom come is their prayer. And with that prayer there is injustice, vice, empty ritual : "Is not Jahveh's day darkness and not light ? Yea, deep darkness, and no brightness therein ?" They say, Upon us hath Jahveh set His eyes ; and Amos answers in Jahveh's name, Behold, I will set mine eyes upon them for evil and not for good. They hold feasts and solemn assemblies and offer sacrifices and peace offerings of fatlings. And Jahveh answers :

> Remove from Me the noise of thy songs ;
> The melody of thy lyres I will not hear
> But let justice roll down as the waters,
> And righteousness as an ever-flowing stream.

And then he points to the future, the coming of the Assyrian, the horrible judgement, the last chance in this eleventh hour :

> Thus saith Jahveh unto the house of Israel :
> Seek Me, if ye would live ;
> But seek not Bethel.
> And Gilgal ye shall not enter :
> For Gilgal shall surely go into exile ;
> And Bethel shall come to trouble.
> Because I will do this unto thee,
> Prepare to meet thy God, O Israel.

Prepare to meet thy God Who still will save thee, Who alone is God to save. Amos brought no message of fate, but a strong crying from a most merciful Judge for His people's repentance. It became nevertheless more and more clear that the divine yearning would be repulsed. Amos tells the stiff-necked people of vision after vision which he has seen, each vision bringing ruin nearer. At last he spoke so plainly that the royal chaplain judged his words treasonable, and bade him go home and draw his tithe like other country parsons, and meddle not with governments. Then Amos turned upon him, and gave him to understand that he was no professional prophet of that kind; that he spoke because he must; that the word was direct from the LORD and would not fail. And he drives the warning home :

> And now hear thou the word of Jahveh ;
> Thou sayest,
> Thou shalt not prophesy against Israel ;
> Thou shalt not drop thy word against the house of Isaac
> Therefore thus
> Jahveh saith,
> Thy wife in the city shall be ravished,
> Thy sons and thy daughters by the sword shall fall
> Thy land by lot shall be divided,
> And thou in a land unclean shalt die.

Thus indeed it used to happen when the Assyrians took a city. But "what a pit is digged for sin ; God's forgiveness, man's forgetfulness." The day would come when all these would be "old unhappy far-off things, and battles long ago." When S. Stephen defended the faith before the Sanhedrin he quoted Amos 5. 27 : "I will send you captive into exile beyond Babylon" instead of "beyond Damascus." The Babylonian exile had ousted the memory of the agony of Samaria. When

A BAS-RELIEF OF THE SERIES WHICH WAS MADE TO COMMEMORATE THE EXPEDITIONS OF TIGLATH PILESER III, THE "PUL" OF 2 KINGS XV. 9, AND SET UP IN THE CENTRAL BUILDING OF NIMRÛD.

(The scene represents the evacuation of a city and the counting of the spoil.)

the words of Amos were collected and edited, the awful sternness and final hopelessness of his message were no longer salutary in their bareness to the imperfect but penitent Jewish Church; and they rounded off the reading with the lovely hymn of hope—a "Jerusalem the golden"—which we read still as the conclusion of the book.

But such a hymn was not for Amos and his times. He was straining every nerve to bring a stubborn nation to their knees. Awful ruin was at their gate. Jahveh was pleading in a terrible present hour—not the hour for lovely dreams. In divers manners and in divers parts these prophets brought each his own contribution to the creed of Israel. Amos' contribution was not the post-exilic hope. But before we formulate that contribution which he did make, we must once more look for a moment at his book.

It opens with judgements on the nations, and so it all but closes. I Who brought thee from Egypt, also brought the Philistines from Caphtor, says Jahveh. Jahveh is the ruler and judge of all the nations, not of Israel alone. That goes beyond Elijah, who had been content to establish the more elementary truth that in Israel Jahveh was the only God. But along this line the great prophets move continuously till at last in the Comfort ye prophecy—the hymn of monotheism as it has been called—we reach the Nicene faith itself in One God the Father almighty, maker of heaven and earth, and of all things visible and invisible. In the Comfort ye that faith is iterated with large illustration in elaborate harmonies. In three passages of this book of Amos we read what seems a first sketch of that full theology, 4. 13, 5. 8 f., 9. 5 f. That indeed would be very natural. Full revelation like finished science is regularly anticipated by flashes of intuition, vernal lights

> before the daisy grows a common flower,
> Before the sun has power
> To scorch the world up in his noontide hour.

But however that may be, enough is clear for us to set out this article as Amos' in Israel's growing creed :— Jahveh, creator and judge of all mankind, will judge his own people Israel most straitly.

CHAPTER 14

THE LOVING-KINDNESS OF JAHVEH

HOSEA followed on the heels of Amos. Amos came from Judah with a stern message to Israel which he delivered and returned home. Hosea's home was Israel, the northerners were his brothers; he brought them the tenderness of passionate affection, and he prophesied a pleading prophecy till the end came and Samaria fell and Israel was blotted out.

The first verse of chapter 3 is an epitome of Israel's temper and Hosea's faith and education as a prophet:

> And the LORD said unto me, Go yet, love a woman beloved of her friend and an adulteress, even as the LORD loveth the children of Israel though they turn to other gods, and love cakes of raisins.

It is still merry Israel with plenty of cakes and ale when Hosea begins to prophesy: but it will be "Samaria shall bear her guilt: they shall fall by the sword; their infants shall be dashed in pieces, and their women with child shall be ripped up," before he ends.

And yet that is not his very last word. For he is the prophet of Jahveh's love, of the loving-kindness of the LORD; and he cannot finally believe that so divine a love will be in vain. He goes on to the last:

> O Israel, return unto the LORD thy God; for thou hast fallen by thine iniquity Take with you words, and return unto the LORD ... for in Thee the fatherless findeth mercy.

And he has learned to believe that God is love by

106 THE LOVING-KINDNESS OF JAHVEH

the saddest private lesson. In that land of joy his wife has gone after lovers. Once and twice she was unfaithful. He bought her back from slavery. He had to keep her prisoner in his own house, so wanderingly lewd had she grown. And yet he loved her still. And as to Amos in the tramp of Assyrian legions, so to Hosea in the sorrow that wrecked his married life, the word of the LORD came. If he loved more the less he was beloved, certainly Jahveh still loves and will love Israel however obstinate Israel is against Him. That is *chesed*,

CAPTURE OF A CITY BY THE ASSYRIANS.

pietas, the natural affection which binds a family together. The article which Hosea added to Israel's creed was: Jahveh loves His people with a love like a husband's or a father's, invincible.

Amos was a moralist, austere. He spoke or wrote in an accordant noble style; plain logical strong terse; he said what he had to say and let it alone. Hosea is a theologian, a thinker about God. He is tender, with profound emotion. He speaks by heart more than head. His logic is the logic of contraries: Jahveh loves Israel so constantly, Israel cannot but repent; Israel will not repent, ruin must ensue. And thus the moods alternate till at last fact cuts feeling short; Samaria was sacked and for aught we know Hosea perished with his paradox unresolved.

These conflicting moods, and the passionate style mingling ejaculation and half-expressions with sustained pleading, render the argument difficult to follow. Much of the difficulty has been laid to the account of the post-exilic editors, who are thought to have softened or corrected the antique "hewing by the prophet" (6. 5) by insertions in another spirit. The last two verses of the first chapter seem indeed an example of such treatment, and this insertion is so awkward that it prepares us to find others. But perhaps there are not many after all. In Jahveh's awful shout of doom in 13. 14 (quoted by S. Paul in 1 Corinthians 15 in an opposite exultant sense, as the good news of Christ's resurrection allows) the difficulty in the first two clauses is removed by making these into questions like the other two. And the last chapter of all (14) is not like the last chapter in Amos, but one of Hosea's own hopeful pieces, placed at the end by the editors for the same reason as made the editor of Mr. Hardy's selected poems in the *Golden Treasury* conclude with the chorus of the Pities from *The Dynasts*. Of course the last verse of all is the editor's own reflection : for all his pains he knows he has given us a difficult book : compare a like reflection at the end of Ecclesiastes.

Yet, difficult though it may be in detail, the drift of Hosea is plain enough. His message is the invincible love of Jahveh. Sometimes he is sure this love must conquer : Israel will repent : the judgement will be stayed. Sometimes he sees too clearly that Israel is not repenting, and that the Assyrians are certain to destroy Samaria. We hear, as we listen to him, the intrigues going on : one wretched king arising after another ; one getting Assyria to back him and selling the nation's freedom to those barbarous imperialists ; another seeking help from Egypt and trying to revolt from the allegiance thus given to Assyria ; Assyria coming to punish the rebellious tributary ; the siege long drawn out but the result not to be doubted as it draws nearer and nearer.

And as we read we enter more and more into the mind of Hosea. We become aware that this is a book of theology. Whom we love or are loved by, we know. To know God is eternal life for Hosea, as for S. John. Jahveh's people are perishing, he says, for lack of knowledge. Amos' robust morality is celebrated for all time in the couplet " Let judgement roll down as waters, and righteousness as a mighty stream." Hosea's theology culminates in the beautiful sixth chapter :

> Come, and let us return unto the LORD : for He hath torn, and He will heal us ; He hath smitten, and He will bind us up. After two days will He revive us · on the third day He will raise us up,

and we shall live before Him. And let us know, let us follow on to know the LORD; His going forth is sure as the morning: and He shall come unto us as the rain, as the latter rain that watereth the earth.

This is beautiful and the beauty is partly due to Hosea's exquisite sense of language. No prophetic book is more rich than his in classic phrases: It shall be, like people, like priest; The wind hath wrapped her up in its wings; Your goodness is as a morning cloud, and as the dew that goeth early away; Ephraim is a cake not turned; Break up your fallow ground; Ye have plowed wickedness, ye have reaped iniquity; When Israel was a child, then I loved him, and called My son out of Egypt; I drew them with cords of a man, with bands of love. There is a touch of academic gentleness about Hosea. He is a scholar, has read history. Amos refers in general terms to the redemption from Egypt; Hosea knows the stories of the patriarchs. He was himself to be a favourite author with another scholar prophet, very

ASSYRIAN BULL.

like in temperament to himself, and who did solve the problem that Hosea left a paradox of love invincible and consequence inexorable ; this was Jeremiah.

One point more must be noticed. Amos was almost contemptuous of ritual : not rites and ceremonies, hymns and worship, but righteous conduct matters. Whether the worship be with or without symbols, or what the symbols are, he was little interested to discuss. But Hosea could not leave it so. He keeps coming back to the shame of calf-worship. Go to the British Museum and look at the winged, monstrous Assyrian bulls, and you will understand his disgust. For Hosea Jahveh was a loving father, religion was to know Him as a son knows a dear father. How could Jahveh, that pure Spirit, be worshipped under the symbol of a lusty bull?

CHAPTER 15

THE HOLY ONE OF ISRAEL

I

SAMARIA was taken by Sargon in 712 B C. The people were carried away. The kingdom of north Israel disappears from history. Meanwhile the Judeans had been ruled in comparative quiet and obscurity under chiefs of the uninterrupted line of David, sometimes in a kind of vassalage to their powerful northern neighbours; preserving a certain simplicity in manners and religion; not very wealthy, not given to change. The book of Ruth belongs to the latest division of the Hebrew Bible. Like the Song of Songs it is one of the five Rolls, or lections for festivals. Like the Song it is a poetic piece, an idyll for a harvest festival, and the picture it presents of early Judah is poetic and ideal. Nevertheless it may not be far from fact and the contrast of its quiet beauty with the violence of Judges and the stirring politics of Samuel, which since the Septuagint have stood on either side of it, corresponds with the general relationship of Judah to the rest of Israel. And now that home-ruled, gradual maturing was to burst into rich fruit. Ephraim has perished : a more fateful kingdom takes its place. Amos and Hosea have been heralds of a far greater prophet, Isaiah son of Amoz of Jerusalem.

The book in which his prophecies are enshrined is the glory of the Jewish Church's scholarship. It is a Life and Times of Isaiah of Jerusalem; his Prophecies and Statesmanship: his Theology and its influence. All that could be recovered of his own words, records of his actions, of the kings he served, of the war with Assyria which was the great historic event of his day, has been collected. Prophecies of the exilic period (which he foresaw) and of later crises which issued from that revolution in Israel's career; modern prophetic pieces in the latest apocalyptic style; hymns of prophetic exultation and hope; all these developments of

ASSYRIAN WARRIORS.

the deepened enlarged faith, the far-reaching impulse to prophecy, which this predominant prophet inaugurated, have been incorporated in The Book of Isaiah. And all has been arranged in a masterly way; with a general plan, simple and easy to follow and remember; suitable for liturgic use; capable of gathering many branching growths under the unity of one idea. The headings to the chapters in the English Authorized Version are an excellent guide to this plan and purpose. They show what the Messianic prophecy of the Old Testament really is; not a series of vaticinations to be concluded by particulars in the history of our Lord and His apostles, but an ever-progressing Spirit, unfolding the new from the old; nothing separate and finished, but Christ and His Church taking form from ancient days as the Holy One of Israel continuously saves, corrects, gladdens His people, brings the nations nearer, and fashions time into accordance with the eternal pattern.

Azariah or Uzziah, king of Judah, overlapped Jeroboam II in Israel. Isaiah's call to prophecy came in the year Uzziah died. Thus the first period of Isaiah's prophetic ministry coincided with the decline and fall of Samaria. Looking now at the book of Isaiah we find that chapters 1 to 5 are a prelude, showing the stirring of Isaiah's conscience before his call. In 6 his call is recorded and from 6 to 12 we have his prophecies during the years that Samaria still stands. From 13 to 27 is the burden of the nations; prophecies belonging to the restless days of intrigue when the nations around Judah were trying to throw off the yoke of Assyria; Sargon the conqueror of Samaria having died and Sennacherib being not yet firm upon his throne. From 27 to 35 are prophecies belonging to the years when, Hezekiah having rebelled, Sennacherib invaded Judah, but was compelled to depart without taking Jerusalem. Then comes a piece of historical prose, partly in the same words as the narrative in Kings (36 and 37) in which this deliverance is recorded. Two chapters follow telling of an illness and recovery of Hezekiah, and of an embassy which came to him from Merodach Baladan, king of Babylon, a rebellious vassal of Sennacherib. This embassy is perhaps out of its place in

ASSYRIAN ARCHERS ATTACKING A FORTIFIED CITY.

the story, being introduced here for the sake of Isaiah's foreboding rebuke :

> Then said Isaiah to Hezekiah, Hear the word of the LORD of hosts.
>
> Behold, the days come, that all that is in thine house, and that which thy fathers have laid up in store until this day, shall be carried to Babylon nothing shall be left, saith the LORD And of thy sons which shall issue from thee, which thou shalt beget, shall they take away ; and they shall be eunuchs in the palace of the king of Babylon
>
> Then said Hezekiah unto Isaiah, Good is the word of the LORD which thou hast spoken He said moreover, For there shall be peace and truth in my days.

These verses prepare for the break of more than a century between chapters 39 and 40. Assyria has failed and fallen. The Chaldeans are now kings in Babylon and masters of the eastern world. Judah has rebelled against these new imperial lords and has been destroyed by them. The monarchy has gone, and the temple, and all freedom. The Judeans have been exiles in Babylonia for fifty years. Cyrus the Persian is on his victorious march, and will soon reach the Chaldeans. And now, in chapter 40, a second Isaiah opens his Te Deum of faith and praise towards the one and only God, his encouragement to the captives :

> Comfort ye, comfort ye My people, saith your God. Speak ye comfortably to Jerusalem, and cry unto her that her warfare is accomplished, that her iniquity is pardoned , that she hath received of the LORD's hand double for all her sins

You are going home, promises this prophet of comfort ; home to a new, most holy life. To his glorious poem we shall return in a later chapter. It is linked in many doctrines with the early doctrine of Isaiah, for instance in this teaching of forgiveness. But it does not come into the story of Isaiah's active ministry, into those days when Assyria was the terrible fact of politics, and the interplay of revelation and politics was producing the immediate prophecies of Isaiah. For the present all our concern is with chapters 1 to 39.

The first chapter of all with its dated title is a preface. Like prefaces in general it stands at the beginning but is a retrospect from the end. It gives a picture of Judah as Judah was left exhausted by invasion, and of the prophet's mind after all the anxiety of experience. Then we go back to his early years. First to his pride in great Jerusalem, so prosperous in the spacious days of Uzziah, so rich in happy holy promise to the world. Then the young enthusiast looks beneath the surface. He sees a less fair sight; the same corruptions, injustice vice and hollow worship, as Amos saw in Samaria. Then he sees, like Amos, that the day of the Lord he hoped for would be a day of humbled pride and dreadful doom. But finally, out of the furnace a new Jerusalem will rise, not grand but really beautiful in holiness, when the Lord shall have washed away the filth and purged the blood by the blast of judgement and of burning. This prelude ends with "a song of My Beloved touching His vineyard," yet cannot quite end thus : Isaiah's heart is not at rest, and he cries his Woes again.

Rest was to come, the peace not of this world which makes prophets indomitable. In chapter 6 he tells how Jahveh called him in the temple to his task. The burning seraphs were there with wings of flame and Holy Holy Holy on their lips. Isaiah, like S. Paul, died and rose to a new life not his own. His lips, his character, were purged with fire. He went forth to bring Jahveh's people through a like fiery mortal trial ; life through death, there was no easier way for them or him. Such was the intensity of a prophet's call, a prophet's work. If his recorded words ever sound too sublime, his vision too far-reaching for modern explanation, we need not be incredulous. No prophet is like other men. The Holy One of Israel really lives and really speaks in His prophets, and none of those prophets is quite so great as Isaiah.

The work soon began. Israel and Damascus were in league against Assyria. They demanded Judah's aid, threatening war if Judah refused. Ahaz the Judean king was frightened. In spite of Isaiah's message of divine command he called Assyria to protect him, thereby selling freedom, entering into vassalage. Isaiah would have had him keep out of the turmoil altogether. Israel and Damascus could do no harm: Assyria would draw their teeth anyhow. Now shame and suffering will be the consequences of Ahaz' base surrender. Isaiah with grim enigmatic language prophesies woe. But he has learned the secret of the divine purpose. It is "God with us" all the way. Out of the woe will spring the real good: "there shall be no gloom to her that was in anguish." And he sees the reign of righteousness, the wonderful divine king, father of the new age, firm on his eternal throne when the short-lived Assyrian tyranny shall have accomplished the purpose of Jahveh. "For unto us a child is born." Did Isaiah utter that Christmas oracle? Many reasonably critical difficulties may certainly be raised, but none are irresistible. Read chapter 9 directly after chapter 6 and consider whether such a prophecy may not well follow such a call.

Chapter 11 is rather different. In later times, when the older prophecy had ceased, a new kind arose of which

Daniel is a type. It is a dream rather than a prophecy, a dream of the end of the world, of the kingdom of heaven rather than of the kingdoms of this world made holy to the LORD. Pieces of such Apocalypse or Revelation are undoubtedly to be recognized in our books of the prophets. In Isaiah each division of the collected volume is concluded by such a piece, itself rounded off by a hymn. Chapter 11 looks like the apocalyptic close of the first division of Isaiah's prophecies, and chapter 12 is the hymn. "The peaceable kingdom of the branch out of the root of Jesse. The restauration of Israel, and vocation of the Gentiles. A joyful thanksgiving of the faithful for the mercies of God": these headings in our Authorized Version fit well with such a view of the arrangement of the book.

SENNACHERIB.

Now began the harder part of the prophet's work. Ahaz had taken his pusillanimous step, and left to his son Hezekiah a throne in vassalage to Assyria. Isaiah would have the allegiance thus promised honestly observed. But the Judeans were a high-spirited people, not inclined to remain in subservience to a suzerain.

The Assyrian king died. His successor Sennacherib came to a troubled throne. The subject states bestirred themselves for freedom. What would Hezekiah do? His neighbours were intriguing all round him, and trying to get him to join their combinations. Egypt, the rival empire, was making the most of all this restlessness for her own ends, promising support, sending embassies; not to be trusted, said Isaiah, Giant-sit-still, a reed which will run into the hand of him who leans upon it.

These movements are vividly pictured in the second division of Isaiah's prophecies. The various nations are characterized in sharp vigorous touches. Sometimes perhaps reflections from a later age are mingled with Isaiah's ancient sentences. Some of these suspected passages may after all be Isaiah's own strange foresight or insight. He is dreaming of a moral future, of Christ's kingdom and an "access that shall grow unto the Church." Hence a rich mystery which satisfies our conscience while it baffles our critical faculty. The section ends with an unmistakably late apocalyptic piece (26 and 27). No one who reads it in the original Hebrew can doubt that. Few will dispute it who have paid attention to the progress of thought that runs through the Old Testament. Our Authorized Version again seems unconsciously to indicate this by the heading to 27, "The care of God over His vineyard. The church of Jews and Gentiles." The seventeenth century scholars who penned that heading felt no incongruity. The Jewish rabbis who inserted the apocalyptic piece did not wish incongruity to be felt. And there is none. This apocalypse, beginning "Behold, the LORD maketh the earth empty, and maketh it waste, and turneth it upside down, and scattereth abroad the inhabitants thereof," and drawing to its close with "Come my people, enter thou into thy chambers, and shut thy doors about thee: hide thyself as it were a little moment, until the indignation be overpast," is a fit development of the burden of the restless nations which precedes it. The propriety of all this interweaving of new with old, this completion of Isaiah's impulse in later theology, is just what makes this bold abundant book the greatest book of the Old Testament.

And these apocalyptic chapters link the second division with the third so admirably. "Behold the LORD maketh the earth empty..." Dwellers in the Cambridge fens have felt a moment like that on days when the sky gathers ominous fantastic heaps of clouds, and the water in the lode turns grey, and a sudden wind blows edges to the solitary trees, and all the large abstract country seems suddenly empty of event—the moment before the storm bursts. That is the moment we have reached in Judah's history. Hezekiah was lured into the rebellion. The Assyrian king soon recovered from his initial embarrassments. He gathered an army and moved westwards, reducing his revolted subjects one by one with horrid reprisals. And Isaiah watched and waited for the turn of Judah. Judah's turn would certainly come. The Assyrian was the staff in the hand of Jahveh. The chastisement was the very means He had revealed to His prophet for recovering His people from their degeneracy. But how far must the chastisement go? How small the remnant that would be left? Judah is obstinate as ever, self-indulgent, trusting in human policy, still (it seemed) with no sort of belief in Jahveh as the living God Who could shape the destinies of nations, and destroy or save.

ISAIAH

Yet as we read we become conscious of a change, a change as it were of atmosphere. As one who has followed the sea all his life, knows when the crisis of the gale is approaching, or the veteran commander realizes that in a few moments the battle will be decided, so Isaiah seems at a certain point to expect repentance and deliverance. We see no sign, as we read, but we see that he has seen it. He begins almost to mock the Assyrian; who still advances, conquering the people as he comes. But Isaiah now all but exults in this clearing of the board. At last all will be gone but the Assyrian and Jerusalem only. Then on the sacred soil of Judah Jahveh will strike in. The Assyrian will have completed his permitted task. Israel will be saved, and he will be broken.

BAKED CLAY CYLINDER OF SENNACHERIB, KING OF ASSYRIA.
Inscribed with an account of his invasion of Palestine and the siege of Jerusalem in the reign of Hezekiah.

So it turned out. Sennacherib invaded and laid waste Judah. He shut up Hezekiah in Jerusalem like a bird in a cage; took tribute from him; and yet, retired. Then he sent back a letter with further, intolerable demands. Hezekiah took the letter to the temple, and (like a child) spread it out for Jahveh to read. He confessed himself at the end of all his resources. He just put himself into the hand of God. A poor, forced repentance perhaps, but it was repentance such as Isaiah had been waiting for. And at once Isaiah sent unto Hezekiah saying,

> Thus saith the LORD, the God of Israel, Whereas thou hast prayed to Me against Sennacherib, king of Assyria, this is the word which the LORD hath spoken concerning him The virgin daughter of Zion hath despised thee and laughed thee to scorn; the daughter of Jerusalem hath shaken her head at thee. Whom hast thou reproached and blasphemed? and against whom hast thou exalted thy voice and lifted up thine eyes on high? even against the Holy One of Israel. I know thy sitting down, and thy going out, and thy coming in, and thy raging against Me. Because of thy raging against Me, and for that thine arrogancy is come up into Mine ears, therefore will I put My hook in thy nose, and My bridle in thy lips, and I will turn thee back by the way which thou camest . .
> Thus saith the LORD concerning the king of Assyria, He shall not come unto this city, nor shoot an arrow there, neither shall he come before it with shield, nor cast a mount against it. By the way that he came, by the same shall he return, and he shall not come unto this city, saith the LORD. For I will defend this city to save it, for Mine own sake, and for My servant David's sake

II

In that magnificent oration Isaiah entitles Jahveh The Holy One of Israel. The same epithet was heard in the seraphic hymn, Holy, holy, holy, is the LORD of hosts. The word in Hebrew signifies apart, separate. Of God, it implies what we mean by transcendent, and this idea exalts the faith of Isaiah above all his predecessors. Jahveh is more, and more wonderful for him: his reverence is more profound. It was much that Hosea should think of Jahveh as loving like a father, but when we remember that he oftener thinks of this love as like a husband's, we perceive that Hosea's 'father' is not quite our Lord's 'our Father which art in heaven.' Hosea is still thinking of God in the likeness of man; as a child might beautifully think. "Do men ever cease to be children? Yes—at all events it is better to suppose so."[1]

So too S. Paul thought, and it is just this growing into the manhood of prophecy that we see in Isaiah. His house of faith has many mansions and it is not so easy as with Amos or Hosea to sum up in a sentence his particular contribution to Israel's creed. Yet this might be done even more shortly. He believed Jahveh to be "very God."

So we find him declaring the presence of Jahveh, as the living God, in politics. Elijah and Elisha had brought about revolutions in the name of Jahveh, and Hosea knew that this had been but an imperfect interpretation of Jahveh's will. Amos and Hosea themselves hardly considered politics, as they hardly considered ritual, at all. The affairs of Israel were hopeless. New life was not to come by statesmanship. But Isaiah's outlook is larger. He has the faith which goes farther than the mystic, which is thought out, disciplined, brought into practical obedience and effect: larger deeper and more wholly true, for he knows God is in the midst of duty and affairs, the more really immanent (as always) in being acknowledged transcendent. Isaiah the prophet was also a statesman, advising kings, raising politics from expediency to courageous trust in the

[1] Henri Poincaré in Charles Nordman's *Einstein and the Universe*, English translation, p. 100. Fisher Unwin, 1922.

living God. Shape policy to the will of God, he said, and fear not what men say or do.

That is difficult. A man may sometimes be found who will transform his private conduct according to the Sermon on the Mount, but to rule a nation and to deal with foreign nations by such a pattern would be so complicated a venture that it is generally refused as not even right to attempt. To a prophet, called, inspired, like Isaiah it seems the only wise way. He really believes in God as living. He is convinced that holiness alone is the welfare of a nation. He has himself died to self, and has been utterly freed from the coil of the use and wont, the inherited corruptions of civilization, and he trusts God's guidance in details as well as generalities. The call of a prophet really was death to self, life in the living God. His will was lost and found in God. His way was plain. He feared nothing. All was simplified. Isaiah possessed that gift of grace in a peculiarly abundant measure. From the impulse of simplicity, he saw how to deal with the complication of facts, and win through to more perfect simplicity. His patience rested on his consciousness of God's eternity. The business of the world was transformed into eternal service. God's transcendence revealed to him not two worlds but one, and that all spiritual.

It may be objected : No, you are reading more into Isaiah than was possible even to him, at that early stage of history. You are interpreting things Isaiah of Jerusalem said by the light of the Comfort ye prophecy which has been bound up with his prophecies. But it is not so. The Comfort ye prophecy is indeed a natural continuation of Isaiah ; the book which we call Isaiah is a unity. But Isaiah himself stands at his own proper place in the continuous movement of revelation. He is the Dante of the Old Testament. He sums up what may be called the mediaeval period in Israel's life and faith. With Jeremiah and Deuteronomy another period is entered. After the exile we find thought still further thought out and developed. Isaiah still works with symbols, and speaks a language of vigorous brevity. Theology is still an art rather than a philosophy; poetry has not yet hardened into prose. It is the free picturesque period of what is termed in critical treatment of the Old Testament J E. Isaiah is so great just because he moves boldly within limitations at which he does not fret. To Jeremiah the temple and all outward rites will be formalities which hinder heart religion and present a painful problem. That problem will be solved for him by the violent break with externalities which the fall of Jerusalem caused. Isaiah knew too well what temple-treading (as he called it) was, the vanities of worship in his day. But he could meet these with his burning awe towards the living God, the Holy One of Israel, whose holy dwelling-place he never doubted the temple to be. And for him that earlier problem of worship was solved by the Assyrian tyranny which humbled Hezekiah into sincerity, and by the deliverance in which Jahveh vindicated the sanctity of His ancient shrine.

The language, the oratory of Isaiah illustrate his theological standpoint. It is the language of a supreme artist. It is more than the absolutely natural strength of Amos. Isaiah cares for how he speaks. He is forcible, can be rough-hewn in style, will now and again shock his hearers into serious attention with a phrase of antique coarseness, calling a spade a spade. But he rises into grandeurs and sustains his height on eagle wings. He knows the joy of noble words : and he knows the artist's secret, that the half is more than the whole : a pregnant phrase, a sacramental picture, needs not to be explained in full : the very God is more deeply adored in figurative sincerities than in careful scrupulous exactitudes. Jahveh is still Jahveh to Isaiah, but Jahveh of Hosts, whose glory is the fullness of all things visible and invisible, the Holy One of Israel in whom " the meek increase their joy and the poor among men rejoice."

The tenderness of that verse (29. 19) is also a note of Isaiah. It too enters into the more complex harmonies of the exilic sequel :

> For thus saith the high and lofty One that inhabiteth Eternity, whose name is Holy I dwell in the high and holy place, with him also that is of a contrite and humble spirit, to revive the spirit of the humble, and to revive the heart of the contrite ones.—57. 15.

Among the early prophecies, Isaiah's own, this tenderness is especially felt in chapter 33. Jerusalem has been delivered from the peril. Isaiah is thankful, but with a thankfulness of prayer, the thankfulness of a tired man, resting and looking back on the destruction he has escaped, yet aware that trouble is not over yet. Jerusalem is safe ; but Judah has been ravaged ; only a remnant indeed survives ; all have been brought very low. "O LORD be gracious unto us ; we have waited for Thee : be Thou their arm every morning, our salvation also in the time of trouble." And so through prayer he rises to fresh hope, a quiet far-reaching hope. But how far-reaching ? Can we believe the vision really shows what we see in it ? The book of Isaiah is punctuated by visions of a most glorious future, of a kingdom, of a king that is to be. After all that skilled and patient critics have done for us—and indeed they have increased the influence of Isaiah upon our consciences a hundredfold—we seem ungrateful if we complain that they have brought doubt upon almost all these great visionary chapters ; are they Isaiah's, or later theology springing from Isaiah ? This is no place to discuss the question. And need the question be confidently answered ? Once allow that the book of Isaiah is one whole ; then it will be of interest to take by themselves those passages which tell the story of Isaiah Jerusalem and the Assyrians, and of what Isaiah said and did with immediate reference to the national crisis : but it is not so necessary to distinguish what Isaiah may have said with reference to a far-off future from what others were led, by virtue of his teaching, to add to his boldly outlined sketch.[1] Indeed there is almost advantage in such vagueness. Few would assign the prophecy about the martyred Servant of the LORD (53) to Isaiah's own lips or pen. But it would spoil the series of these kingdom-visions if they were not completed by that martyrdom and its issue. In the first part of the book the notable chapters are 7 (Immanuel) 9 (the Christmas Child) 11 (the sevenfold Spirit) 32 and 33. All these have been explained

---

[1] The children of light may learn wisdom from the children of the world, and will forgive a quotation from Scott's *Pirate* which surely displays much critical sagacity —"I just ca'ed him the Captain, replied Bryce Snailsfoot , for I make it a rule never to ask questions of them I deal with in the way of trade ; for there is many an honest captain, begging your pardon Captain Cleveland, that does not care to have his name tacked to his title , and as lang as we ken what bargains we are making, what signifies it wha we are making them wi', ye ken ?" "Bryce Snailsfoot is a cautious man," said the Udaller laughing , "he knows a fool may ask more questions than a wise man cares to answer."

as referring to the happy reign of Hezekiah or his successor when the judgement shall be over and Judah, free from Assyria and purged by fiery trial, shall dwell in peace and holiness. But it is impossible to rest satisfied with such explanations. The Child in 7 and 9 is mysterious and glorious : the King in 32 and 33 is no ordinary king of mortal line. Hence a later school of critics, feeling this mystery, have given a full meaning (Messianic as we say) to the passages, but have supposed they must be products of post-exilic faith, for indeed there was an intense expectation of that kind in one party of the later Jewish Church. But others, again, who have extended the study of "apocalyptic" religion and mythology over a wider field than the Hebraic and back through long tracts of time, have found this hope of a redeeming hero for sinful and suffering mankind implanted in the almost primeval mind of men, and have shown that such language as these prophecies present might be less astonishing to Judeans in Isaiah's period than had been supposed. Of course it is far purer deeper language than the parallels these scholars bring from early paganism. And of course the most astonishing thing about it is the likeness it bears to the Gospel of our Lord Jesus Christ. But yet again ; students of Hebrew prophecy have revived our perception of the intensity of these prophets' calls.[1] Their

[1] See especially *The People of God*, vol 1, Israel, by H. F. Hamilton (Frowde, 1912), or the smaller version of this book which Dr. Hamilton published in 1915 (Longmans) with the title *Discovery and Revelation*. The best general introduction to the Prophets from Samuel to Jeremiah is still Robertson Smith's *Prophets of Israel*, a noble book which made the prophets live again to a generation growing weary of them. But to turn from the *Prophets of Israel* to Dr Hamilton's chapters on the prophets is also a revival and conversion.

passage (like S. Paul's) through death to life; their utter loss of self and finding of God; their unique experience raising mind and will to heights far above other men; all this is a warning against prejudice as to what it is likely the divine Spirit might or might not utter through them. Prophecy is indeed the eminent example of what the Old Testament proclaims throughout, the unexpectedness of the operation of God Who really lives.

This does not mean that we should not read critically, that is with attention, with an open mind, comparing one writing with another, weighing the authority of each. One reason for supposing that Isaiah himself had something to do with these Messianic chapters is the development which may be observed in them, such a development as might befit the progress of his ministry. The Immanuel prophecy (7) springs forth as an indignant response to Ahaz' folly and subterfuge. It shows the good that might have been, the evil that now must be; and then, as with a recollection of the recent call, the new purified hope emerges, with difficulty, not clearly. In chapter 9 there is the same progression from foreboding to new hope; but the hope comes sudden and distinct, in gorgeous picture-language. In chapter 11 the picture is less clear but the sense is more profound. Not as a glorified king like one of David's sons, but as a person whose features are shadowly discerned, while the inward spirit moulds his character and flows forth through him pervading and civilizing all creation, is this "branch of Jesse" delineated. Then in 32 and 33 the present and the future are mingled. The scene is set in Judah just freed from the army of occupation, worn and weary. The king is there, very

K

THE SEA OF GALILEE.

personal again but in a quieter way. And as his solitary figure defines itself against this background, it at once begins to detach itself and recede from nearness to vague distance : and this dissolving impression is at a particular moment fixed in the memory by a striking phrase : "Thine eyes shall see the king in his beauty : they shall behold a land of far horizons."

It is as though Isaiah climbed the hills about Jerusalem, and first stayed and looked from a moderate height upon the city, and saw all sharp and clear in detail, very bright and splendid. Then climbed higher and looked again not at Jerusalem only, but over all the country, with the scars of its war softened in luminous haze. Then climbed, higher than any of the hills round about Jerusalem would let you climb : city and fields were no longer to be discerned : for a while his mind's eye presents only too clearly the spectacle of the ravaged, yet saved land : and then another memory or dream comes to him from the secret communions God has cheered him often with, and leagues or centuries away beyond the pencilled horizons of visionary hope, he sees not but knows that some shall see—that King Whom some did see with their eyes nineteen centuries ago, but Who is now again seen by some as it were far off blurred by the mist of history, while others find Him nearer than senses or history can bring, by His Spirit manifest in present joys and trials : the miracle of prophecy is repeated.

CHAPTER 16

BETHLEHEM EPHRATAH

WHILE Isaiah was prophesying in Jerusalem, Micah the Morasthite was prophesying in the country ; and, strange to hear, he was contradicting Isaiah. Isaiah at the worst never said Jerusalem should perish. Micah said it should and evidently wished it should.

> Thus saith the LORD concerning the prophets that make My people to err ; that bite with their teeth and cry Peace ; and whoso putteth not into their mouths, they even sanctify war against him. Therefore it shall be night unto you that ye shall have no vision, and it shall be dark unto you that ye shall not divine. . . . But I truly am full of power by the spirit of the LORD, and of judgement, and of might, to declare unto Jacob his transgression, and to Israel his sin Hear this, I pray you, ye heads of the house of Jacob, and rulers of the house of Israel, that abhor judgement and pervert all equity. They build up Sion with blood, and Jerusalem with iniquity. The heads thereof judge for reward, and the priests thereof teach for hire, and the prophets thereof divine for money yet will they lean upon the LORD, and say, Is not the LORD in the midst of us ? No evil shall come upon us. Therefore shall Sion for your sake be plowed as a field, and Jerusalem shall become heaps, and the mountain of the house as the high places of a forest.

There is no mistaking what that last verse meant. To become heaps, is the regular phrase of the period for the utter destruction of a captured city. Isaiah never expected that for Jerusalem : Micah is positive that it shall be so.

We need not suppose that Micah was thinking of

Isaiah in what he said so fiercely about the greedy prophets who promised peace for the sake of popularity. It would have been very unjust if he had. Isaiah by no means courted popularity. Except for the last declaration of doom for Jerusalem, all that Micah utters here might have come from Isaiah himself. Indeed Isaiah said such things more boldly than Micah; for he said them to the kings' and princes' own faces, Micah in the comparatively safe distance of Moresheth Gath among a country folk who shared his indignation. Micah was a fine denunciatory prophet, but Isaiah was greater still. He knew the difficulty of governing; and the large purpose of God for kings. He knew Ahaz and Hezekiah in daily life, knew their wish to do right and all the complicated circumstances that thwarted them. Moreover Jerusalem was his own romantic town: he believed it was divinely destined for the salvation of men; and he believed this because he had seen the LORD. The enthusiasm of one converted and called, combined with the statesman's patient trust in working out ideas to immortalize hope for Jerusalem, is Isaiah's mind.

But in the country failures in government were felt in rudest consequences, poverty extortion desolation hopeless toil. Presently, when the Assyrian did come, the people in Jerusalem had hardship, but the farmers in the country were slain, burnt out, ruined. They took a simple view of kings and viziers, and a shrewd one: authority means responsibility, and rich men are better off than poor men. Micah thought so too, and his hope for the future was a thorough break with the evil that had been growing ever since Solomon became magnificent. Let us return to our shepherd kings, and, rid once for all of contaminated Jerusalem, let the village of our shepherd king be the seat of government.

> Sion shall be plowed, and Jerusalem shall become heaps. . . But thou, Bethlehem Ephratah, which art little to be among the families of Judah, out of thee shall one come forth unto me that is to be ruler in Israel ; whose goings forth are from of old, from ancient days. Therefore will he give them up, until the time that she which travaileth hath brought forth . then the residue of his brethren shall return unto the children of Israel.—5. 2 ff

Notice " until the time that she which travaileth, etc." This may be compared with Isaiah's " Behold the maiden shall conceive and bear a son . . . for before the child shall know to refuse the evil, and choose the good, the land whose two kings thou abhorrest shall be forsaken." Both prophets appear to be simply foretelling a short time of trial, which shall end as quickly as it will take some child just coming to the birth to grow to years of intelligence. But Isaiah continues in such strange sublime ambiguous manner as compels us to doubt whether that is all he means. And here Micah does the same :

> And he shall stand, and shall feed his flock in the strength of the LORD, in the majesty of the name of the LORD his God . and they shall abide ; for now shall he be great unto the ends of the earth. And this man shall be our peace : when the Assyrian shall come into our land, and when he shall tread in our palaces, then shall we raise against him seven shepherds, and eight princes among men. . . . And he shall deliver us from the Assyrian. . . . And the remnant of Jacob shall be in the midst of many peoples as dew from the LORD, as showers upon the grass , that tarrieth not for man, nor waiteth for the sons of men. And the remnant of Jacob shall be among the nations, as a lion among the beasts of the forest. . . . Let Thine hand be lifted up above Thine adversaries, and let all Thine enemies be cut off.

There is a primitive savagery in the holiness of that which marks the difference between Micah and Isaiah, but it does seem primitive, the sort of thing Micah himself would say. Not unfairly may we infer that both Micah and Isaiah had a vision of more than immediate, more than temporal promise: they looked for a Redeemer who through Israel would reconcile all nations to Jahveh the very God. Micah differs also from Isaiah in his vaguer handling of the theme. His idea is in the air: he does not stay to consider the discipline of fact. That is his inferiority. Isaiah is really simpler because he has a more complex faith. Through existing facts in all their stubborn variety he hears the simplifying call of the duty lying near, the unifying assurance of God's promise. Micah lacks the urbanity of education, and is therefore too quick a despairer, too facile a satirist, too short in his theology.

But in the ground of the heart, where revelation springs, Micah and Isaiah are at one, for all their dispute about the fate of the existing, builded, royal Jerusalem. And Micah's simplicity gives him an eminence of his own: from his plain pen comes the classic celebration of religion as pure morals:

> Wherewith shall I come before the LORD, and bow myself before the high God? shall I come before Him with burnt offerings, with calves of a year old? Will the LORD be pleased with thousands of rams, with ten thousands of rivers of oil? shall I give my firstborn for my transgression, the fruit of my body for the sin of my soul? He hath showed thee, O man, what is good; and what doth the LORD require of thee, but to do justly, and to love mercy, and to walk humbly with thy God?

And how exquisitely does the book close. It is once

more the old idea, camels and tents, a people apart, not competing in the commerce of civilization :

> Feed Thy people with Thy rod, the flock of Thine heritage which dwell solitarily, in the forest in the midst of Carmel : let them feed in Bashan and Gilead, as in the days of old. As in the days of Thy coming forth out of the land of Egypt will I show unto him marvellous things. . . . Who is a God like unto Thee, that pardoneth iniquity, and passeth by the transgression of the remnant of His heritage ? He retaineth not His anger for ever, because He delighteth in mercy. He will turn again and have compassion upon us ; He will tread our iniquities under foot : and Thou wilt cast all their sins into the depths of the sea. Thou wilt perform the truth to Jacob, the mercy to Abraham, which Thou hast sworn unto our fathers from the days of old.

Like Mr. Wilfrid Blunt, that lover of the Arabs, misliking empires, so Micah dreams of

> A home-ruled kingdom of primeval wood

CHAPTER 17

THE JUST SHALL LIVE BY HIS FAITH

AFTER the deliverance of Jerusalem from Sennacherib and the Assyrians we hear no more of Isaiah except in doubtful legend. The next great prophet was Jeremiah, by whose time important political changes were coming upon the eastern world. Hezekiah was succeeded by his son Manasseh. Josephus says more than Kings or Chronicles, but even from the Bible it is clear that Manasseh was all but an apostate from the faith of Jahveh. He brought in pagan rites, cruel and impure. He persecuted those who held to the teaching of Isaiah : it may be he murdered Isaiah. His long reign finished, his son Amon walked still in his ways. Then Josiah came to the throne, a child of eight years old, brought up under better influences. Jeremiah was his friend. Together they did something to restore faith and morals. But to those who took short views they seemed to fail. Jeremiah outlived his master, and saw the nation degenerating more and more under the last four kings, till Jerusalem was taken, the temple burned, and the people carried away captive in 586 B.C., rather more than a century after the deliverance in 701.

It was not the Assyrians who did this. Josiah died in battle at Megiddo, refusing passage through his land to the king of Egypt who was advancing northwards to dispute with the waning power of Assyria the dominion of the world. But the battle he fought at Carchemish, in which he was defeated, was not with Assyria. By that time the Chaldeans (with some help from allies) had taken Nineveh, the Assyrian capital on the Tigris, and had got possession of the whole ancient empire of Babylon. Let us remind ourselves that Babylon was as it were the Rome of this old eastern world. Her military ascendancy had vanished long ago. Now one now another fierce barbarian people seized the empire which still preserved its name and prestige. The Assyrians were the lords of Babylon in Isaiah's day : now these Chaldeans from the coast of the Persian Gulf destroy them and take their place ; more thoroughly perhaps and audaciously, for the Chaldean monarch actually appropriated the venerable name, and was called king of Babylon.

The fall of Nineveh looms obscure in history. Exactly how it came about we do not know. But Nahum the Elkoshite in his Burden of Nineveh has made the ruin unforgettable. Jahveh whose way is in the whirlwind and the storm, and the clouds are the dust of His feet, hath at last taken vengeance on the wicked one ; he shall no more pass through the land of his victims ; he is utterly cut off. We see the armies in their steel and scarlet ; the chariots rage in the streets and jostle one against another in the broad ways; rattling wheels, prancing horses, jumping chariots, no end of corpses. And the dreadful day draws to twilight and night, and the fugitives are heard stealing away and scattering over the mountains, while "thy shepherds slumber, O king of Assyria ; thy worthies are at rest."

Habakkuk comes rather later. He sees the new Chaldean power asserting itself throughout the earth even more effectively than Assyria. Ruthless are these Chaldeans, that bitter and hasty nation, who march though the breadth of the earth, to possess dwelling-places that are not theirs ; their horsemen spread themselves, and they gather captives like the sand. He scoffeth at kings, princes are a derision unto him : his might is his god.

Habakkuk appeals to the true God : Art Thou not from everlasting, Jahveh my God, mine Holy One ; Thou that art of purer eyes than to behold evil ; dost Thou hold Thy peace when the wicked swalloweth up the man that is more righteous than he ? dost Thou make men as the fishes of the sea, the helpless prey of this Chaldean net ?

And the word of the LORD comes to him in the patience of faith :

> I will stand upon my watch, and set me upon the tower, and will look forth to see what He will speak with me, and what I shall answer concerning my complaint And the LORD answered me and said, Write the vision and make it plain upon tables, that he may run that readeth it. For the vision is yet for the appointed time, and it panteth toward the end, and shall not lie though it tarry wait for it ; because it will surely come, it will not delay. Behold, his soul is puffed up, it is not upright in him but the just shall live by his faith.

Alas, the prophet's faith, his trust, was disappointed. In half a century or so the Chaldean did indeed fall before Cyrus. But the people of the prophet, the people of Jahveh this pure promiser, what had happened to them in the meantime ? Jerusalem ravaged, temple burned, monarchy cut off, freedom for ever abolished ; that was the life which sprang from such a faith. Habakkuk would think otherwise. When S. Paul chose this as his faith-text, it was no neat catchword that attracted him. Doubtless the rude trust of an Old Testament saint was different from the faith of the New Testament. In the New Testament itself there is distinction between the faith of Paul, of James, of the Epistle to the Hebrews. But to distinguish is not to separate. Now hope, now loyalty, now philosophy, now morality adds a particular colour to that serenity of union in God's will which we call faith. But that, the essence of faith, abides unchanged through all faith's varied forms. And S. Paul quotes Habakkuk because Habakkuk more than any other prophet of the Old Testament knew what S. Paul knew; to be crucified with Christ and so to live the life that is Christ in man, is well. Nothing else matters. The luck of prosperity may go which way God wills: there is a peace that passeth understanding. Happy are the people, says a psalmist, whose oxen bring forth thousands and ten thousands in their leas? Nay rather, happy are the people who have the LORD for their God.

Habakkuk too is a psalmist: at least his book ends with a psalm which gathers up his doctrine into a burning mystic's poem. It is barely comprehensible in our English version or even in the Hebrew. Mr. St. John Thackeray has penetrated by help of the Septuagint to something like the true original text. Canon Dalton made a version of his own when he restored this poem to the worship of the Church in his *Book of Common Prayer, an edition containing Proposals and Suggestions.*[1] In this lucid translation the ode so perfectly sums up and explains Habakkuk's idea of faith, that every man will surely be grateful to Canon Dalton for his permission to print it here in full.

[1] Cambridge, at the University Press, 1920

O LORD, I have heard what Thou hast done of old : and I am filled with awe.

O LORD, revive Thy work in the midst of the years, in the midst of the years make it known : in wrath remember mercy.

Lo! the Almighty is coming from Teman : and the Holy One from Mount Paran.

His splendour doth cover the heavens : with loud acclaim resoundeth all the earth.

His brightness is as the Light, whereof flashes ray forth from His hand : and there is the secret storage of His power.

Before Him goeth the livid glow of His burning : and fiery bolts burst forth at His feet.

He stood, the earth did quake : He looked, then trembled the nations.

The ancient mountains are shattered, the everlasting hills bow low :—His goings forth are as of old.

Is the LORD displeased against the mountains : is Thine anger against the rivers? or Thy wrath against the sea,

That Thou dost ride upon the storm-wind, Thine horses : and the storm-clouds, Thy chariots of salvation?

The mountains saw Thee, and reeled in pangs : the downpour of waters swept on ;

The deep uttered his voice : and lifted up his hands on high.

The sun grew dim, the moon waxed pale : at the splendour of Thine arrows as they sped abroad, at the glancing of Thy glittering spear.

In indignation dost Thou march through the land : in anger dost Thou thresh the nations.

Thou art come forth for the salvation of Thy people : for the deliverance of Thine anointed.

They came out as a whirlwind to scatter me : and their rejoicing was as to devour the poor secretly.

Ah ! the uproar of many peoples : which roar like the roaring of the sea ;

Thou has trodden that sea with Thine horses : their tumultuous surge of waters.

I heard, and my heart was sore affrighted : my lips quivered at the thunder of Thy voice ;

With the faintness of terror enfeebled was my frame : and I shuddered where I stood.

But I will quietly wait through the day of trouble : when He cometh up against the people which invadeth me with troops.

For though the fig-tree may not blossom : and there be no fruit upon the vines,

Though the labour of the olive fail : and the cornfield yield no grain ;

Though the flock be cut off from the fold : and there be no herd in the stalls ;

Yet I will rejoice in the LORD : I will exult in the God of my salvation.

The LORD God is my strength, and He will set me free : as the gazelle at large upon the high places of mine own homeland.

CHAPTER 18

REFORMATION

BEFORE Nahum sang the dirge of fallen Nineveh Zephaniah had seen the ruin coming :

The LORD will destroy Assyria and make Nineveh a desolation . . . herds shall lie down in the midst of her . . . the pelican and the porcupine. . . . This is the joyous city that dwelt carelessly, that said in her heart, I am, and there is none else beside me : how is she become a desolation, a place for beasts to lie down in ¹ every one that passeth by her shall hiss and wag his hand

Thus Zephaniah in the second chapter of his book. But he immediately goes on to speak of another rebellious polluted and oppressing city, whose princes are roaring lions, her judges evening wolves, her prophets light and treacherous, her priests have profaned the sanctuary and done violence to the law. But the LORD in the midst of her is righteous : He hath a judgement to execute. There is no doubt what this city should be called. It is Jerusalem, defiled with vile and foreign worships, Baal Malcam and the abominations of the Chemarim ; with superstition luxury and injustice. " I will search Jerusalem with candles," says Jahveh, " and I will punish the men that are settled on their lees, that say in their heart, The LORD will not do good, neither will He do evil." But Zephaniah is no hopeless prophet of wrath. The earliest prophets "hew" a stiff-necked unrepenting people with doom and terror. After the exile the note changes : Comfort ye My people, saith the LORD then, they have received double for all their sins. In Habakkuk, and now in Zephaniah, we hear something midway between these extremes : Judah is perverse and vile, but there is a change to be expected even now : " I will leave in the midst of thee an afflicted and poor people, and they shall trust in the name of the LORD. The remnant of Israel shall not do iniquity, nor speak lies ; neither shall a deceitful tongue be found in their mouth : for they shall feed and lie down, and none shall make them afraid. . . . In that day it shall be said to Jerusalem, Fear thou not : O Zion, let not thine hands be slack. The LORD thy God is in the midst of thee, a mighty One Who will save : He will rejoice over thee with joy, He will rest in His love."

The explanation of this may be found in 2 Kings 22 and 23 : Josiah's good reign ; he taketh care for the repair of the temple ; Hilkiah findeth the book of the law ; Josiah causeth the book to be read ; he reneweth the covenant of the LORD, and destroyeth idolatry. The book of Kings is the history of the reformation of religion in Israel. In Samuel worship goes on in the high places, sacrifices are merry feasts, there is no organized priesthood ; and no fault is found, on the whole the practice of this religion is at least decent and salutary. Samuel offers sacrifice at the high place of his city, and seems to have tolerated even images, teraphim, with indulgence. But in Kings there is a difference. These things go on, and the historian does find fault. And he shows that he is right to find fault. He shows that these practices were ensuing evil. They were the issue of superstition and engendering vice and cruelty. He shows that conscience was waking against them. Elijah and prophets in the north were forbidding them.

JOSIAH

The best kings in Judah, Asa Hezekiah, tried to reform manners and rites. But they accomplished little. At last Josiah did accomplish what these had essayed. The pagan reigns of Manasseh and Amon had perhaps encouraged reaction. Certainly Josiah did presently set about the restoration of the ancient faith and worship. The temple has fallen into decay and part of his work was the restoration of its fabric. In the course of the work a book appeared; we are not told how, only that " Hilkiah the high priest said unto Shaphan the scribe, I have found the book of the law in the house of the LORD." And Hilkiah delivered the book to Shaphan, and he read it. And Shaphan told the king and read it before the king. And the king when he heard the words of the book rent his clothes. And he sent to Huldah the prophetess to inquire of the LORD about this matter. And Huldah said " Thus saith the LORD, the God of Israel : Tell ye the man that sent you unto Me, Thus saith the LORD, Behold, I will bring evil upon this place, and upon the inhabitants thereof, even all the words of the book which the king of Judah hath read : because they have forsaken Me, and have burned incense unto other gods that they might provoke Me to anger with all the work of their hands." But mercy is promised to Josiah ; he shall be gathered to his fathers in peace, and his eyes shall not see the evil of the future.

Josiah might have learned, perhaps had learned from Jeremiah that divine prophecy is not blind fate, and that all dooms are alterable by repentance. He used his respite royally. He called the people together, read the book to them, " made a covenant before the LORD, to walk after the LORD, and to keep His commandments, and His testimonies, and His statutes, with all his heart and with all his soul, to perform the words of this covenant that were written in this book : and all the people stood to the covenant." Then the king set about the task of reformation. He destroyed all the implements of the worship of Baal, the Asherah, the host of heaven : put down the idolatrous priests : defiled Topheth, "that no man might make his son or his daughter to pass through the fire to Molech." At Bethel he slew priests and defiled sepulchres. Then he commanded a passover as it was written in the book : "Surely there was not kept such a passover from the days of the judges that judged Israel, nor in all the days of the kings of Israel, nor of the kings of Judah ; but in the eighteenth year of king Josiah was this passover kept to the LORD in Jerusalem."

Read the short code of law in Exodus 20–24. Then read Deuteronomy, and you will see that Deuteronomy repeats that short code with modifications and additions. The cardinal modification is that whereas in the former code the LORD promises to meet His people in many places of worship, in Deuteronomy there is to be but one place of sacrifice : "Take heed to thyself that thou offer not thy burnt-offerings in every place that thou seest : but in the place which the LORD shall choose in one of thy tribes, there shall thou offer thy burnt-offerings, and there shall thou do all that I command thee." That is the rule which will be necessary when the children of Israel are settled in Canaan ; for Canaan is impregnated with pagan tradition and its sacred places are unfit for the worship of Jahveh. "Ye shall surely destroy all the places, wherein the nations which ye shall possess served their gods, upon the high mountains, and upon the hills, and under every green tree : and ye shall

JOSIAH

break down their altars and dash in pieces their pillars, and burn their Asherim with fire ; and ye shall hew down the graven images of their gods ; and ye shall destroy their name out of that place. Ye shall not do so unto the LORD your God. But unto the place which the

THE MOUND OF MEGIDDO: FROM THE SOUTH-EAST.

LORD shall choose out of all your tribes to put His name there, even unto His habitation shall ye seek, and thither thou shalt come" (12. 1 ff.). And so the commands proceed with iterated detail. And the commands are incorporated in a sermon which now promises, now denounces, full of love yet very stern. Well might such commands, such promises, such threats, move the heart of Josiah.

Read 2 Kings 22, 23. See how Josiah's works of reformation correspond step by step with the commands in Deuteronomy. Look at the denunciations in Deuteronomy of evil to come if these commands be neglected, and compare the words of Huldah. Notice the stress upon the covenant which Josiah made and the people stood to. Notice how the very trick of deuteronomic style, the ciceronian amplification, the amplification which distinguishes the reformers' part in our English Prayer Book, is caught in 2 Kings 23. 3 : "made a covenant before the LORD, to walk after the LORD, and to keep His commandments, and His testimonies, and His statutes, with all his heart and all his soul."

This resonant deuteronomic style is one of many reasons against believing Moses to have written Deuteronomy. But indeed there is no reason at all for believing that. The book itself professes by its form to be another's record of what Moses said when the wandering was over and Israel was about to enter Canaan. May it not be really that? Surely yes; on the whole, substantially. Jewish tradition itself makes Deuteronomy the book which Hilkiah found; Moses' directions for life and worship in Canaan, given on the plains of Moab, since then lost for long. Later criticism has modified that naive presentation, but after all has kept what matters of it. Prophets took the ancient law, shaped and enlarged it for the need which life in Canaan had only too obviously created, and repeated the fervour of Moses' exhortations in their own sermonizing language. The newest critics are inclined to make our book of Deuteronomy a later product, the record of Josiah's reforms instead of the impulse. But that is chiefly a question of detail : there is no advantage to any one in deciding that Deuteronomy itself was found by Hilkiah. What comes out from all theories alike is this : in Samuel's day the faith and practice of the early law and the first prophetic teaching was Israel's rule of life. This presently proved insufficient and throughout the progress of the monarchy a developed faith and law pressed for recognition. This development we may broadly designate deuteronomic : and at last it entered effectively into the nation's history at the reformation of Josiah.

And now we can guess the secret of Zephaniah's gentle hope. In his day the good king Josiah was on the throne. Reform was in the air. Proud tyrants, luxurious princes, superstitious bigots were not the whole people : most of them were anxious for better ways if they could find them ; the people were ready to stand to the covenant. Zephaniah saw a day of the LORD coming in national repentance and reform : the blood and burning of judgement by warfare was not so soon to be repeated. And he believed that this was the word of the LORD, that the LORD Himself had taught him, and bidden him teach to others this confidence.

But was he right? There is a bitter contrast between Zephaniah's gladness and Huldah's gloom. And the tide of history, the decline and fall of Jerusalem, was with Huldah.

Here again we perceive, what the variation between Isaiah and Micah indicated, that there are degrees in prophecy. The prophet cannot but interpret the word while he repeats it, and interpretation is affected by time place education, all that has formed the interpreter's character. Zephaniah was, we may infer it from the deeper things in his book, a nobler prophet than Huldah.

There was a contemporary, grander than either, Jeremiah. We may, without offending much, suspect that the historian of Kings has touched his very brief report of Huldah's response with a tinge of recollection of the event. He has taken a stranger liberty than that. Nowhere does he mention Jeremiah in his history. Perhaps he had a reason.

It is often supposed that Jeremiah in the eleventh chapter of his book, where he talks of "this covenant" and of the LORD's command to him to proclaim this covenant in the cities of Judah and in the streets of Jerusalem, refers to Hilkiah's book of the law and to Josiah's reformation. At first sight this may appear a large piece of guesswork, but careful reading of Kings Jeremiah and Deuteronomy will make it more and more probable. But if so, the whole course of Jeremiah's prophecy, as recorded in his book, will convince us that he was no ardent reformation man. He may have hoped something from the reforms at first, but Josiah's reforms were—what else can kings and parliaments do?—but external, institutional, matters of law, and the only reform that Jeremiah cared about was of the heart. The nerve of Josiah's new religion was the unique sanctity of the temple. The temple of the LORD, cries Jeremiah, The temple of the LORD: you can all say that. But I tell you, and this is the true word which the LORD saith, that there is no security in the mere temple. Nay, unless you change your hearts, and with heart religion turn to the LORD, this very temple will perish in ruin like Shiloh.

Thus Jeremiah. But the historian of Kings was a historian not a theologian. He took the reformation simply and sincerely. He believed that all good dated from it. Even the downfall and the exile did not shake that very gallant confidence. To him, it might be, Jeremiah was far too academic, peculiar, Laodicean. There was no place for him in his story.

And yet Jeremiah was a more genuine reformer than any : at least he was if this reformation had any touch of kindred with the book of Deuteronomy. Through modern criticism Deuteronomy has lost and gained a throne. The deuteronomic law of the one sanctuary is the pivot of pentateuchal development. Here, just at this point, you see conspicuously the law of Moses entering into the general history and its gradual expansion and composition explained in the light of the whole history. Critically valued Deuteronomy is just the law of the one sanctuary.

But what is that? Some old-fashioned pious reader may respond : the law of the one sanctuary ; I never noticed that ; I always thought Deuteronomy was the book of the love of God.

That is just what Jeremiah would say. Deuteronomy has perhaps other things besides the law of the one sanctuary which Jeremiah would not care for very much. He did not value sacrifices highly, and was not dismayed when the exile stopped sacrificial worship. But Deuteronomy in its length and breadth—" to love the LORD thy God, to obey His voice, and to cleave unto Him : for He is thy life, and the length of thy days. . . . The eternal God is thy home, and underneath are the everlasting arms "—why this is Jeremiah himself, Jeremiah and his heart religion, simple profound unalterable by circumstance.

CHAPTER 19

IN THEIR HEART I WILL WRITE IT

BUT Jeremiah claims a chapter to himself. He may not be put above Isaiah, who is the greatest of the prophets. But Jeremiah is the deepest and kindest, the most like our Lord Jesus Christ.

According to the title-verses of his book he came of priestly stock; his family had an estate at Anathoth in Benjamin. Priestly men are naturally conservative, so are scholars; they like the quiet life of old. Jeremiah was a lover of books: see how he has read and thought upon Hosea, how he looks to history for his mind's food. The LORD said to him, Stand ye in the ways and see, and ask for the old paths, where is the good way, and walk therein, and ye shall find rest for your souls. But Judah would not have it so, and this retiring scholarly lover of libraries had to turn puritan and street preacher, and declare what was accounted novelty, and earn the reputation of a free thinker, a subverter of the patriotic doctrine of Isaiah, a Chaldaizer, when all the manhood of Jerusalem was astir for freedom or dogged in a last resistance to the foreign tyrant.

All this Jeremiah dared and endured. He longed for a lodge in the wilderness but he stayed where the LORD set him, in Jerusalem. He grumbled, sometimes agonized, but he obeyed with a delightful simplicity. Simple indeed he always was. How different the scenery of his prophetic call from the fire and ritual of

Isaiah's vision in the temple. Conscience had pricked him, but indolence held the scholar back. Then one spring day he marks the almond blossom. *Shaked* the Hebrews call it, the Waker; for it is the first of the year to wake. 'Tis a sign, thought Jeremiah: the LORD is waking, I may not linger any longer. And so he received his troublesome commission—" over the nations and over the kingdoms, to pluck up and to break down, and to destroy and to overthrow; to build and to plant."

He began with his history and his gentle bookish reminiscences: " Thus saith the LORD, I remember the kindness of thy youth, the love of thine espousals; how thou wentest after Me in the wilderness, in a land that was not sown. Israel was holiness unto the LORD, the first-fruits of His increase " : but now " art thou turned into the degenerate plant of a strange vine." And he goes on with the sins of Israel, the injustice luxury and vice which all the prophets had so long denounced, only there is worse now. That word " degenerate " just hits the mark. Baalim and superstition have again infected religion itself. " Return, O backsliding children, saith the LORD. . . . This is thy wickedness; for it is bitter, for it reacheth unto thine heart."

The gentleness and bookishness fall away. Once started Jeremiah was carried passionately on. " My bowels, my bowels! I am pained at my very heart; my heart is disquieted in me; I cannot hold my peace; because thou hast heard, O my soul, the sound of the trumpet, the alarm of wars. . . . For my people is foolish, they know me not; they are sottish children, and they have none understanding: they are wise to do evil, but to do good they have no knowledge. . . .

A wonderful and horrible thing is come to pass in the land; the prophets prophesy falsely, and the priests bear rule by their means; and my people love to have it so: and what will ye do in the end thereof?"

These pitying boding sentences, culled from the first six chapters, impress one with degeneracy. There was a fierce spirit still in the nation. The resistance they were so obstinately to maintain against the new tyrant of Chaldea showed courage which we cannot but admire. But this was not the high spirit of Isaiah's day. It needs an effort to accept the austere truth of Jeremiah, but a purged mind does accept it: these Judeans were no longer fighting on the side of the LORD; acquiescence in the empire of the Chaldeans was the nobler policy. No politics indeed but a fresh conversion of the heart at home was the only chance of life for Israel now. "As a well keepeth fresh her waters, so Jerusalem keepeth fresh her wickedness; violence and spoil is heard in her; before Me continually is sickness and wounds. Be thou instructed, O Jerusalem, lest My soul be alienated from thee; lest I make thee a desolation, a land not inhabited."

And these complaints prove how unpopular Jeremiah was becoming. As his words grew plainer, so he was lonelier, 'alienated' as he says of Jahveh. Beautiful but rather awful it is to observe how intimately his mind is coalescing with Jahveh's. "The whisper of the LORD, the whisper of the LORD: so they keep *neumming neum*," he says of the demagogue-prophets, coining a verb in scorn. But for himself Jahveh's whisper was the one reality. He is the first of the Old Testament saints to pray without ceasing. Strange prayers indeed he often prayed: they help us to understand that

JEREMIAH 155

sometimes bitter music of the Psalter. He poured out his heart to God. He would come in dispirited from the insults of street preaching, and tell about it, and call for payment to these adversaries. But he had a "through Jesus Christ" to end his collects: he would sum up, "LORD Thou knowest." And one day a special answer was borne in: "Be thou converted and I will convert thee; in My presence shall thou firmly stand: and if thou wilt take forth the precious from the vile thou shalt be as My mouth; they shall be converted unto thee, thou shall not be conformed unto them" (15. 19).

From henceforth Jeremiah's course is a continual taking more and more the precious from the vile. The inward battle between ambition and the absolute was won; what remained was an ever more loyal service, a profounder dying into life eternal, finding firm will by losing private will. In the Jewish Church's arrangement of his book (which we follow) there is beauty in the position of that short chapter 45. Jerusalem has fallen. Jeremiah has refused honourable ease in Babylon. He has chosen to share the hardship of the remnant left in Palestine. Then came the murder of Gedaliah, the panic of the depressed remnant of Judeans, their decision to escape into Egypt. Against that decision Jeremiah's wrath blazed: the old temper awoke in him, and he hewed them with a prophecy in the old style. And after that storm those gentle editors place, out of chronological order,[1] what the master had

---

[1] Dr Skinner thinks that "we can best appreciate the tone and significance of this chapter if we hold that it stands in its proper chronological place at the close of Baruch's biography, and contains the last words of Jeremiah to his devoted disciple. It reads like

said to Baruch in the reign of Jehoiakim. Jeremiah had dictated to Baruch, his friend and scribe, a book of prophecies up to that date delivered. The princes had them read to Jehoiakim. The gloomy king cut up the roll and burned it. The princes bade Baruch keep out of the king's way : it was as much as his life and Jeremiah's life were worth to brave his displeasure. But Jeremiah bade Baruch trim his pen and write all out again, adding more. Baruch naturally hesitated. But Jeremiah thus encouraged him :

> Thus saith the LORD, the God of Israel, unto thee, O Baruch : Thou didst say, Woe is me now ! For the LORD hath added sorrow to my pain ; I am weary with my groaning, and I find no rest. Thus shalt thou say unto him, Thus saith the LORD Behold, that which I have built will I break down, and that which I have planted will I pluck up ; and this in the whole land. And seekest thou great things for thyself? seek them not . for behold, I bring evil upon all flesh, saith the LORD and thy life I will give unto thee for a prey in all places whither thou goest.

Jeremiah had heard of that breaking down and plucking up at his call. He saw the need of it in his intercourse with the people. How it would come he could foretell from the politics of his day, the overbearing empire of Babylon, the intrigues of the subject nations to get free, the part which the fierce nobles

a farewell oracle, perhaps even a death-bed charge. The last verse strongly suggests that the friends are about to separate, and that Baruch will tread a lonely and perilous path through life, deprived of the guidance on which he had so long leaned." *Prophecy and Religion: studies in the Life of Jeremiah*, p 346 (Cambridge University Press, 1922). This book is a "spiritual biography," based on great scholarship, pastoral, very beautiful ; a worthy sequel to Dr Cheyne's brief, pointed, *Jeremiah · His Life and Times* (Nisbet, 1888). Both of these books are kindled by Jeremiah's own heart religion.

of Jerusalem were taking in those intrigues. He knew Judah would rebel, and he knew Babylon would be too strong for Judah, and the punishment would be the downfall of the monarchy. He had also been learning more and more clearly that the ruin might somehow meet the need. Fond of common things, interested in all the arts and occupations of men as well as in the ways and instincts of birds and beasts, he delighted in recognizing signs from the LORD in homely matters. So in the potter's house (18) he learned how the divine potter certainly meant to make a vessel of His people Israel to His liking, but if the clay flawed on the wheel He would break it up and begin again. Thus when the end drew nigh, he was prepared to take the meaning of another sign.

Zedekiah had been forced by his warlike nobles into rebellion. Nebuchadrezzar had sent an army to repress and punish. Jerusalem was under siege. Jeremiah was in prison as a traitor. To him, in prison, as to the head of the family Hanamel came with a legal document about the sale of a bit of land which was at that moment actually occupied by the besieging army. There, thought Jeremiah, is the sign : the Chaldeans and the siege is not the last word : we shall still be delivered.

For understanding the sequel we may, somewhat daring, rearrange chapters 31–33. That is not so outrageous a daring after all. The book of Jeremiah is like the corner of a library where a variety of documents have been collected to serve as material for a " Life Times and Theology " of a famous person. There are records of Jeremiah's acts words and sufferings : genuine pieces of his prophecy, some in grand poetic style, some in the conversation of every day. There are poems and prayers, perhaps in Jeremiah's own handwriting. There are notes of the impression made by him on other people. There are long passages of historical narrative. There are theological interpretations and expansions of his teaching. All this waits final ordering and use. One attempt was made by the Palestinian Jewish Church : that attempt is the base of the Hebrew and our English Bible. In the Septuagint we have the very different arrangement of the Jewish Church at Alexandria. Commentators still try new combinations. Let us then be permitted to try our hand modestly on these three chapters, and read them in this order : (*a*) 31. 1–30, (*b*) 32–33, (*c*) 31. 31–40.

Chapter 31 begins with a meditation on the prophecy of Hosea. Jeremiah may be imagined as solacing his captivity by applying the bygone sorrow and the ancient faith to the lost hope of Judah. Hosea indeed saw no issue from his paradox, but Jeremiah quiets himself with a doubtful hope of restoration after ruin. Then in chapter 32 Hanamel comes about the sale. Jeremiah reads this as a sign : "Thus saith the LORD of hosts, the God of Israel : Houses and fields and vineyards shall yet again be bought in this land." He can hardly believe it, but again came the word of the LORD, saying, Behold, I am the LORD, the God of all flesh : is there any thing too hard for Me ? And he thinks it out, his thought and divine revelation helping each other to clearness. Certainly Jerusalem will fall : but surely Israel will be gathered home again ; "for I will cause their captivity to return, saith the LORD."

That is a significant phrase. In later Jewish theology it was used in a spiritual sense like our "conversion" : to turn captivity was to convert the soul. And in

JEREMIAH

chapter 33 Jeremiah lets his hope run higher. He utters a poetic exultation: the throne of David, the temple ritual, all the bright popular luxuries of religion are in it. But all are figures of deeper feeling: the two families which the LORD did choose, hath He cast them off? His covenant, can He forget it? No: "I will cause their captivity to return, and will have mercy on them."

So for the time the LORD's word ends: unless indeed we may take the uncorrected reading of the Hebrew text[1] and find a more austere yet tender promise therein: "in their captivity I will return to them." That would be something like what Ezekiel said (11. 16): "Whereas I have removed them far off among the nations, and whereas I have scattered them among the countries, yet am I a little sanctuary to them in the countries where they are come." But finally Jeremiah went farther still. In 31. 31 ff. we have his prophecy of the new covenant, the issue of all his meditation on the sign of Hanamel. He has no doubt now whether Jerusalem will be taken, whether anything will be saved of the old order. He does not ask whether there will be a restoration of prosperity, of independence. He faces the prospect of utter loss of all such goods, and he believes that the loss will be the gain of all that is really worth wishing for.

> Behold, the days come, saith the LORD, that I will make a new covenant with the house of Israel, and with the house of Judah: not according to the covenant that I made with their fathers in the day that

---

[1] The masoretic or traditional text of the Hebrew Bible has been unchangeably fixed since the ninth century at least. But a large number of authorized corrections had by that time been admitted to the margin Some of these are obvious and necessary, many give smoother easier sense. In this verse (*Jer* 33. 26) R.V. and A V. text follows the masoretic correction, R.V. margin the Hebrew text.

I took them by the hand to bring them out of the land of Egypt ; which My covenant they brake, although I was an husband unto them, saith the LORD   But this is the covenant that I will make with the house of Israel after those days, saith the LORD ; I will put My law in their inward parts, and in their heart will I write it , and I will be their God, and they shall be My people · and they shall teach no more every man his neighbour, and every man his brother, saying, Know the LORD : for they shall all know Me, from the least of them unto the greatest of them, saith the LORD : for I will forgive their iniquity, and their sin will I remember no more.

This covenant is not new in terms. I will be their God, they shall be My people : that is the covenant which God makes from the first and renews to the end. The newness is in the means. I will write it in their heart. All the outward props and forms were vanishing : throne temple, priesthood sacrifice, the old prophetic faith in Jerusalem secure, the home of Jahveh inviolate. It was as though from us church creed and sacrament were ravished. And now says Jeremiah true religion will be set free : heart religion, real communion with God, real forgiveness and a fresh start. It was what he had longed prayed laboured for : in vain, it had seemed ; no, after all it was coming now. In part it did come. In the exile the Jewish Church grew up, to take the place of the Hebrew monarchy. When we remember that the Psalter was the Prayer Book of the Jewish Church, we measure the immediate fulfilment of Jeremiah's hope. Yet we remember other things also, and are too well aware that his hope was no quicker to be realized than the best hope of any former prophet. Six hundred years later the author of the Epistle to the Hebrews, writing when some break and parting of the ways was imminent, and—perhaps through another capture of Jerusalem—the young church of Jesus Christ

was facing loss and gain much like the loss and gain
of Jeremiah and the Judeans, then in that letter to the
Hebrews he quotes Jeremiah's new covenant at length.
There had been renewal already, at the Last Supper,
through the Cross and Resurrection. Still the hope had
not yet been realized: and yet again, then, the writer
expects it to be realized by desperate sacrifice. And he,
that very author, while his own austere hope ran so high,
teaches that in every generation, in each believer's life,
the sacrifice must be re-enacted. He says of the
Mediator of that last new covenant that He is able to
save to the uttermost those who, one after another as
their turn comes round, draw near through Him to God;
seeing He ever liveth to make intercession for them.
The historian of the Maccabees tells (2 *Macc.* 15. 14)
what Onias the good high priest said to Judas Maccabaeus in his dream: " This is the lover of the brethren,
he who prayeth much for the people and the holy city,
Jeremiah the prophet of God."

CHAPTER 20

THE VISION OF THE SCRIBE

THERE is a certain pleasantry, which we appreciate to-day as we pass from the nineteenth to the twentieth century, in Jeremiah's "they shall teach no more every man his neighbour and every man his brother." We fancy him rather weary of the superior persons, the didactic *longueurs* of a deuteronomic period. He liked simplicities and directnesses, almond blossoms and potters and baskets of figs and a good talk with give and take. Ezekiel too was not so much for teaching, certainly not for the many masters; but the simplicity he liked was authority: with Ezekiel the Law began to enter effectively into Jewish life, "The book of the law of Moses which the LORD had commanded to Israel."

Ezekiel was a priest and a nobleman. He had been carried to Babylonia with Jehoiachin and the court and that first band of stately captives whose dignified acceptance of Chaldean rule Jeremiah had so offensively commended to the militant populace left in Jerusalem. Two baskets of figs he said he had dreamed of: one good, very good, and those were now in Babylonia; the other bad, so bad that they could not be eaten, and these were his neighbours in Jerusalem. Among those good men Ezekiel was of the best. He dwelt for years in the skirts of the storm which Jeremiah saw from Sion as it gathered and drew on: deep answered deep, says Dean

Stanley, across the Assyrian desert. And he used the years with their quiet security in priestly pastoral offices, feeding the flock entrusted to him. "And they shall know that I the LORD their God am with them, and that they, the house of Israel, are My people, saith the Lord GOD. And ye My sheep, the sheep of My pasture, are men, and I am your God, saith the Lord GOD." So he writes in chapter 34.

So he writes: for Ezekiel is himself a scribe. Jeremiah did not write his own prophecies: he dictated to Baruch who was a scribe. Isaiah wrote a name, a sentence, on a board for those who ran to read; so also Habakkuk: but we hear nothing of these earlier prophets writing books. Of course they could write: in Judges we read of a country boy who wrote down certain names when he was asked. But it is one thing to write a scrap like that, or a letter to a friend, quite another to write a book. And it is in every way probable that Isaiah Micah Amos Hosea Jeremiah wrote little or nothing. Others wrote the prophecies they heard them utter. Some of their utterances were known by heart and so passed on from mouth to mouth, from generation to generation. That would be the easier in that their great deliverances were poems, not merely poetic in language but really composed in formal rythm. You can test this to some degree by reading our English version aloud. In Dr. Box's Commentary on Isaiah, or Mr. Edgehill's Amos, the Hebrew rythm (and sometimes rime) is preserved in translation. Here then was part of a store of material for composing a book of Isaiah or Amos, but it is unlikely that there ever was a book written by Isaiah or Amos.

Ezekiel's book is very different. There are no passages like the last chapter of Amos or the lyrical pieces in Isaiah, which at least appear to many to be derivative and not original. All bears the plain impress of one mind. The dates and personal statements with which the prophecies are punctuated must come from the prophet himself; unless the whole were an elaborate and most skilful work of fiction, which is a preposterous hypothesis. And above all the whole is arranged, not merely with clearness, but in a masterly imaginative authoritative plan, as by one who has thought out his experience, is in earnest about his purpose, sees from the beginning how he will set out everything to the end, and has succeeded in fashioning a book easy to read, hard for the conscience, destined to mould the faith ritual and morals of the Jewish Church which Ezekiel was determined should presently be born.

It is a kind of narrated drama; perhaps nearer a miracle play than a Greek or modern drama. The scenes are long chantings by the prophet, but they represent what has happened, is happening, or shall be performed, and his peculiar skill in language is to make the listener see things with the eye. There are four acts:

I   The removal of the LORD, 1–24.
II The pomp of the nations, 25–32.
III The resurrection of Israel, 33–39.
IV The return of the LORD, 40–48.

The first act opens with the magnificent and complicated vision of Ezekiel's prophetic call: the wheels, the living creatures, the Spirit and the voice of many waters, the throne and above the throne the likeness as the appearance of a man. Then, as in the apocalypse of S. John, a voice, an angel, guides him, calling him always Son of man. In the Spirit (like S. John) he is transported in time and place. He sees the abominations of Jerusalem. Then he sees a ghastly scenic symbol of the Chaldean victory and the divine judgement (9). Six men come, slaughter weapon in hand, from the way of the upper gate, and one in the midst clothed in linen with a writer's inkhorn by his side. The command is given and they go forth to slay, beginning with the ancient men before the house, then smiting throughout the city. The prophet cries for mercy but in vain: the answer of the LORD is pitiless. And the man with the writer's inkhorn reported the matter, saying, I have done as thou hast commanded me. Meanwhile "the glory of the God of Israel was gone up from the cherub, whereupon it was, to the threshold of the house."

That was the first step in the LORD's removal. A little while after in chapter 11 the removal is completed: "Then did the cherubim lift up their wings, and the wheels were beside them; and the glory of the God of Israel was over them above. And the glory of the LORD went up from the midst of the city, and stood upon the mountain which is on the east side of the city." This is removal but not absolute. The pitiless response in chapter 9 was not cruel. All this first act in Ezekiel's drama is very stern, but there are gleams of hope, and interludes of love. Ezekiel has no doom for Israel in the lump: as later by S. Jude so now by Ezekiel God says "Of some have compassion making a difference." In this eleventh chapter a gracious message is sent to Ezekiel's parish on the Chebar, and it is a message which represents the very heart of all his doctrine :

> Thus saith the Lord God : I will gather you from the countries where ye have been scattered, and I will give you the land of Israel. And they shall come thither, and they shall take away all the detestable things thereof. And I will give them one heart, and I will put a new spirit within you ; and I will take the stony heart out of their flesh, and I will give them an heart of flesh that they may walk in My statutes, and keep Mine ordinances, and do them : and they shall be My people and I will be their God.

But the immediate woe is determined. This first division of the book closes with the date of the siege, and the prophet waiting in silence for the news of the fall of Jerusalem.

And while he waits a procession goes by, as on a half stage while behind the curtain the agony of Jerusalem is being consummated ; a procession of nations which have betrayed Judah to her fate ; Ammon, Moab, Edom, the Philistines, Tyre, Egypt. Splendid beyond all imagining is Ezekiel's presentation of Tyre and Egypt. But on all alike there is the livid hue of death ; all of them uncircumcised, slain by the sword.

Then (33. 21) the announcement arrives :

> And it came to pass in the twelfth year of our captivity, in the tenth month, in the fifth day of the month, that one that had escaped out of Jerusalem came unto me, saying, The city is smitten.

It is the turning-point in prophecy. Hitherto each true prophet had stood all but alone, thundering against, "hewing" a rebellious unrepentant people. Henceforth Israel is repentant, trustful, needing consolation and receiving it. Before the fall "Woe to the rebellious children" is the Lord's word by the prophets : after the fall it is "Comfort ye, comfort ye My people, saith the LORD." In his parish on the Chebar Ezekiel has indeed had gentler treatment than Jeremiah had among the war party in Jerusalem. But the indifference had been as hard to resist. "Lo, thou art unto them as a very lovely song of one that hath a pleasant voice, and can play well on an instrument : for they hear thy words, but they do them not." Now that also will be changed : "When this cometh to pass (behold it cometh) then shall they know that a prophet hath been among them."

A few more stern things have to be said of those who have brought the silly people to such misery. Read the accusation of the shepherds in 34: it is a good example of the peculiar magic Ezekiel uses with plain words ; plain words, phrases repeated like a lawyer's, monotony; then a sudden touch, a vivid picture, that wakes you just as you are nodding, by the shock to the eye : ". . . as a shepherd seeketh out his flock in the day that he is among his sheep that are scattered abroad, so will I seek out My sheep ; and I will deliver them out of all places whither they have been scattered in the cloudy and dark day."

The accusation of the bad shepherds quickly passes into the diligent affection of the Good Shepherd. The day of consolation is due. In chapter 37 Ezekiel launches forth on his vision of resurrection, the vision of the valley of dry bones. A vision indeed : none reads of that valley without seeing it ; none who has once seen it has ever lost sight of it again. ". . . Then said He unto me, Prophesy unto the wind, prophesy, son of man, and say to the wind, Thus saith the Lord GOD : Come from the four winds, O breath, and breathe upon these slain, that they may live. So I prophesied as He commanded me, and the breath came into them, and they lived, and stood up upon their feet, an exceeding great army." This is not of course the resurrection of the body, as in our creed. The prophets have a doctrine of the life of the world to come for each and all; but this is not the place to look for that. This is the restoration of fallen Judah, new life from the death of the captivity. And astonishingly does Ezekiel proclaim it. He has no doubt and yet he has had no outward sign for hope. The "Comfort ye" prophecy fifty years later was a welcome to the conqueror Cyrus. He was advancing and all might surmise that his advance would do something for the victims of Babylon. But Ezekiel sees nought like that. When he spoke it was midnight with never a glow of dawn. Yet he is undaunted positive precise. So he passes on to the last act of his drama: the return of the LORD; the restoration of the temple; the ordering of civil and religious life in the revived community; the holy Levitical Jerusalem; the Jewish Church.

He saw it all, precise, with that quiet inward eye of his. "In the five and twentieth year of our captivity, in the beginning of the year, in the tenth day of the month, in the fourteenth year after that the city was smitten, in the selfsame day, the hand of the LORD was upon me, and He brought me thither. In the visions of God brought He me into the land of Israel, and set me down upon a very high mountain, whereon was as it were the frame of a city on the south." Then guided by "a man, whose appearance was like the appearance of brass, with a line of flax in his hand, and a measuring reed," he surveys the house of the LORD its courts and sanctuary, measuring and establishing every detail, till presently

> he brought me to the gate, even the gate that looked toward the east and behold, the glory of the God of Israel came from the way of the east. and His voice was like the sound of many waters and the earth shined with His glory . And the glory of the LORD came into the house by the way of the gate whose prospect is toward the east And the spirit took me up, and brought me into the inner court ; and behold the glory of the LORD filled the house. And I heard one speaking unto me out of the house , and a man stood by me. And He said unto me, Son of man, this is the place of My throne, and the place of the soles of My feet, where I will dwell in the midst of the children of Israel for ever . and the house of Israel shall no more defile My holy name, neither they nor their kings by their whoredom . . now let them put away their whoredom, and the carcases of their kings far from Me, and I will dwell in the midst of them for ever

The LORD had returned, to be a presence and a holiness more deeply interfused with the new life of His people than ever before. The idealists of the past had put forth their sublimities ; it seemed in vain. Now Ezekiel, this legalist, will realize their truth and righteousness. Law too is, he knows it, Spirit ; the Spirit of God caring for detail, for the several souls and the several duties of men. The kings of Israel had gone their selfish headstrong way : now there shall be no more kings. Rich men and nobles had annexed the land and oppressed the poor : now the whole land shall be divided fairly ; held by the whole nation, from the God of Israel, guarded from change by law. There had been cheating in trade, exploiting of the simple : now not so much as a pair of balances shall be left without inspection. God's commonweal ; therein justice shall at last be secure.

Worship too : how bad that had been. 'Temple

treading' pompous ritual with insincerity was ill indeed. But Ezekiel was not inclined to do away with ordered worship because it did not always find pure hearts to use

JERUSALEM: SHOWING THE GIHON CATTLE MARKET.

it. Purity comes by discipline to many, and the many (for each of whom this pastoral man cared) do need rules and order if they are to make anything of worship. The grave evil had sprung from the unregulated worship of the high places which, it seems from Ezekiel's complaint, even Josiah's reformation had not thoroughly cured. Of all such considerations the outcome was that Ezekiel saw in his vision of the new church a temple with regular priesthood and authorized sacrifices. He

SACRIFICES: NEAR THE GATES OF JERUSALEM.

carried sacrifice to a higher plane : and he did that as prophet quite as much as priest.

The deepest saying about sacrifices in the Old Testament is in Leviticus 17. 10 f. :

> And whatsoever man there be of the house of Israel, or of strangers that sojourn among them, that eateth any manner of blood ; I will set My face against that soul that eateth blood, and will cut him off from among his people.

So far we read a primitive taboo, older far than Moses.

Then follows a reason which is hardly less antique : "for the life of the flesh is in the blood." That was the primitive belief; the blood was the life, the actual blood that streamed forth from the wound was the life, the soul : the two words are one in Hebrew.

Now comes the transformation of the primitive taboo in the sacerdotal theology of the Jewish Church :

> For the life of the flesh is in the blood : and I have given it to you upon the altar to make atonement for your lives for it is the blood that maketh atonement by reason of the life.

Sacrifice is an affair of life not death. The death of the victim is but the means of setting free life, life still living, for action upon life.

God is the author of this decree of restoration. God has not to be reconciled propitiated atoned ; His love is unchangeable ; from His unfailing goodwill to His people comes the means of restoration of their broken alienated lives.

The Hebrew word for atone is a strange one. It seems in common Hebrew to mean 'cover'; but that scarcely makes sense in many places where it is used. More likely the word has the same ritual meaning as the kindred 'kupparu' has in Babylonian ritual, to cleanse. Cleansing is the essence of sacrifice throughout the epistle to the Hebrews, the Leviticus of the New Testament. So it would seem thought Ezekiel. He too looks on sacrifice as the grace of God Who always loves poor sinners. He too is full of the idea of life not death as God's desire purpose operation. And the hope of cleansing is his perpetual solace and the key to his ordinances of sacrifice : life provided by God to be consecrated to God shall cleanse the ruined lives of each and all His people. Ezekiel's vision sweeps on past the sacrifices of the altar to a universal, out-door sacrament, the cleansing of the whole country by that river of water of life which S. John too saw in his apocalypse :—And he brought me back unto the door of the house ; and behold, waters issued out from under the threshold of the house eastward ... it was a river, waters to swim in, a river that could not be passed through. . . . Everything shall live whithersoever the river cometh . . . and by the river upon the bank thereof, on this side and on that side, shall grow every tree for food, whose leaf shall not wither, neither shall the fruit thereof fail : it shall bring forth new fruit every month, because the waters thereof issue out of the sanctuary : and the fruit thereof shall be for food, and the leaf thereof for healing.

> East the forefront of habitations holy
>   Gleamed to Engedi, shone to Eneglaim ·
> Softly thereout and from thereunder slowly
>   Wandered the waters, and delayed, and came.
>
> Then the great stream, which having seen he showeth,
>   Hid from the wise, but manifest to him,
> Flowed and arose, as when Euphrates floweth,
>   Rose from the ankles till a man might swim.
>
> Even with so soft a surge and an increasing,
>   Drunk of the sand and thwarted of the clod,
> Stilled and astir and checked and never-ceasing
>   Spreadeth the great wave of the grace of God.
>
>   (F. Myers, *S. Paul*)

CHAPTER 21

COMFORT YE

EZEKIEL'S hope of faith sprang out of mere darkness, God's gift to a masterful soul. The years of exile passed and presently it became evident that the hope might be fulfilled. Cyrus was leading his army on that career of victories which was to make him king of Persia; and the empire of Babylon already stood within his danger. The air was full of the rumour of his advance, and a prophet was inspired to interpret the rumour to the exiles of Israel, to encourage them and prepare them for return.

We have seen how the first thirty-nine chapters of Isaiah are a record of Isaiah's prophetic ministry in Jerusalem in the latter half of the eighth century B.C. when the fear of Assyria was on Israel and Judah. Isaiah and the leading persons of the time are frequently named, particular prophecies are dated by events. Later prophecies and poetry are interspersed, but generally by way of liturgical punctuation, marking the divisions of Isaiah's life and teaching. His own style of utterance is so vivid that even by that alone we are able to distinguish the main original prophecy from the additions. At chapter 40 something quite different begins. Isaiah is never named nor any other man until Cyrus in chapter 45 is entitled the LORD's Anointed or Christ who is to send Israel home. The style, sublime in fluency, is very unlike the rugged sublimity of Isaiah. The background is evidently Babylon during the last years of the captivity. "Comfort ye, comfort ye My people" is the theme. Israel is going home. A new life is to begin, an absolutely happy holy life in purity of faith and spiritual worship.

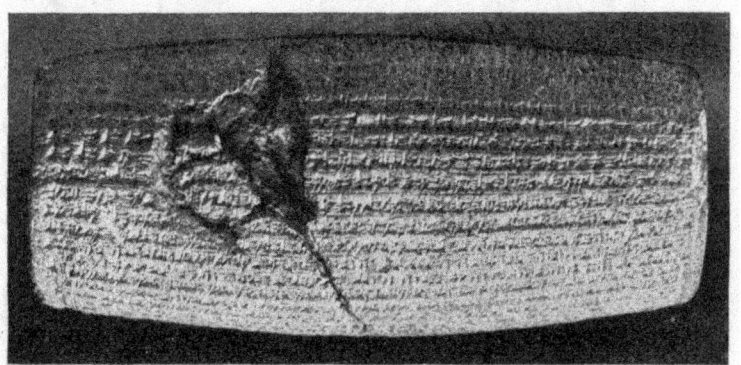

BAKED CLAY CYLINDER INSCRIBED WITH AN ACCOUNT OF THE CAPTURE OF BABYLON BY CYRUS, KING OF PERSIA, 538 B.C.

An unnamed prophet speaks in these chapters. He stands in the great idealist line of Isaiah and Jeremiah. No legal ordinances are here; no temple; no sacrifices: the vision is quite another than Ezekiel's. When "My sabbaths" are commemorated in chapter 56 you feel an incongruity: this and the following ten chapters must be reconsidered by themselves; the Comfort ye prophecy stands apart, rounded and complete in 40–55. And what a glorious piece it is; a Te Deum, or Hymn of monotheism as it has been called by Sir George Adam Smith.[1] You are going home, it says, you thought

[1] *The Book of Isaiah*, in two volumes: vol. ii Isaiah 40–66 with a sketch of the history of Israel from Isaiah to the Exile. The Expositors, Bible. Hodder & Stoughton. Thirteenth edition, 1907.

you were forgotten and forsaken, the promises to the fathers broken, Jahveh a defeated God. So Israel had despaired; but it was not so. Jahveh had kept His word, as He kept it to the children of Abraham in Egypt, when what seemed desertion issued in a mighty rescue. That rescue had been described as redemption. This prophet takes up the word and fills it with a deeper meaning, with theology: it is from his use that S. Paul draws the still larger doctrine of redemption in the New Testament. So too with the name Jahveh. The Redeemer is to him still Jahveh God of Israel. The tie between Jahveh and His people Israel is closer than ever. But it is closer because it is more spiritual than ever had been known before. And the free range of true spirit transcends all that is merely national. Jahveh is here adored as the one and only God Who fills all time and space. Matthew Arnold was for rendering Jahveh into English as The Eternal, and there is beauty and truth in such a rendering. But it is not suitable for those earlier passages of the Old Testament in which the primitive genius of Hebrew thought asserts itself; with its naive idea of person, its bold language of art which adumbrates mystery by frank imagery from scenes of earth and the affairs of men. Still greater is the difficulty where fierce zeal takes faith by storm—when you read of Elijah at Carmel triumphing over Baal and slaying Baal's prophets at the brook Kishon, you cannot translate the antique name; presently, with the still small voice, The Eternal would be almost right. But now this prophet of the exile has finished with all those limitations and imperfections. As in the Gospel according to S. John we perceive how the title Christ comes to the evangelist with too strait associations of

merely national import, and he is feeling after some
larger phrase to fit the Saviour of the whole world, so is
it with this prophet. But as finally the Church kept the
title Christ and enriched it with the Johannine fullness
of the Word, so this prophet keeps the time honoured
name Jahveh and deepens it as he uses it, till it includes
all that is confessed of godhead in the Nicene Creed:
"I believe in one God, the Father all-ruling, maker of
heaven and earth, and of all things visible and invisible":
"I even I am Jahveh; and beside Me there is no Saviour.
... Yea, since the day was I am He; and there is
none that can deliver out of My hand. ... I am the
first and I am the last; and beside Me there is no God.
... Is there a God beside Me? Yea, there is no Rock;
I know not any. ... That they may know from the
rising of the sun, and from the west, that there is none
beside Me: I am Jahveh, and there is none else. I form
the light, and create darkness; I make peace, and create
evil; I am the Jahveh, that doeth all these things. ...
There is none else, there is no God. Verily Thou art a
God that hidest Thyself, O God of Israel the Saviour."

This is not monotony; though compared with the
oratory of Isaiah it might appear monotonous. The
eloquence is like music in which a theme is constantly
repeated, constantly varied, and each repetition carries on
the movement. This is music, a Te Deum. And it
rings with the joy of a Te Deum. Those lyrics which
are intertwined with the earlier half of the book are part
and parcel of the whole wreath. All nature is revived
and glad, as in the psalms of the "new song":

> Let the heavens be glad, and let the earth rejoice;
> Let the sea roar, and the fullness thereof,
> Let the field exult, and all that is therein;

> Then shall all the trees of the wood sing for joy ;
> Before the LORD, for He cometh ;
> For He cometh to judge the earth
> He shall judge the world with righteousness,
> And the people with His truth
>
> *Ps.* 96.

But the prophet has a keener vision than the psalmist, and overflows with sounding titles of particular trees, or delineations of particular loveliness—"and they shall spring up among the grass, as willows by the watercourses." More noticeable than such artistic graces is his frequent mention of "the isles." The psalmist looks beyond Israel with his "people," but the prophet looks in a particular direction, to the isles of the Aegean and the indented coasts of Asia, to those Hellenic people who now, as the sixth century draws on, are about to start on their career. In his theology Jahveh, The Eternal, is the God of Aeschylus and Plato as well as of Isaiah. New vistas open ; yet these might not have seemed too strange to Isaiah himself. That prophecy in chapter 19 is confined in terms by the politics of an earlier generation, but its inspiration is all one with "Comfort ye" :

> In that day shall there be a high way out of Egypt to Assyria, and the Assyrian shall come into Egypt, and the Egyptian into Assyria ; and the Egyptians shall worship with the Assyrians.
> In that day shall Israel be the third with Egypt and with Assyria, a blessing in the midst of the earth : for that the LORD of hosts hath blessed them, saying, Blessed be Egypt My people, and Assyria the work of My hands, and Israel Mine inheritance

There is a unity in the whole succession of Isaianic theology as represented in this complex book of Isaiah :

taken altogether it is the greatest theology in the Old Testament.

And it reaches its height in 52. 13–53, that description of the Servant of the LORD who dying saved his persecutors. Critical controversy surrounds the passage: is it all of a piece with the rest, or is it later? Do the other three Servant Songs—42. 1 ff., 49. 3 ff., 50. 4 ff.—go with it, or are they parts of the original prophecy which have been completed by this even deeper inspiration from another age? For the present we leave it, not because of the critical question: this is one of those rare pieces about which we scarcely care to attend to criticism. Whenever, by whomsoever written, whatever its immediate intention may have been, it shows us our Lord Jesus Christ, illuminating the whole Old Testament. But we are not yet ready to comprehend that illumination thoroughly. We shall appreciate this hymn of hymns when we can look back upon our completed study: Law History Prophecy Wisdom Psalter, all are summed up and interpreted by it.

We leave it then for the present, disclaiming critical prejudice. Yet critical considerations will intrude upon readers who are really interested in what they read, and we must just glance at the last eleven chapters of the book of Isaiah, and recognize that here again there is a difference: the Comfort ye prophecy ends with chapter 55; what follows is another collection of various prophetic utterances. Some seem to belong to the time of Nehemiah and Ezra and may be compared with the book called Malachi. Some might fit an earlier period of the restored temple, and be compared with Haggai and Zechariah. The last chapter has the flavour of Daniel and the Maccabees and the apocalyptic dream.

Many parts of this appended collection are most tender or solemn or splendid. In 57 we have that inimitable verse:

> Thus saith the high and lofty One that inhabiteth eternity, whose name is Holy: I dwell in the high and holy place, with him also that is of a contrite and humble spirit, to revive the spirit of the humble, and to revive the heart of the contrite ones. . . . Peace, peace, to him that is far off and to him that is near, saith the LORD. and I will heal him.

And there is "Arise shine" (60); and our Lord's text at Nazareth (61):

> The Spirit of the Lord GOD is upon me; because the LORD hath appointed me to preach good tidings unto the meek: He hath sent me to bind up the broken-hearted, to proclaim liberty to the captives, and the opening of the prison to them that are bound; to proclaim the acceptable year of the LORD—

but then, in another spirit from our Lord's and from the evangelic prophet, it goes on—" and the day of vengeance of our God."

"Who is this that cometh from Edom, with dyed garments from Bozrah?" (63). To us, who know the chapter as an Epistle in the liturgy of the sacred Passion, it is glory and beauty: but turn to it in its context and are you quite ready to suppose that the evangelic prophet of comfort would fiercely contemplate his Redeemer marching knee deep in Idumaean blood? This grim poem runs on indeed to a strain of incomparable tenderness in "I will make mention of the loving kindnesses of the LORD"—what consolation it brought to troubled hearts during the dreadful days of war. This might be in the spirit, though surely not in the manner of the Comfort ye prophet; but what of the last verse of the whole book? That verse is so terrible that the Masoretes made a note, still printed in Hebrew Bibles: Go back and finish by reading again the last verse but one.

It is no use calling things simple when they are not. A good deal of the objection against recognizing two Isaiahs (as it was often expressed) must have arisen from the feeling that the new dogma was too simple to fit the facts. All analytic criticism of an ancient book is beset with uncertainty: we are groping in the abyss of the past: dogma is excluded. But to recognize the complexity of the problem is only sensible. Once accept the book of a prophet as no book composed by himself throughout, but the Life, Remains and Theology of the prophet as edited by the Jewish Church, and there is no difficulty in imagining it to consist of a copious variety of elements.

CHAPTER 22

THE FIRST CHURCHMEN

IN 538 B.C. Cyrus took Babylon and made a decree:

> Thus said Cyrus king of Persia, All the kingdoms of the earth hath the LORD, the God of heaven, given me; and He hath charged me to build Him an house in Jerusalem, which is in Judah. Whosoever there is among you of all His people, his God be with him, and let him go up to Jerusalem, which is in Judah, and build the house of the LORD, the God of Israel (He is God,) which is in Jerusalem. And whosoever is left, in any place where he sojourneth, let the men of his place help him with silver and with gold, and with goods, and with beasts, beside the freewill offering for the house of God which is in Jerusalem.

Accordingly a number of the exiles did return to Jerusalem under Sheshbazzar their prince. They carried with them the sacred vessels, which Cyrus restored. At once they set up the altar, and offered sacrifice: next year they laid the foundation of the holy house.

Then came a check. There were adversaries of Judah and Benjamin, who at first were for building with them. That was repugnant to the exclusive zeal of the pure and reborn Jews. The adversaries, thus repulsed, hired counsellors against the Jews, and when Cyrus died in 525 B.C., wrote spiteful letters to his successors, advising them of the rebellious history of Jerusalem and of the mischievous ambitions this present building enterprise cloaked. Then ceased the work of the house of God which is at Jerusalem: it ceased unto the second year of Darius, who became king of Persia in 521 B.C.

Under Darius relief came. The sober tradition of Jerusalem was that the prophets Haggai and Zechariah encouraged Zerubbabel the prince of Judah and Joshua the high priest, and set the people boldly building again. Then the Persian governor inquired of their right to do this, and the Jews appealed to the decree of Cyrus. The governor wrote a fair and sensible letter to the king; search was made in the records of the kingdom; Cyrus' decree was found: and Darius ordered the building to be permitted, with facilities granted, and horrid penalties for any who disregarded the royal command. The tradition of the Grecian Jews of Alexandria was more picturesque. After a very splendid feast in the palace three young men of Darius' bodyguard proposed a kind of wager for themselves: "Let every one of us say one thing which shall be strongest: and he whose sentence shall seem wiser than the others, unto him shall Darius the king give great gifts, and great honours in token of victory: as to be clothed in purple, to drink in gold, and to sleep upon gold, and a chariot with bridles of gold, and a head tire of fine linen, and a chain about his neck: and he shall sit next to Darius because of his wisdom, and shall be called Darius his cousin" (1 *Esdras* 3): a gaudy ambition, but the destined victor had a better in his mind.

They wrote their sentences and laid the writings under the king's pillow. He read when he woke, and called the young men to defend each his thesis publicly, which they did with spirit. The first had written, Wine is the strongest: the second, The king is strongest: the third, Women are strongest; but above all things Truth beareth away the victory. This third, after saying somewhat about a lady of the court which caused the king and the nobles to look one upon another, began to speak concerning truth, and ended thus :

> Wine is unrighteous, the king is unrighteous, women are unrighteous, all the children of men are unrighteous, and unrighteous are all such their works ; and there is no truth in them ; in their unrighteousness also they shall perish But truth abideth, and is strong for ever , she liveth and conquereth for evermore. With her there is no accepting of persons or rewards ; but she doeth the things that are just, and refraineth from all unrighteousness and wicked things; and all men do well like of her works. Neither in her judgement is any unrighteousness , and she is the strength, and the kingdom, and the power, and the majesty, of all ages Blessed be the God of truth.
>
> And with that he held his tongue And all the people then shouted, and said, Great is truth, and strong above all things.

Magna est veritas et praevalet. The champion of truth won the prize, and the king would have him sit next himself and be called his cousin. But this young guardsman was Zerubbabel, and he spoke up again for truth and for his people. "Remember, he answered Darius, thy vow, which thou didst vow to build Jerusalem, in the day when thou camest to thy kingdom : thou didst also vow to build up the temple, which the Edomites burned when Judaea was made desolate by the Chaldeans. And now, O lord the king, this is that which I require, and which I desire of thee, and this is the princely liberality that shall proceed from thee : I pray therefore that thou make good the vow, the performance whereof thou hast vowed to the King of heaven with thine own mouth."

And so a great band of exiles returned to Jerusalem with Zerubbabel. And Zerubbabel and Joshua and Haggai and Zechariah set the building on, and the temple was rebuilt, and dedicated with glad ceremony. But, say they who tell the story, many of the priests and levites and heads of fathers' houses, the ancients who had seen the first house, wept with a loud voice, while many shouted aloud for joy: so that people could not discern the noise of the shout of joy from the noise of the weeping of the people: for the people shouted with a loud shout, and the noise was heard afar off.

"Ezra."

There was reason for low spirits. Those were the brave days of Zerubbabel and Darius. Fifty years or so pass and we are in the reign of Artaxerxes (465–425 B.C.), and in the meantime Jerusalem has not prospered. These are the days of Ezra and Nehemiah when the Jewish Church was founded as men build a lighthouse on a rock at sea, amid waves and storms, redeeming the time, obstinate for their purpose with a great faith.

Nehemiah was cupbearer to Artaxerxes. In the twentieth year of the king's reign one came from Jerusalem and told Nehemiah how the remnant left of the captivity then in the province were in great affliction and reproach, the wall of Jerusalem broken down, and the gates thereof burned with fire. The king noticed his servant's grief; he had not been beforetime sad in his presence—which tells us something of Nehemiah's character. He got leave to visit Jerusalem, and liberal aid for his enterprise. He came to Jerusalem and rested three days after his long journey. Then he rode round the walls by night, saw how bad things were, and cheerfully called upon the leaders of the people to work and build. "I told them, he says, of the hand of my God which was good upon me; as also of the king's words which he had spoken unto me. And they said, Let us rise up and build. So they strengthened their hands for the good work."

Nehemiah was a capital organizer, and there was encouragement in his presence. The people laboured according to their clans and families, each in the appointed place; and the work went forward. But a sort of rascals, represented by Sanballat the Horonite, and Tobiah the servant the Ammonite, and Geshem the Arabian—these stand pilloried in Ezra's history for all time—first mocked, then devised odious and dangerous methods of hindrance. But Nehemiah was undaunted. He made from his labourers relays of guards. Their readiness foiled the first attack so that it was never delivered. "And it came to pass from that time forth, that half of my servants wrought in the work, and half of them held the spears, the shields, and the bows, and the coats of mail; and the rulers were behind all the house of Judah. They that builded the wall and they that bare burdens laded themselves, every one with one of his hands wrought in the work, and with the other held his weapon ; and the builders, every one had his sword girded by his side, and so builded. And he that sounded the trumpet was by me " (*Neh.* 4). And so he went on till no breach yet remained in the wall ; only the doors had still to be set in the gates.

Then Sanballat and Tobiah and the Arabian and the rest plotted against Nehemiah's person. They invited him to conference. But he sent them a good answer and repeated it four times : I am doing a great work, so that I cannot come down : why should the work cease, whilst I leave it, and come down to you ? Then one of his own friends was for taking refuge in the temple ; " for, said he, they will come to slay thee ; yea, in the night will they come to slay thee." But Nehemiah was too stout for that. " And I said, Should such a man as I flee ? and who is there, that being such as I, would go into the temple to save his life ? I will not go in. And I discerned, and lo, God had not sent him : but he pronounced this prophecy against me : and Tobiah and Sanballat had hired him." No, such a man was not to be tricked nor frightened nor discouraged, and so the wall was finished in the twenty and fifth day of the month Elul, in fifty and two days.

A fine success : the more so, since Nehemiah was worried with ills at home as well as from without. There was a great cry of the people and of their wives against their own brethren among the Jews. The poor had to borrow money. They had to sell their children into bondage for their debts. Then I was very angry, says Nehemiah. Very angry, but very spirited and kindly too. He told the rich nobles roundly that they were exacting usury and doing a wicked thing. But he saw that use and wont were hard to escape: "I likewise, he said, my brethren and my servants, do lend them money and corn on usury." The touch of nature made all kin. He won the hearts of all, and insisted on restoration and a solemn dramatic promise for the future. And he ends his little story with a reckoning of the liberal table he kept, as we might be sure such a labouring prince would do, and so he concludes with his favourite and well-earned prayer: Remember unto me, O my God for good, all that I have done for this people (*Neh.* 5).

"NEHEMIAH."

Then he had trouble about the Sabbath; treading wine presses, bringing in sheaves, lading asses, carrying wine grapes and figs into Jerusalem on the Sabbath day: he testified against all this. The Tyrians with their sale of fish, the nobles conniving; it disturbed him much. But he had the gates shut and remonstrated with the traffickers when they lodged outside, expecting to be let in. And he commanded the levites to purify themselves and come and keep the gates and sanctify the Sabbath. And once more, sticking to his point, he seems to have won the day. Remember unto me, O God, he says, this also, and spare me according to the greatness of Thy mercy.

It is likely that part of the difficulty was in the novelty of Nehemiah's strictness. However to be accounted for, Sabbath keeping seems to have been taken easily hitherto at home in Judaea. The Law of Moses was first observed with scrupulous precision by the exiles in Babylonia. Nehemiah had to get the home keepers to submit to an unaccustomed yoke. And in this task he found a notable supporter. Ezra had gone in the seventh year of Artaxerxes from Babylon to Jerusalem. He was a ready scribe in the law of Moses, interested in pedigrees—he enjoyed a long one of his own—in priesthood rites and rules, the very man Nehemiah needed. He had brought some exiles with him, especially priests and levites. He had set his heart on teaching statutes and judgements in Israel (*Ezra* 7). Nehemiah called him forth and gave him a great opportunity. " All the people gathered themselves together as one man into the broad place that was before the water gate ; and they spake unto Ezra the scribe to bring the book of the law of Moses, which the LORD had commanded to Israel. And Ezra the priest brought the law before the congregation, both men and women, and all that could hear with understanding. And he read therein before the broad place that was before the water gate from early morning until midday, in the presence of the men and the women, and of those that could understand; and the ears of all the people were attentive unto the book of the law." He read from a pulpit lifted up above the people. Dignitaries stood beside him. When he opened the book the people stood up. He blessed the LORD, the great God. And all the people answered, Amen, Amen; lifting up their hands, bowing their heads, and worshipping with their faces to the ground. He read a second day the ordinance of the feast of tabernacles, and they went and fetched olive branches and branches of wild olive and myrtle and palm and of thick trees, and kept the feast as it had never been kept since the days of Jeshua the son of Nun unto that day. And there was very great gladness. And still day by day, from the first day unto the last day, Ezra read the law to the people. This was the third main act in the giving of the law. First with the thunders of Sinai Moses had spoken to Israel the words of Jahveh. Then at the reformation of Josiah the deuteronomic completion of those primitive words was introduced effectively into Israel's life. Now all the priestly ordinances which had been observed some more some less, some at one holy place some at another, are rehearsed, codified by the learning and diligence of the exiled scribes, and the full Levitical law enters effectively into Israel's life.

A sketch of this effective order is given in Nehemiah 9-12, prefaced by one of those prayers, part prayer part sermon, which are characteristic of this earnest liturgic period, when Israel, formerly perverse and stiff-necked, bows before " our God, the great, the mighty, and the terrible God, Who keepest covenant and mercy"; to whom it would not seem little " all the travail that hath come upon us, on our kings, on our princes, and on our priests, and on our prophets, and on our fathers, and on all Thy people, since the times of the kings of Assyria unto this day"; this day when they return at last to "a God ready to pardon, gracious and full of compassion, slow to anger, and plenteous in mercy," Who never forsook them.

There is the kindly, heart-deep spirit of the law : not one jot or tittle of that will ever pass away. This is law as Ezekiel taught it, or Richard Hooker, law that cares and hopes for the several souls of men, not for nations in the mass or classes in the abstract :

> Behold, all souls are Mine ; as the soul of the father, so also the soul of the son is Mine ; the soul that sinneth, it shall die. . . . When the wicked man turneth away from his wickedness that he hath committed, and doeth that which is lawful and right, he shall save his soul alive . . . Yet saith the house of Israel, The way of the LORD is not equal   O house of Israel, are not My ways equal ? are not your ways unequal ?   Return ye, and turn yourselves from all your transgressions   Cast away from you all your transgressions, wherein ye have transgressed , and make you a new heart and a new spirit   for why will ye die, O house of Israel ?   For I have no pleasure in the death of him that dieth, saith the Lord GOD . wherefore turn yourselves, and live.

Doubtless there was another temper in the law, jealous transitory ; considering the malpractices of Nehemiah's adversaries we may excuse it. Yet it were to be wished he had not been so stern to the Jews who had married women of Ashdod Ammon and Moab. We think, and perhaps some thought then of Ruth the Moabitess, and told again her story. And Ashdod : Professor Macalister in his book on the Philistines,[1]

---

[1] *The Philistines, their history and civilisation*, by Professor R A Stewart Macalister.   Schweich Lectures, 1911   Published for the British Academy by H. Milford, Oxford University Press

showing how the Philistines were emigrants from Crete, cousins to the Greeks, quotes that pathetic verse, " and their children spake half in the speech of Ashdod and could not speak the Jews' language," and says that perhaps the last accent of the noble ancient language of Homer still lingered on those children's lips, and Nehemiah quenched it.

One important result this suppression of the mixed marriages had. One of the sons of Joiada, the son of Eliashib the high priest, was son-in-law to Sanballat the Horonite: therefore, says Nehemiah, I chased him from me. And we learn from Josephus that this was the origin of the Samaritan schism: the Samaritans were not Horonites and Arabians but Jews whose fathers had been chased from Jerusalem.[1]

[1] *The Samaritans, the earliest Jewish sect; their history theology and literature,* by James Alan Montgomery Philadelphia, 1907

CHAPTER 23

THE LAST PROPHETS

EZRA is a shadowy person. Some have doubted whether there ever was such a person, pointing out the obvious connexion between Chronicles Ezra and Nehemiah ; how all seem to have one author ; how that author was exactly like the Ezra of Ezra and Nehemiah, fond of ritual priesthood genealogies, and entertaining the prejudices which correspond to those tastes ; how Ezra may be just a fancy portrait of himself. Jesus the son of Sirach (who wrote the book we call Ecclesiasticus) seems to come strangely near such critics ; for in his praise of famous men he includes Nehemiah but has not a word to say about Ezra. However where all is guessing let us guess more timidly, though our guess falls far short of accounting for all the ins and outs and inconsistencies of these two books, which with Chronicles are the last books in the Hebrew Bible, and seem to have gained tardy admittance as being but romantic history. Their position too is further complicated by the existence of 1 Esdras in the Septuagint and in our Apocrypha. From that variant version of the story the account of the three guardsmen was taken in our last chapter, which is less generally known now than it used to be. For we should remember that the Septuagint was the Bible of the early Christian Church ; and therefore that the Christian Church did not for some time accept the history of the return and of the beginnings of Judaism to which we are accustomed.

However let us formulate our modest guess. Ezra was a real person who came with a party of exiles from Babylon to Jerusalem in the reign of Artaxerxes. He was a deep student of Jewish law and religion and brought with him the Law of Moses with all the complete Levitical rubrics which he and his fellow scribes had written out fair in Babylon. He was eager to teach all this to the Jews of Jerusalem, but a scholar is not the man to impress the multitude, and he did in fact pass a "shadowy" obscure life in Jerusalem till Nehemiah came, found him useful and brought him forward. He was dry formal, yet formless as a writer; he had the tedious diligent genius of the compiler; and after the stirring events were finished he compiled a history of them. He knew little about the outside world, and his references to earlier Persian history are extremely vague: yet we should not lay great stress on that, for the information we derive from the Greeks, Herodotus Ktesias Xenophon, is romantic and contradictory also. He had Aramaic documents, letters to the Persian kings, etc., which he placed in his narrative as well as he could. He had genealogical lists which he also placed as seemed con-

DARIUS.

venient. And he had a memoir of his hero Nehemiah written by Nehemiah himself which he could appreciate, and it gave indeed life and spirit to his ill-arranged book. But ill-arranged though it be, Ezra was in earnest, and he was a strong obstinate good man, and his book dominated consciences. It went far towards the founding of the Jewish Church. It made the Law of Moses the rallying point of all parties. Expanded afterwards into Chronicles it imposed a view of the early history of Israel which superseded Kings till the revolution of modern critics.

The Greek Esdras, however that came to be composed, was indeed a rival. In Esdras Zerubbabel is the hero ; in Ezra-Nehemiah the hero is Nehemiah. Esdras is recommended by its conformity to the contemporary prophets Haggai and Zechariah. At least those prophets belonged to the days of Zerubbabel and he was their hero too. Prophecy had changed from its old grandeur when these spoke or wrote. Yet these are still prophets and their fine sayings must be interpreted prophetically : when Haggai rises to his height with " the desire of all nations" we must consider whether he a prophet, still continuing the majestic inspiration of Isaiah, may not be credited with the full glory of the phrase.

Haggai seems to belong to that elder generation who wept remembering the former temple. His first task was to urge the dispirited people and the indolent nobles to build the house of the LORD. Then he turned to cheer his friends who compared the present with the past. Thus came the word of the LORD :

> Speak now to Zerubbabel the son of Shealtiel, governor of Judah, and to Joshua, son of Jehozadak, the high priest, and to the remnant

of the people saying, Who is left among you that saw this house in its former glory? and how do ye see it now? is it not in your eyes as nothing? Yet now be strong, O Zerubbabel, saith the LORD; and be strong, O Joshua, son of Jehozadak, the high priest; and be strong, all ye people of the land, saith the LORD, and work : for I am with you, saith the LORD of hosts.

Then recalling the mercies of past history he strikes a louder note :

Fear not. For thus saith the LORD of hosts : Yet once, it is a little while, and I will shake the heavens, and the earth, and the sea, and the dry land; and I will shake all nations, and the desire of all nations shall come, and I will fill this house with glory, saith the LORD

" Desire " is the literal translation of the Hebrew word. It might signify, if the context required it, " desirable things," as our R.V. renders. That makes sense here of a kind : I will shake all nations and compel them to contribute riches for the restoration of this temple. But how flat a prophecy that would be. And surely the following verses are against it :

The silver is Mine, and the gold is Mine, saith the LORD of hosts. The latter glory of this house shall be greater than the former, saith the LORD of hosts : and in this place will I give peace, saith the LORD of hosts.

Not gold and silver : those are the LORD's already. He has something better in view. It is the old undying spirit of " camels and tents." The nations prosper; Israel knows a profounder peace. Only here the desire of the nations themselves is embraced. They too are waiting for their light : the glory of the Israel of God is a missionary glory : from Isaiah to Malachi that grows in clearness, and it is especially characteristic of this post-exilic age : the LORD of hosts will be the LORD

of the heathen now, and Israel His Servant is His
messenger to them.

Zechariah is the prophet of the younger generation,
who shouted for joy over the new temple. He sees the
nations shaken and his head is turned with visions of
Israel's restoration to far more than has come about

SEAL OF DARIUS.

yet. For him Zerubbabel is the LORD's anointed in a
fuller than the older sense. Will he revive the royal
state ? set a king on David's throne again ? Faith and
politics intermingle in Zechariah's dream. But faith
prevails. The LORD's anointed, the Messiah, Christ :
that is a vast idea which here reaches a stage in its
realization. And again the missionary spirit breathes :
Thus saith the LORD of hosts : In those days it shall
come to pass that ten men shall take hold, out of all the
languages of the nations, shall even take hold of the
skirt of him that is a Jew, saying, We will go with you,
for we have heard that God is with you.

Thus ends chapter 9 and with it the prophecy of Zechariah. What follows (9–14) is in an utterly different style. Presently we find ourselves in that Greek period which began with Alexander's victory and the fall of Persia in 333 B.C.: "I will stir up thy sons, O Zion, against thy sons, O Greece." We think of the Maccabean wars, and indeed these chapters are in the apocalyptic vein which runs through that time of struggle. Apocalypse is always rich in phrases of mysterious beauty, and no apocalyptic piece is fuller of such than these last chapters of the book of Zechariah : Behold thy King cometh ... lowly, riding upon an ass ; Turn ye to the strong hold ye prisoners of hope ; The thirty pieces of silver ; The wounds between the arms with which I was wounded in the house of my friends ; At evening time there shall be light. That last is part of the solemn scene of Jerusalem's final peril and salvation, the very peace and consummate holiness of apocalypse : "And the LORD shall be king over all the earth : in that day shall the LORD be one, and His name one." Yet how gladly do we turn back to the simpler apocalyptic of Zechariah himself:

> And Jerusalem shall be called The city of truth , and the mountain of the LORD of hosts The holy mountain. Thus saith the LORD of hosts : There shall yet old men and old women dwell in the streets of Jerusalem, every man with his staff in his hand for very age. And the streets of the city shall be full of boys and girls playing in the streets thereof

It is not surprising that the book of Zechariah should be thus composed of two prophecies and periods. There is connexion : the apocalypse runs out of the new Messianic strain. But besides that, these twelve minor prophets, as we call them, are in fact one book, the Book of the Twelve,[1] divided into chapters, and the division is here and there rather artificial. The last book or chapter of all is entitled Malachi ; which may be a proper name, but Malachi means in Hebrew My angel or My messenger, and it may simply be a title taken from the opening words of Mal. 3, " Behold I send My messenger, and He shall prepare My way before Me : and the LORD, whom ye seek, shall suddenly come to His temple."

If Haggai and Zechariah are the prophets of Zerubbabel, Malachi is the prophet of Ezra and Nehemiah, the prophet of the priesthood and the law : " For the priest's lips should keep knowledge, and they should seek the law at his mouth : for he is the messenger of the LORD of hosts : " " Remember ye the law of Moses My servant, which I commanded unto him in Horeb for all Israel, even statutes and judgements." But Malachi is a prophet still and Ezra and Nehemiah are ecclesiastics. There is a fire in what follows which we cannot fancy burning even in the stout and genial Nehemiah : " Behold I will send you Elijah the prophet before the great and terrible day of the LORD come. And he shall turn the heart of the fathers to the children, and the heart of the children to their fathers ; lest I come and smite the earth with a curse."

And Malachi would have had more feeling for the foreign wives than Nehemiah had : see how indignant he is in chapter 2 against a man's treacherous dealing with the wife of his youth. And he is not exclusive

[1] See *The Book of the Twelve Prophets commonly called the Minor*, by George Adam Smith, D D., etc. 2 vols. : The Expositor's Bible Hodder & Stoughton. Eighth edition, 1905.

but a brother in religion to the nations; for here as in Haggai prosaic interpretations must be rejected :

> I have no pleasure in you, saith the Lord of hosts, neither will I accept an offering at your hand. For from the rising of the sun even unto the going down of the same My name is great among the Gentiles ; and in every place incense is offered unto My name, and a pure offering . for My name is great among the Gentiles, saith the Lord of hosts.

CHAPTER 24

THE MANIFOLD WISDOM OF GOD

FROM Ezra onward the children of Israel may properly be called the Jews. That was not their proper designation before the exile. Jew is short for Judean : northern Israel could never have been Jews. But Jew means more than that. It means that the people live according to the fully-developed law and priesthood, that they are now a church rather than a nation. Jerusalem is but a subject city to foreign empires. Her children are scattered among the nations, once more pilgrims and sojourners on the transitory earth. Sion in a mystic sense is their home. The LORD, the one true God, is their only king : now when we may call them Jews, we may call their constitution a theocracy. Now the Messianic hope takes form ; it was but adumbrated in the old prophets ; for their visions the phrase was hardly suitable, it is Jewish. It is the Jews, not ancient Israel, who are the people of the Book : the monarchy had no Bible, the Bible is the product of the Jewish Church, the witness of the Jewish Church's faith.

No longer now do we see prophets withstanding single-handed a stiff-necked half-pagan nation, but a whole people confessing the prophetic creed. They have repented, accepted the divine idea, are set to work it out in faithfulness ; failing often and backsliding, but humble—at least before God if not before men—and recovering. No longer do we hear prophets with a general message to a nation in the mass, but a law is in operation of which the essence is pastoral care of all the several souls of men and women, the performance of a divine message already known by all, a charity which binds together all the divine brothers of the one spiritual family, a charity which is generous, liberal, careful of the weak and about small courtesies. That is the law on its human side : on the other, it brings Israel, "the children" of Israel, near to the one, transcendent, awful, holy God, all-ruling with a place in His majestic will for all the diverse wills of men.

The Jewish Church was like the church S. Paul describes in Ephesians, a diversity in unity. The four centuries between Malachi and the birth of our Lord has sometimes been pictured as a period of dry legalism, even a gradual petrifaction of religion. That view sprang from the domination of Ezra and Nehemiah's account of things. Modern criticism has cleared a larger and truer view. And as in former stages of our inquiry so here : it is not necessary to go far into criticism to recover this larger view. Turn simply from the English to the Hebrew Bible with its arrangement of the books under Law, Prophets, Writings. Look at the books included in the Writings, the latest division, the repository of the products of these latest centuries. There are Daniel, Job, Ecclesiastes, the completed Psalter. These books represent three characters of faith which belong to the Jewish Church of those latest centuries : those three characters are far from legal. The remarkable point is that, the Jewish Church being founded upon the Law, it still had room for such divergent types. The Law is the centre of

THE JEWISH CHURCH AFTER THE EXILE

the faithful, but round it many sorts of faithful rally : the Law is the ground and upon it notes of various tone and quality move harmoniously.

This variety may be simplified by distribution into four types :

1. There is the Law. This is the ground and centre, but good Jews, loyal to the Law, held to it in differing mode and measure ; and some were men of the Law in a special way. Using a rough analogy from our own time and place, we may say that there were parties in the Jewish Church as there are in the church in England, and one of these was the high church party of the Law.

2. The book of Daniel is an apocalypse. Apocalypses were a development of ancient prophecy. They were consolations for the saints and covenanters who stood for the pure faith when persecution raged against it. These apocalypses or revelations promised the triumph of God over the forces of the world, the coming of the kingdom of the saints or of heaven in the last days, or when things were at the worst ; the end of the world ; the reign of Messiah. These apocalypses are the voice of another party in the Jewish Church, the saints, the puritans, the enthusiasts.

3. Job and Ecclesiastes are books of criticism. In Job the problem of man's sorrow and suffering is discussed, and bold protest is made against the dogma of popular religion that suffering is the judgement of God upon sin. The discussion goes deeper than that ; the book appealed to profound thinkers, and is often exceedingly subtle in argument. But it is, speaking broadly, a criticism, a protest against received opinion, an inroad of reason upon faith. And Ecclesiastes is of the same

kind. A scholar faces the difficulties of faith. Some think he gives way before them. We shall find cause to dispute that judgement; but it is the excessive frankness of the speaker's criticism which has made it possible so to judge him. Both Job and Ecclesiastes represent a rational, latitudinarian, broad church party; modernists they might be styled to-day.

4. In the Psalter is the bond of union : the Law is the centre but the Psalter is the heart. It was the Prayer Book of the Jewish Church, a book of devotions drawn from many sources, many periods ancient and modern. But gathered into the Psalter, the Psalms show the very heart of the Jews, their real religion, their theology or intercourse with God. This is indeed no party book. Law, saintly hope, new law of liberty, sacrifice of praise without the blood of beasts, penitence and new life, reasonings of mind and conscience on creation providence atonement fate freewill; delight in nature child-like and meditative too; all the real emotion reason obedience daring of all the parties come together in the Psalter : the LORD throned on the praises of Israel, the children of Israel on their knees.

Here is a summary which we will work out as far as may be in our following chapters. For the present let us conclude with a few remarks upon it in general.

Some would consider Jewish Church a misnomer. The Jews got near the idea, but never quite formed a church : so it has been said. Well, there is no need to dispute about titles. Anyhow they did get very near. For look again at S. Paul to the Ephesians. See how his missionary period was full of fightings without and fears within; how the care, the anxiety,

THE JEWISH CHURCH AFTER THE EXILE

of all the churches in their several kinds and places wore him ; how gallantly he managed, as best he could, the rebellions and heresies and quarrels of the growing Christian community. Then compare with that the work of the prophets during the monarchy of Israel and Judah. S. Paul's missionary period ended with his arrest, and the leisure and peace of captivity succeeded ; leisure and peace, yet a trial was before him at Rome which might cost him life. In that quiet time the idea descended upon him, as from another world, the idea of the one church the body of the Christ, the body with its diverse living members, the unity in variety of the church, the "mystery" or sacrament of "the manifold wisdom of God." Does not the exile of Israel correspond to S. Paul's captivity? Do we not see the idea descending there too, as from another world, and all the warring impulses of earlier days brought together in this one living body, this "church" with its unity in diversity?

And to S. Paul the destined idea brought an enlarged outlook. The expectation of the Advent, which in Thessalonians he looked to see in a few years at most, changed and grew during the season of captivity. In Ephesians the church has a long vista before it. Christ is being all in all fulfilled. Instead of coming in the clouds to-morrow, He is through His body the church to grow and gather all, "till we all attain unto the unity of the faith, and of the knowledge of the Son of God, unto a full grown man, unto the measure of the stature of the fullness of Christ." The history of the nascent Jewish Church in the four centuries before our Lord was born, is a kind of first essay of such enlargement. Mere national ambitions were laid aside : the dispersion carried the faith over the wide world : hope soared into new regions of the Spirit. "When the fullness of the time came," not when faith had shrunk and hardened in the shell, the Lord, whom they sought, suddenly came to His temple.

One last word. The idea, we said, descended as from another world. What is commonly called the Ideal is such an idea in operation. The church is such an idea in operation ; not yet, or not here, in completion. Here it is always imperfect, falling short in holiness truth unity of its idea or heavenly pattern. But the pattern not the imperfection is the character, the real self of the church. Therefore the church is never satisfied with expediency or compromise ; though she has to bend to these limitations in operation, the idea may never be reduced. Therefore the Jewish Church insisted, Be ye holy as the LORD is holy in the midst of you. Therefore our Lord said, Be ye perfect as your Father in heaven is perfect. Therefore we confess One holy catholic apostolic church. The portrait drawn above of the post-exilic Jewish Church seems too pure : the Jews were often very far from such purity and charity. The portrait is like a creed, according to the idea ; the history is but the idea in operation : yet it makes all the difference between men of the world and churchmen whether there is the idea from which and into which they grow. The Septuagint translation of Ezekiel ends thus :

> And the name of the city · from the day in which it comes to be —when its idea shall be realized—it shall have its name.

CHAPTER 25

DISCREET AND LEARNED MINISTERS OF GOD'S WORD

THIS church was provided with its form in Babylon. Form, says Plato, is that which always follows colour. There had been plenty of colour, summer blue and blood red, in the days of judges and kings: form followed in the scholarship of the exile. Ezra is a type of the Jewish scholars from Babylon. Far down into the Christian centuries Jewish scholarship flourished eminently in Babylon.

Thus the Bible was made for the church. The people needed it, partly for their reading, still more for their worship. The Bible services of the synagogue, which superseded at last the sacrificial worship of the temple, germinated in the exile. Scholars and ritualists were in alliance. They collected selected and combined, they rewrote and edited the histories which they inherited from the simpler writers of former times, which those earlier writers had adapted from the lips of story-tellers, the first historians of all, rude vigorous, as story-tellers most accomplished, their stories glowing with colour. The Babylonian scholars composed new histories too of their own, extracting copying compiling: compare Chronicles with Samuel and Kings and you will perceive the method. But the stiff later work added something to the free early work. Naturally the exilic writers looked upon ancient events in the light of their changed tradition and experience: they saw the tabernacle and the worship of Solomon's days through the window of their own elaborate ritual and law and wrote accordingly. But more important is the reverence and splendour of mature faith which they brought to bear upon the rude past. Read for instance David's blessing in 1 Chron. 29 when he leaves to Solomon all he has prepared for the temple that shall be built; or Abijah's oration before the battle with Jeroboam in 2 Chron. 13 : we must doubt whether either belongs to strict history, and we may prefer the franker piety of the prophets ; yet there is something in this post-exilic devotion of the Chronicler which we would not willingly let die.

Legend and folklore were also admitted. The later taste was rather for miracle, startling and prosaic; the supernatural instead of the mystic. But these editors had scholarly consciences, and in their preservation of old work they were faithful to the older spirit. Sometimes perhaps we discern a tinge of contemporary Babylonian influence, but the utter contrast with Babylonian extravagance impresses us far more. With still more delight we recognize a kindly sympathy with simple readers in these rabbis, their care for the little children. Of course they put the Garden of Eden into their Bible, but perhaps there was discussion about the Tower of Babel : but the tower which was to reach to heaven fascinates a child's imagination ; it must come in. Only they took care to set the solemn theological Hymn of Creation on the first page of the Torah. There is the deep true faith of the church : all that comes after, Tower of Babel, jealous God, smelling of sacrifices, must be interpreted or even corrected by that opening celebration of God Who made heaven and earth and made all very good; Whom no man sees, Who speaks and it is done, Who passes understanding yet creates man in the image of God.

PLOUGHING IN THE VALLEY OF AJALON.

And the rabbis were themselves of a learned simplicity. They liked to use dialogue and story for the setting forth of ineffable things. Their successors in Talmudic days called such stories Midrash. Jonah is a regular midrash, an allegory, a parable. It is rather surprising to find Jonah among the Prophets : it seems to hail from quite a later age. But there it is, and its position in this second division of the Hebrew Bible shows that the rabbis were no innovators ; their traditions grew up gradually from far-off beginnings. Anyhow the vulgar difficulties of our days about Jonah would have seemed strange indeed to a Jew of Ezra's time. He would have read the psalm in chapter 2 and the story in chapter 1 as two presentments of the prophet's despairing and revived spirit, and thence would pass gladly on to the large doctrine of repentance forgiveness and charity in the parable of the gourd. So too with Balaam and the ass: he would recognize the working of a troubled conscience expressed in dialogue, all the more touching in that a poor beast might be God's intermediary and her master's friend. The Jew loved marvels, but did not take them so literally as we do. And being never flippant, he never spoiled his faculty of grave enjoyment. Reverence, wonder, quickness in the uptake, delight in a good story, hence springs the charm of Genesis for its readers. It is "manifold wisdom," but we must add "of God." The storytellers and the listeners were sincere in piety: they really loved God, though "knowing" God might seem to most of them presumptuous.

Ezra seems a dry prosaic person, but doubtless there were other kinds among his peers. It is remarkable how rich the Old Testament is in poetry. The older prophets declaimed their oracles and exhortations in thorough form of poetry. To that impressive and remembered form is due the preservation of much of the older prophecy. The rythmic strophes were repeated by ear before they were written out. Thus the rabbis had a good store of genuine material, the very words of the prophet, to start from. They added biographic notices ; kindred pieces of theology were appended ; the primitive denunciations were joined, sometimes fused, with post-exilic consolations. Isaiah is not the book Isaiah wrote, nor the book Isaiah wrote which has been enlarged afterwards : [1] it is "The Life Prophecies and Theology of Isaiah edited for the use of the Jewish Church." Thus too with Jeremiah, and The Book of the Twelve so much of which is anonymous. The whole collection of Prophets and prophetic histories must have been completed before the Maccabean struggle in the second century ; else we should expect to find Daniel included therein. We do include it : so did the Jews at Alexandria in their Greek Bible. But Daniel is one of those Writings which were being produced contemporaneously with the labours of these first editors or Bible makers : Bible Biblia that is The Library the Scriptures, means just that, an edition of documents furnished with titles punctuations and all the literary conveniences available at a given period.

In the Injunctions which were sent to Cambridge University and other Foundations Queen Elizabeth not only ordered a sermon to be preached on the commemoration day, but (as became Tudor learning) provided the heads of it : [2]

> The preacher shall declare the munificence of the Founder . shall show the value of good scholarship, and how much they are to be

---

[1] See *Isaiah 1–xxxvii*, by G. Buchanan Gray, D D., etc , in the International Critical Commentary. T. & T. Clark. The hundred pages of introduction to this excellent commentary gather into one readable essay what elsewhere is scattered in various writings of the latest criticism, and set the prophetic books in clearer light than ever before.

[2] *Visitation Articles and Injunctions of the period of the Reformation*, vol. II, pp. 210, 220. Alcuin Club Collection XV. Longmans, 1910.

praised who by their liberality give an impulse to studies: what an ornament it is for a kingdom to possess learned men who can judge well in matters of controversy: how honourable are the holy scriptures, how superior to all authority of men, how useful is the teaching of them to the commons, how widely the influence extends how excellent and royal a thing it is (for to the Ruler God has committed the cure of the whole People) to labour for a good supply of ministers of the Word, and to take care that these be respectable and erudite.

The sermon might be Ezra's own: it has as much the flavour of the fifth century B.C. as of the Elizabethan settlement. And indeed we owe the trustworthiness of the Old Testament to the scholarship of the Jewish Church: ancient things faithfully preserved, progress in revelation not obscured, new thought fearlessly admitted yet tempered by a reverent continuous tradition, the church tradition, the rule of faith and morality.

CHAPTER 26

THE TWO-EDGED SWORD OF THE SAINTS

THE book of Daniel has been glanced at several times in preceding chapters. It is not included among the Prophets in the Hebrew Bible, and it is not prophecy of the old kind. But it does represent a new form of prophecy which became conspicuous in the centuries between Malachi and the birth of our Lord. This is called Apocalypse or Revelation, and it enters as an original contribution to the theology of the Jewish Church.

Its roots were doubly in the past. It was an imitation of the ancient prophecies, and it was a revival of that undying fire of Israel which is typified by the camels and tents of the patriarchs; the sojourning on earth and the home with God; the peace of God better than the corn wine and oil of civilization. The world well lost for an idea: that has been given as a definition of romance. It might be a description of the apocalyptic temper, and more or less with lulls and storms it is characteristic of Israel from origin till now.

But it was again and again newly roused by persecution. It was the stern faith, the enthusiasm of saints or covenanters who stood for freedom and a national religion both pure and fierce against foreign arrogance and corruption or lukewarmness at home. Saints and covenanters: the terms are frequent in the psalms and histories, and a good way to understand the significance of them would be to read Scott's *Old Mortality* and ponder the language temper deeds and sufferings of those Scotsmen of the seventeenth century who prayed and fought on the mountains and called their brethren the saints and upheld a noble narrow faith under the form of the Covenant.

These centuries of the Jewish Church are rich in fruits of theology but not in historical events. Now and again we catch a rumour of oppression. Ezra told of Sanballat's malice. Something is heard of one Bagoses as a persecutor in the latest Persian times. But in the second century B.C. there was a persecution and a glorious resistance of which we know a good deal. The Persian empire fell before Alexander in 333 B.C. Soon after he died and his empire was divided between his generals. Egypt was held by the Ptolemies, Syria by the family of Seleucus many of whom were called Antiochus. The Jews were subject sometimes to Egypt sometimes to Syria. In 168 B.C. they were subject to Syria and an Antiochus of a very strange character : he called himself Epiphanes, the Splendid ; some called him Epimanes, the Madman. He came to his throne in Syria from Rome where he had lived as a hostage, and he came with a large and simple idea in his head : "he wrote to his whole kingdom, that all should be one people, and that each should forsake his own laws " ; he would hellenize the east. There were many among the Jews who shared his hellenizing taste. But it was clean contrary to the genius of Israel ; it was a "forsaking of the holy covenant." And presently Antiochus was defied.

Mattathias, son of John, son of Simeon, a priest of the sons of Joarib from Jerusalem, dwelt at Modin.

He had five sons, John who was surnamed Gaddis ; Simon who was called Thassi ; Judas who was called Maccabaeus ; Eleazar who was called Avaran ; Jonathan who was called Apphus. He saw the blasphemies that were committed in Judah and Jerusalem, and he said, Woe is me ! wherefore was I born to see the destruction of my people, and the holy city given into the hand of the enemy, the sanctuary into the hand of aliens ? Indeed he had cause for grief. Antiochus had forbidden the lawful worship, had "builded an abomination of desolation upon the altar" and turned the house of the LORD into a pagan temple. He was hanging and heading men and women, mothers and children : Jerusalem had "become a bond woman instead of a free woman." And Mattathias did more than cry woe.

The king's officers, who were enforcing the apostasy, came to Modin and summoned the people to sacrifice, urging Mattathias to set the example. But Mattathias made a spirited answer, and when he saw a Jew coming in the sight of all to sacrifice according to the king's commandment, "his zeal was kindled, and his reins trembled, and he showed forth his wrath according to judgement, and ran, and slew him upon the altar." He pulled down the altar and killed the king's officer also. Then he cried out in the city with a loud voice, Whosoever is zealous for the law, and maintaineth the covenant, let him come forth after me. And he and his sons fled into the mountains, and forsook all that they had in the city.

So the war began, a rebellion of highlandmen in their mountains, covenanters who forsook all for the faith. Mattathias intended to win, and after an unresisted slaughter of innocents who would not fight on a sabbath, he tempered such zeal and disciplined his band. They became a terror to unworthy Jews, and "they pursued after the sons of pride, and the work prospered in their hand." Mattathias died leaving Judas Maccabaeus captain in his room. And all his brethren helped him, and so did all they that clave unto his father, and they fought with gladness the battle of Israel. And he gat his people great glory, and put on a breastplate as a giant, and girt his warlike harness about him, protecting the army with his sword. The lawless shrunk for fear of him, and he angered many kings, and made Jacob glad with his acts, and he was renowned unto the utmost part of the earth, and he gathered together such as were ready to perish.

Antiochus sent generals and armies in vain. Apollonius, Seron, Lysias, Gorgias were all defeated. And after a short three years of fighting, Judas and his brethren could say, Behold, our enemies are discomfited: let us go up to cleanse the holy place, and to dedicate it afresh. They held the temple though not yet the rest of Jerusalem. And they did cleanse the temple, restore the worship, and inaugurate that feast of the dedication which was ever afterwards kept "from year to year by the space of eight days, from the five and twentieth day of the month Chisleu, with gladness and joy."

But fighting still went on. No longer mere guerilla warfare in the mountains the battle rolled far and wide over Edom, Ammon, Gilead, Galilee. The star of Antiochus began to set, and he died ingloriously in Persia, remembering all he did to Jerusalem, and confessing that "on this account these evils are come upon me, and behold, I perish through great grief in a strange land." His son Antiochus reigned under the regency of Philip, one of the king's Friends and renewed his father's hostility to the Maccabees. There was a great battle with a Syrian army of foot and horse and elephants, in which Eleazar died in the performance of a brave exploit. Four sons of Mattathias were now left, but another was presently to go.

Peace was arranged with the young Antiochus. But his right to the throne was disputed by Demetrius. This was the beginning of a tangle of disputed successions. The Maccabees generally held by the lawful line of descent, as far as it is possible to distinguish that. At this time Judas held by Antiochus, and in a battle against Demetrius' general Bacchides he was killed: "Judas fell and the rest fled. And Jonathan and Simon took Judas their brother and buried him in the sepulchre of his fathers at Modin. And all Israel mourned many days and said, How is the mighty fallen, the saviour of Israel! And the rest of the acts of Judas, and his wars, and the valiant deeds which he did, and his greatness, they are not written; for they were exceeding many."

So ends the history of Judas in 1 Maccabees, a Greek book of the Alexandrine Bible, which must have been drawn from nearly contemporary record, if it was not actually composed soon after the events. This first part, 1–9. 22, is a stirring story, plainly told, with grand touches here and there. The rest of the book is not quite so readable, but that is chiefly because the ins and outs of Syrian politics are so confusing; few will read the history of Judas without wishing to follow the fortunes of his brother Jonathan, who regained the whole of Jerusalem, was high priest, supported the true heir of the Syrian throne, was taken prisoner by the usurping Tryphon and put to death by him in cold blood; his brother John having already perished in something like the same way: then of Simon who succeeded Jonathan as high priest and leader of the people, gave them peace and prosperity, and was treacherously murdered by another would-be usurper, Ptolemy the son of Abubus. With a brief notice of John, who succeeded his father Simon, 1 Maccabees concludes.

It is a fine book, too little studied in the English Church. Let us read oftener in it: *cras amet qui numquam amavit quique amavit cras amet.* If there be any whose historical imagination must have modern aid, let them read *Jerusalem under the High Priests*[1] which is commonly and justly held to be as good as a novel only more true.

But at least two chapters ought also to be read from 2 Maccabees, a later Greek book of the Alexandrine Bible, and perhaps not quite without the element of romance; but it is certainly consecrated romance. The author of the epistle to the Hebrews had made 2 Maccabees part of his favourite reading. The Greek Church celebrates the festival of the Maccabean "martyrs before the martyrs." The glory of these proto-martyrs is set forth in 2 Maccabees 7. They were a mother and her seven sons. All seven resisted unto blood dying for the faith with cruel tortures, encouraged by their mother who herself died last of all, and testifying to their trust in a joyful resurrection and the ultimate triumph of the saints: "Women received their dead by a resurrection: and others were tortured, not

[1] *Jerusalem under the High Priests*, by E. R. Bevan. Arnold.

THE MACCABEES

accepting their deliverance ; that they might obtain a better resurrection" (*Heb.* 11. 35).

And no one who cares about immortal art can be content to leave 2 Maccabees 3 unread. It tells of the days of Onias the good high priest, and how Heliodorus the king's officer came to spoil the temple

HELIODORUS AND THE HEAVENLY RIDER

treasury, and of the grief of priests and people, and of the deliverance :

> While therefore they called upon the Almighty Lord to keep the things entrusted to them safe, Heliodorus went on to execute that which had been decreed. But when he was already present there with his guards over against the treasury, the Sovereign of spirits and of all authority caused a great apparition, so that all that had presumed to come in with him were sore afraid. There was seen a horse with a terrible rider upon him, and he rushed fiercely and smote at Heliodorus with his forefeet, and it seemed that he that sat upon the horse had complete armour of gold Two other also appeared unto him, young men notable in their strength, and beautiful in their glory, and splendid in their apparel, who stood by him

on either side, and scourged him unceasingly And when he had fallen suddenly to the ground and great darkness had come over him, his guards caught him up and put him into a litter, and carried him that had just now entered with a great train and all his guard into the treasury, himself now brought to utter helplessness, manifestly made to recognize the sovereignty of God.

It is noteworthy that none are said to have seen these apparitions except Heliodorus and his attendants; a testimony to the writer's honesty.

CHAPTER 27

THE KINGDOM OF HEAVEN

IF Maccabees were more read Daniel would be better understood. Daniel begins with the adventures of Daniel and his three companions at Babylon during the exile : their abhorrence of foreign luxury and faithfulness to the true God exactly illustrates the uncompromising practice of the Maccabean covenanters. At chapter 7 visions begin. These Daniel is told to "shut up" for they belong to future days (8. 26, 10. 14) : whenever the book was written, it was to be read in troublous times to come. As we go on studying it we see that those times were the times of Antiochus Epiphanes and the Maccabees. In chapters 7 and 8 we are told that the beasts of the vision are the empires of Media Persia and Greece : the horn is the first Greek king, that is Alexander ; and the four horns which rise out of it are his successors. "And in the latter time of their kingdom, when the transgressors are come to the full, a king of fierce countenance, and understanding dark sentences, shall stand up. And his power shall be mighty, but not by his own power ; and he shall destroy wonderfully, and shall prosper and do his pleasure : and he shall destroy the mighty ones and the holy people. And through his policy he shall cause craft to prosper in his hand ; and he shall magnify himself in his heart, and in their security shall he destroy many : he shall also stand up against the prince of princes ; but he shall be broken without hand ... and arms shall stand on his part, and they shall profane the sanctuary, and shall take away the continual burnt offering, and they shall set up the abomination of desolation. And such as do wickedly against the covenant shall he pervert by flatteries: but the people that know their God shall be strong, and do exploits ... and when they fall they shall be holpen with a little help ... and it shall be for a time times and a half; and when they have made an end of breaking in pieces the power of the holy people, all these things shall be finished" (8, 11, 12). In these last chapters the whole career of Antiochus is figured, but his death is foretold vaguely and not as it actually happened. The "time, times and a half" are the three and a half years which Judas Maccabaeus and his band, the "little help" will take to recover the sanctuary: they seem to have succeeded even sooner.

The natural inference from all this would be that Daniel was written as well as read in Maccabean times, before Antiochus died, and before Judas recovered the sanctuary. There are many other indications that this was so: part is written in Hebrew, part in the Palestinian Aramaic (not the Babylonian) which began to be the language of the people in the last centuries before Christ; the Chaldeans are a special class of wise men, whereas in the captivity they were the whole of the ruling nation at Babylon; and much more which would be strange in a book written during the captivity may be found clearly set out in Dr. Driver's excellent plain commentary in the *Cambridge Bible for Schools.*

If the Maccabean intention of the book is recognized the date of its writing need not be hotly disputed.

Yet the later date does add to its significance in the faith of the Old Testament. For if it is of late date, a prophecy disguised in symbols, put forth in the person of a hero of older time, it takes its place among those Apocalypses which nourished the popular hope of the kingdom of heaven and the coming Messiah during the three or four centuries in the middle of which our Lord was born. The labours of Dr. Charles especially have opened this strange world of thought to us in the last twenty years, and have thrown a flood of light on the Old and New Testament.[1] The book or books of Enoch, referred to in the epistle of S. Jude, is the most important. This is a series of prophecies set forth in the name of Enoch, and that is the regular fashion in Apocalypse, a literary convention not meant to deceive. They contain story and vision, express their prediction by symbols often bizarre. They console and encourage in times of trouble. The old prophets rebuked the sinful nation, pleaded for repentance, warned of judgement at hand, and promised a happier time when judgement had issued in purification. The Apocalypses console the saints, and promise them the kingdom of heaven. And the promise, at least in its fullness, is for "the last days." Daniel declares that deliverance from the tyranny of Antiochus will come speedily through the Maccabean warriors; but the reign of righteousness is not to be assured so quickly. The vision is extended. This present order of the world will come to an end. At that tremendous day "shall Michael stand up, the great prince which standeth for

[1] Translations of many of these Apocalypses are published at small price by the Society for Promoting Christian Knowledge.

the children of thy people : and there shall be a time of trouble, such as never was since there was a nation even to that same time : and at that time thy people shall be delivered, every one that shall be found written in the book. And many of them that sleep in the dust of the earth shall awake, some to everlasting life, and some to shame and everlasting contempt. And they that be wise shall shine as the brightness of the firmament ; and they that turn many to righteousness as the stars for ever and ever" (12).

In the splendid chapter 7 it is this final kingdom that the nearer vision of deliverance runs out into. And in that chapter we are shown not only the Ancient of days throned with ten thousand times ten thousand before Him, the judgement set, the books opened : " I saw in the night visions," Daniel goes on to say, " and, behold, there came with the clouds of heaven one like unto a son of man, and he came even to the ancient of days, and they brought him near before Him. And there was given him dominion, and glory, and a kingdom, that all the peoples, nations, and languages should serve him : his dominion is an everlasting dominion, which shall not pass away, and his kingdom that which shall not be destroyed." This Son of man appears again in one of the Enoch visions, and in Enoch he is described almost definitely as divine, pre-existent in heaven. All the Jewish Apocalypses proclaim the kingdom. Here in Daniel and Enoch, and in some of the rest, is the Messiah or Christ, as king of the kingdom. And the conception is far more distinct than anything in the old prophets. It was the hope of the Apocalypses, growing out of and bringing sharp outline to ancient prophecy, which seethed in the heart of the Jews when our Lord was born. He came from the wilderness after baptism with the startling announcement that the day of fulfilment had at last arrived : The kingdom of God is at hand : repent and trust this good news. That was His good news, His Gospel. No wonder the multitudes gathered round Him, regarded Him with awe, wondered if He could Himself be the Christ ; and if so, whether He would be a political leader or, as some expected, God from God divine. The drama of the Gospel is our Lord's deepening and purifying of this nascent trust, of the tragic disappointment of popular expectation, of the tragic fulfilment of His promise in death and defeat. The rest of the New Testament is the gradual stripping away of traditional apocalyptic scenery, the trumpet and the clouds ; the gradual revelation of what our Lord's Christhood, Deity, Advent essentially mean ; His Messianic Spirit leading deeper into His own truth. The apocalyptic scenery fades but the apocalyptic mystery is not merely the background of the Gospel : it is its heart.

Teacher or Redeemer ? It might seem that this light from the Apocalypses has revived belief in Christ as Redeemer for a generation that tended to reverence Him merely as a teacher. But the two offices are blended into one. The sermon on the mount is as apocalyptic as the Lord's answer out of Daniel to the high priest. " Lay not up for yourselves treasures upon the earth, but in heaven where neither rust nor moth doth consume . . . Take not thought for your life, what ye shall eat or drink or put on, for your heavenly Father knoweth that ye have need of all these things. But seek ye first His kingdom and His righteousness." All for the kingdom : all passing away, passing away : life lost is found : we know that we have passed out of death into life, because we love the brethren. . . . Even so : come, Lord Jesus. From camels and tents to Thy kingdom come, from patriarchs to scribes and Maccabees and our Lord and His disciples and the poor in spirit of all generations, there is one Christian faith and it is always a heart in heaven and a revolutionary morality—impossible except in Christ.

That phrase " in Christ " is explained by the Apocalypses. In Daniel 7 the kingdom given to the Son of man, is the kingdom given to the saints : the Son of man includes the saints. So to S. Paul the Christ is not just our Lord Jesus, but Jesus Christ including in His Christhood all who belong to Him : He is " all in all being fulfilled,"[1] through His growing body the church, till at last " we all attain unto the unity of the faith, and of the knowledge of the Son of God, unto one fullgrown man, unto the measure of the stature of the fullness of Christ " ; a proper hope if as Dr. Hort said, the church is " mankind knowing and fulfilling its destiny."

That large hope is in the Apocalypse of S. John the Divine, the consummation of the apocalyptic series, but even there it is obscured by visions of fearful judgement : in the Jewish Apocalypses judgement upon the enemies of faith is conspicuous. It is part of their doctrine of resurrection, a notable development of the doctrine of eternal life in Old Testament. The patriarchs lived on earth as sojourners with God : when they died they went to God, and that was enough to know. For our Lord too it was enough,

[1] The right translation of Eph 1. 23 : see Dr Armitage Robinson's Commentary (Macmillan, 1903)

and when He was tried by hard questions about resurrection He quoted the passage of the Burning Bush: "That the dead are raised Moses shewed when he called the LORD the God of Abraham, and the God of Isaac, and the God of Jacob. Now He is not the God of the dead, but of the living: for all live unto Him" (*S. Luke* 20). And that is our Lord's teaching in S. John : to know God is eternal life ; I am the resurrection and the life. This, the simplest and the deepest doctrine of eternal life, runs all through Old and New Testament from beginning to end. But this alone did not satisfy all at all times. The sorrows and injustices of life on earth compelled men to ask further questions, and answers were sought along another line which had its beginning in the Sheol of Israel's pagan ancestors and cousins among the Semites. In Sheol, the pit or hell, the dead still lived a shadowy life, cut off from the care of God : so held the Israelites in their popular religion. But the prophets declared with increasing certainty that there is but one true God, and that there is no place or state outside His care : if that were the meaning of Sheol, there is no such thing. And in their hostility to the superstition of Sheol the prophets kept silence about a life beyond the grave. They kept silence about a life beyond the grave ; they preached no doctrine of resurrection ; but who can read Isaiah and see how he lived in the living God, and doubt his profound faith in life eternal ? The prophets won the victory of faith at last, and the language of Sheol came back with altered import. The pagan despair, the being cut off from the care of God was impossible to the settled faith of the Jewish Church. It might still appear sometimes in the popular religion which inveterately lowers the best of faiths, and it might still be allowed in the passionate poetry of a psalmist, sympathizing with the bitterness of a soul when it was overwhelmed with the immediate blow of grief. But such psalms are completed by juxtaposition with psalms of another kind, and popular superstition was no longer dominant in those church centuries.

But on the other hand the old doctrine of Sheol was corrected and raised to a doctrine of resurrection and of judgement. We see this in its earlier vague poetic form in the apocalyptic piece in Isaiah 26 : "Thy dead shall live ; my dead bodies shall arise. Awake and sing ye that dwell in the dust : for thy dew is as the dew of herbs, and the earth shall cast forth the dead." And in the last chapter of Daniel we find it hardened into a dogma, the bold faith of persecuted saints, of martyrs : a faith which will flow into the New Testament to meet and coalesce with the other faith in life eternal, spiritual, now ;—cleansing its streams as it runs to the sea.

CHAPTER 28

ESTHER

IN the Writings, the third and latest division of the Hebrew Bible, there is a group of books which are called The five Megilloth or Rolls. These were read at certain feasts or fasts; Canticles at Passover, Ruth at Pentecost, Lamentations the 9th of the month Ab when the destruction of the temple was commemorated, Ecclesiastes at the feast of Tabernacles, and Esther at Purim. Purim was both fast and feast. A fast was kept on the 13th, a feast on the 14th and 15th of Adar, the last month of the year, i.e. the month immediately before New Year's Day in spring. The first two Rolls are well suited for their seasons and the third for its anniversary. And for Purim too a good story was appointed to be read, a story tragic in its opening but exultant at the end, telling of "the days wherein the Jews had rest from their enemies, and the month which was turned unto them from sorrow to gladness, and from mourning into a good day : that they should make them days of feasting and gladness, and of sending portions one to another, and gifts to the poor."

Once upon a time King Xerxes, or Ahasuerus as the Jews called him, feasted his princes for a whole six months, and ended with an especial entertainment of his courtiers in Shushan the palace. When all had well drunk he sent for queen Vashti to display her beauty to the company. But the queen had the good taste to refuse. Great was the indignation of the Persian lords. Queen Vashti was deposed and a new queen sought by a competition of maidens in worth and beauty. A Jewish orphan Esther, trained by her uncle Mordecai, won the prize. Soon after her promotion Mordecai saved the life and throne of Xerxes by discovering the plot of two chamberlains against him.

But Xerxes had a vizier named Haman whom Mordecai treated with dignified contempt. Haman vowed vengeance. " In the first month which is the month Nisan, in the twelfth year of king Ahasuerus, they cast Pur, that is, the lot, before Haman from day to day, and from month to month, to the twelfth month, which is the month Adar." Then he spoke to Xerxes about the Jews, a peculiar people whom he showed to be a peril to the empire, and against whom he advised the king to order a *pogrom* through the length and breadth of his dominions. Xerxes made no objection and the massacre was arranged for the thirteenth day of the twelfth month, which is the month Adar. " And the king and Haman sat down to drink ; but the city of Shushan was perplexed." Mordecai then sent to Esther bidding her put a stop to this. Esther replied that it was beyond her power and indeed it was death to approach the king without being invited to do so. Mordecai by plain speaking roused her to a more heroic spirit. "Think not, he said, with thyself that thou shalt escape in the king's house more than all the Jews. For if thou altogether holdest thy peace at this time, then shall relief and deliverance arise to the Jews from another place, but thou and thy father's house shall perish : and who knoweth whether thou art not come to the kingdom for such a time as this ? Then Esther bade them return answer unto Mordecai, Go, gather together all the Jews that are present in Shushan, and fast ye for me, and neither eat nor drink three days, night or day : I also and my maidens will fast in like manner ; and so will I go into the king, which is not according to the law : and if I perish, I perish."

With that brave word Esther began to show her worth. She proceeded carefully and cleverly. First she begged the honour of entertaining the king and Haman. Then in the genial hour she asked permission to give a second party next day when she would name the boon which the first feast had induced the king to promise recklessly. Chance, or some deeper " lot " than Haman's, aided her management of the royal reveller. Xerxes passed a wakeful night and read the annals of his reign. He found Mordecai's good service to the throne recorded and heard that he had received no reward. Determining to set that right he asked Haman what should be done for the man whom the king delighted to honour. Haman, supposing himself to be the lucky person, asked for ornament wealth and authority on a royal scale.

A yet grimmer irony was working in events. Stung yet again by Mordecai's contempt, he was advised by his wife and friends to hang the fellow, and had set up a gallows fifty cubits high for the purpose. When Xerxes put his question to him Haman had actually come to ask permission to hang Mordecai. Now he had to drop that scheme and at once do public honour to Mordecai. Sorrowful he returned to his house. Gloomily his wife Zeresh predicted his fall. Then came the second banquet, and Esther asked her boon. She told Xerxes of Haman's wicked design against the king's benefactor Mordecai and all Mordecai's people. Xerxes was very angry. He went to walk in the garden and to consider. Returning he found Haman begging for his life from Esther and with suspicious jealousy his wrath ran over. "As the word went out of the king's mouth, they covered Haman's face." He was taken away and hanged on his own gallows.

Then there was an orgy of retribution. Repeal of the decree was bettered. The Jews were bidden to defend themselves and make reprisals. Panic seized their adversaries. In Shushan the palace and far hence throughout the wide empire the Jews slew and slew. Ever after the happy days were kept, the day of doom, the days of vengeance. The whole festival of fast and revelry was called Purim in memory of Haman's "lot."

But it is an odd name. There is no word Pur in Hebrew. Scholars cannot agree on any word in any other language which will suit in sound and sense. There is a word something like it in Persian or Babylonian which means assembly. It is used in old mythology for the assembling of the gods on new year's day to fix the lots or fates of the opening year. It seems as though the Jewish Church in Persian times may have assimilated a Persian Saturnalia, itself an assimilation of a Babylonian mystery, to some day of rejoicing of their own. And in *The Golden Bough*,[1] Sir James Frazer points out curious coincidences between the narrative of Esther and the practices of this ancient new year's festival. The moral of *The Golden Bough* is the cruelty of superstition, and cruel indeed this festival seems to have been in its origin. It was nothing less than the murder of the king who, worn out with his

---

[1] *The Golden Bough, a study in magic and religion* (3rd edition), by J. G. Frazer. Part vi, *The Scapegoat*, p. 360 ff. (Macmillan, 1913.)

magical regality, could no longer be depended upon to ensure the prosperity of land and people and must make way for a younger victim. In later times there was mitigation. The king lived on but the ancient rite was represented in mockery. A criminal was made king of revels for a term of days : then, his dreadful license ended, was put to death ; an ironic reversal of the "lot," like Haman's.

Is this folk-lore too ingenious ? One is loth to say so, after reading such a fine story-teller as Sir James Frazer. Yet the book of Esther is finer still in its large simple moving Hebrew style, the style of Holy Scripture. By the quality of style at least Esther vindicates its claim to a place in the sacred canon.

But is that enough ? Can we really think Esther to be in its proper place by the side of Job, Psalms, Lamentations ?

Is the story true ? Not wholly we must confess. Ahasuerus is not the Xerxes of history. The dates in the narrative are not so vague as reckless : you jump a hundred years without noticing it. Does the narration ring like history at all ? Not so to a trained ear. And yet ; does that matter so very much ? The books of the Old Testament are of various kind. Genesis is like the Gospels : Job is like a grand religious drama of the Greeks : the Wisdom of Solomon is like Plato or the Epistle to the Hebrews : Isaiah 40–55 is a Te Deum. May we not accept Esther as akin to the Legends of the Saints in the mediaeval Breviaries ?

Perhaps: but there is a difference. Those legends are edifying. Is Esther edifying ? God is not so much as named. Fasting is mentioned but never prayer. And yet—" If I perish, I perish "—that gallant decision of an inexperienced girl; the dignity courage and obstinate patriotism of Mordecai; lives there a man with heart so dead as to read this brave tale and not be stouter-hearted for the reading? And though God be not named, who is it that directs, unseen unheard, that ever deepening mystery of the " lot "?

The fierce close is repellent. Not more so than are certain Psalms, or those terrible last verses of the book of Isaiah, or even the last chapter of Daniel; for does the reward of the just blot out the awfulness, to conscience, of that last judgement on the persecutors?

On the persecutors: wait a moment and consider that. The festival of the month Adar, " Mordecai's day," is first mentioned outside the book of Esther at the end of 2 Maccabees. It seems not improbable that it was instituted in commemoration of the Maccabean victory over Nicanor. That would not forbid our also supposing that some Jewish custom of new year's jollity was adapted, consecrated, to a new connexion. But if the Maccabean memory tinges the ritual and scripture lesson for the day, we may partly excuse the vindictiveness. Read 1 Maccabees 1–7 and learn charity toward persecuted and therefore bitter covenanters. They have not the perfection of Isaiah's Servant of the Lord, but they do not stand before the bar of our poor judgement. They suffered and they smote; for the Lord, for the faith, for the nation. Mordecai thought perhaps of all three: Esther of none of the three but only of gratitude and obedience to her guardian; and is that less admirable, an ignorant child risking life, planning wisely, in her simplicity?

The book of Esther tells of souls devoted to high duty; it is not lacking in devotion. Nor is it without a brooding sense of divine though secret providence. But it has not the accent of piety. This was added in the Greek version of the Septuagint, as may be read in the Apocrypha of our English Bible in "The rest of the chapters of the Book of Esther, which are found neither in the Hebrew, nor in the Chaldee." Here is a piece from Esther's prayer before she intruded upon the presence of King Xerxes:

> Remember, O Lord, make Thyself known in the time of our affliction, and give me boldness, O King of the gods, and holder of all dominion Give me eloquent speech in my mouth before the lion and turn his heart to hate him that fighteth against us, that there may be an end of him, and of them that are likeminded with him . but deliver us with Thine hand, and help me that am desolate and have no other helper but Thee, O Lord Thou hast knowledge of all things; and Thou knowest that I hate the glory of the wicked, and abhor the bed of the uncircumcised, and the sign of my high estate, which is upon my head in the days wherein I shew myself Neither had Thine handmaid any joy since the day that I was brought hither to this present, but in Thee, O Lord, the God of Abraham. O God that art mighty above all, hear the voice of the forlorn, and deliver us out of the hands of the mischievous, and deliver me out of my fear "

Not without beauty, this. But it is not the prayer our high-spirited natural joyous Esther would have prayed. There is more sentiment in the Greek, more honesty in the unadorned Hebrew.

CHAPTER 29

THE SPIRIT OF MAN IS THE CANDLE OF THE LORD

THIS verse was a favourite with the seventeenth-century Cambridge Platonists and will serve as a motto for a party not unlike them in the Jewish Church, the Wisdom writers. The verse is from Proverbs (20. 27), and represents the more philosophic vein of that shrewd, broadly pious book. For the Hebrew Wisdom corresponds to the philosophy of the Hellenic world and like it has two modes, gnomic sentences of homely penetration, and critical speculative thinking. In Prov. 8 there is a notable example of that speculative theology, the hymn of Wisdom in which Wisdom is a person, the assessor of God at the creation, His messenger to the spirits of men; almost a Person within the Godhead. This hymn gave impulse to the Greek book called The Wisdom of Solomon, to Philo the Jewish philosopher of Alexandria, to the Epistle to the Hebrews and the prologue of the Gospel according to S. John. The rest of Proverbs is racy of the soil:

> Where no oxen are, the crib is clean.
> But much increase is by the strength of the ox —14. 4.

conversant with the affections of ordinary men:

> The heart knoweth its own bitterness.
> And a stranger doth not intermeddle with its joy —14 10.
> A friend loveth at all times,
> And a brother is born for adversity.—17. 17.

As cold waters to a thirsty soul,
So is good news from a far country.—25 25.

liberal and generous :
He that hath pity upon the poor lendeth unto the LORD.—19. 17
The liberal soul shall be made fat .
And he that watereth shall be watered also himself.—11. 25

good mannered :
The discretion of a man maketh him slow to anger
And it is his glory to pass over a transgression.—19. 11.

Be honest, diligent, stand in the old ways : 'tis a rough world but a good man can make it happy : yet do not count on yourself too much, the LORD appoints, and the LORD disappoints the confident : that is the gist of Proverbs, and that kind of Wisdom is continued by Jesus son of Sirach in his book of Wisdom, which we commonly call Ecclesiasticus.

Solomon is the patron of Hebrew Wisdom. The first collections in the book of Proverbs bear his name. Other collections with other titles are included in the complete book. It ranges far and wide, and illustrates three characteristics of all the Wisdom writers : they are not precisians for law or sacrifices ; they look beyond the limits of Israel and begin to be citizens of the world ; they criticize conventions, and are by no means all conservatives—in chapter 30 Agur the son of Jakeh is a bold freethinker, but he is answered by a wise man who still thinks the old is good.

Agur was perhaps one of the fools who said there is no God. Job was never foolish and never spoke an obvious irreverence like that. But he was a bold freethinker, a titanic protestant. At least the Job who suffers argues and at last comes home to God in the book that is named after him, is such a character. This book is a dramatic meditation on a traditional story. The author seeks an answer to the whole problem of life. Milton's prayer in *Paradise Lost* might be his:

>What in me is dark
>Illumine; what is low raise and support;
>That to the highth of this great Argument
>I may assert th' Eternal Providence,
>And justifie the wayes of God to men.

Indeed Job is comparable with *Paradise Lost*. In both an ancient story is retold with modern reflexion. Both might be styled renascence works: they both come from an age in which men look back upon a long process of thought, while a new way of regarding faith and experience is newly opening: no longer can they be content to picture God as ruling from without, they find God more within their own conscience hopes fears action and sufferings.

There is a certain resemblance between the Satan in Milton and in Job. Following his tradition Milton says that Satan is very evil. Yet how noble he has made him; not only is he the most interesting, he is almost the grandest figure in the poem. God is immutable in power and peace, but Satan lives with a life like ours. Often Satan is John Milton himself, and John Milton in his faulty best, not in his worst. So in the prologue of Job this Adversary enters grandly, sinister yet curiously sympathetic with Job; Job tried to the uttermost yet enduring; yet, as the Satan declares, doomed to fail at last. And the Satan is no rebel angel, but eminent among the servants of the LORD; his antagonism brings the calmly supreme God into the struggling progress of men. The Satan is bidden to try Job, and

"When the Almighty was yet with me; when my children were about me."

he tries him horribly. Bereaved, sick unto death, he presently gets comfort that is worse than misery from his three friends. Job argues against their cruel conventional theology. They turn upon him more and more severely, judging him proved a sinner by his suffering, which must be deserved; for thus they justify the ways of God to men. Job answers wisely impatiently fiercely; yet again and again checks the fierceness as though some flash of deeper understanding renewed his endurance; sweetened his temper. Yet more than once or twice he comes near to despair. His friends' iteration of what they suppose God to be, the more terrible character which his own appeal to the facts of life obliges Job to assign to God, overwhelms him. Each time however the spirit within him asserts itself and saves him. He turns from all these outward baffling testimonies and calls upon God Who is hiding His real Godhead, Who yet is real and yet is God: where is God, can He too be within?

At last the weariful dispute ceases. As by a chorus to the drama a lyric praise of Wisdom is sung. Where can wisdom be found? How can such questions as Job asks be answered? The old traditional response is given: Man has no wisdom but to fear God, man can never find answer to these questions. But, as always in this transporting book, subtle novel harmonies beset the accustomed tune. That resigned impotence is not the last word. There is a spirit in man which still keeps him searching: can it be that the search progresses?

Then what seems an excrescence in the book appears. One Elihu, not mentioned as yet nor afterwards, makes a long speech, finding fault with both Job and his friends, yet not unkindly. The author has drawn his story and his ideas from many sources. Here he brings it something different in language and intellectual power from anything else he includes. With the almost arrogant carelessness of a masterly artist he troubles not to fit the alien patch neatly in. He puts up with its inferiority; for he has a purpose to serve with it. He is enlarging the story of Job into a story of mankind. The friends are the bitter representatives of popular orthodoxy wearing stale. Job is the undying spirit of humanity protesting, and (so to say with reverence) discovering God anew. Elihu is the younger man—so he describes himself—the younger generation in a time of transition, rather conceited, unwitting of what deeper thinkers have already shown, yet having something to say which no wise man will ignore, the average something of the vernacular of the day. Elihu is hard to follow, for he has not got his thought clear. But he is trying to think: he fashions a number of illuminating phrases: he prepares us for a solution which would not have occurred to either Job or his friends.

In a great storm it comes. Out of the storm Jahveh, the God of the patriarchs, thunders. He opens a vast vista of life before Job prostrate in adoration. Job's sufferings, the friends' cruelties, Elihu the bright youth quite forgotten, all are but parts in a whole which is no scheme of justification, but all life itself, and all of it divine. There is comfort in all large views. But it would be foolish to say that Job's comfort came just so, or that a mere large view will ever mend a broken heart. The Hebrew writers of Wisdom or of anything else were only quasi-philosophers: the fiery particle was always disturbing them: God was reality to them, and the only hopeless trouble they knew was to be cut off from God

—as Job had come near to feeling himself—the only peace to be in communion with God. The humble spirit, the contrite heart; wisdom protest critical questioning might be among the means of renewing such a spirit, but the renewal was the only thing that mattered; and the renewal came ultimately from God Himself. So was it at last with Job. In that awful hour when the voice of Jahveh rolled over him, he became again as a child who, crying, knows his father near. He was left feeble but reborn. His communion with God was restored, secured.

On this grand poem many great commentaries have been written.[1] There is a famous essay by Dr. Mozley. Dr. Cheyne's *Job and Solomon* is rich in theology, scholarship, humanity. Dr. A. B. Davidson wrote years ago one of the best commentaries that we have on any book of Scripture, a simple one in the *Cambridge Bible for Schools*. Dr. Driver began and Dr. Buchanan Gray completed, a fine full commentary in the International Critical series. Last year Dr. Ball's translation and notes won the gratitude of Hebrew students. Job in the Revised Version is almost a new interpretation, for splendid as the language of the Authorized Version is, it leaves the argument of the drama all but incomprehensible.

[1] *Essays Historical and Theological* By J. B. Mozley, D D. Vol. ii. Rivingtons, 1878.
Job and Solomon, by T. K. Cheyne. Kegan Paul, 1887.
A critical and exegetical Commentary on the Book of Job together with a new Translation, by the late Samuel Rolles Driver, D.D, and George Buchanan Gray, D.D T. & T. Clark, 1921
The Book of Job, a revised text and version, by C. J. Ball, with preface by C. F Burney. Oxford at the Clarendon Press, 1922.

CHAPTER 30

VANITY OF VANITIES

"THE words of the Preacher, the son of David, king in Jerusalem." This first verse is the title prefixed to the book we call Ecclesiastes. Ecclesiastes is the Greek for the Hebrew word we render Preacher. The Hebrew is a feminine participle, and according to the usage of the Hebrew language (in which there is no neuter) it might mean Debating in the abstract, or perhaps Debater (rather than Preacher) *par excellence*, the Great Debater. The literary fiction that Solomon is the debater is not kept up after the first chapter. The innocent conventionality, or picturesqueness of this fiction may be understood by comparing the Wisdom of Solomon in the Alexandrine Bible and our Apocrypha. That book is written in Greek, in which language no one ever supposed Solomon would have written. The Hebrew of Koheleth or Ecclesiastes is almost as far as Greek from the tongue of Solomon. It is Hebrew of a markedly late style, the classic language breaking down into rabbinic. The concluding verses show what the book really is. This "Preacher" was one of the learned men who met in what is called "the house of instruction" in Ecclesiasticus 51.23. In earlier chapters we have sometimes called them rabbis, though it was an anachronism to do so, for rabbis belong strictly to a later period: it was a picturesque convention, like the author of Ecclesiastes calling his master Solomon. This author was a pupil who attended the debates of the great men. His master sat eminent among the rest for his wisdom and his boldness in facing the difficulties of faith. The pupil has here preserved a record of his master's words. He adds a few of his own (12. 9–14). He says that his master was not only a subtle talker in the schools, but a plain teacher also of the people : he did not puzzle the ordinary people with his academic difficulties. The pupil professes his admiration for those deeper " words of the wise " : the purity of a progressive faith depends on such frank scholarship, especially when it is raised and unified by the commanding intellect of " one shepherd " such as his master was. But he himself and his readers must not be presumptuous. These high debates they may be interested in but had better not meddle with. For them, to fear God and keep His commandments is the end of the matter. Nor is that modesty irksome : of making many books there is no end, and much study is a weariness of the flesh.

We are the more grateful to him for making us this book. No doubt it attracted readers at once. It is pretty clear that new editions were called for and that the independence of the original has been infringed in the edition we now use. The last verse of chapter 2—except the very last words—cannot have come from the Preacher. "For to the man that pleaseth Him God giveth wisdom and knowledge and joy : but to the sinner He giveth travail, to gather and to heap up, that He may give to him that pleaseth God " : that is average piety, not the Preacher's grip on things, and indeed it contradicts him ; the later ecclesiastical editors inserted that for edification. But such insertions are very few. Some passages which have been thus explained can well be co-ordinated with his thought. In some places modern translation has disguised the genuine meaning. Thus the verse 3. 21 is a question not a statement: who knows that the spirit of man is better than the beast's? In 10. 12 we should translate : " The words of a wise man's mouth are gracious ; but the lips of a fool will swallow him up," not "swallow up himself," bitter fact not moral propriety. Elsewhere inconsistencies appear, but such inconsistencies as belong to the progress of an honest mind, going back and forth upon itself. Thus in 9. 10 the Preacher applies the popular idea of Sheol to the general vanity of life : " Whatsoever thy hand findeth to do, do it with thy might ; for there is no work, nor device, nor knowledge, nor wisdom, in the grave, whither thou goest " ; but in 12. 7 he moves onward and inward to a deeper conception of the change that comes through dying : " And the dust return to the earth as it was, and the spirit return unto God Who gave it."

"Vanity of vanities, all is vanity." In one breath with that remarkable recovery of patriarchal faith, that anticipation of our Lord's " Father, into Thy hands I commend My spirit," this ambiguous theologian repeats his creeping refrain. Is it cynicism, or is it the narrow way of faith at last ? Faith, surely. See what has gone before. All is vanity, he began, there is no new thing under the sun. Pleasure is vanity, and so is wisdom. But he soon begins to modify that last complaint : come what may, let us reverence wisdom, he says more and more frequently ; let us trust reason wherever it leads. Then in chapter 3 he looks more curiously into the cause of vanity, and finds that God "hath made everything beautiful in its time : yet also He hath set eternity at the heart of things, so that man cannot find out the work that God hath done from the beginning even unto the end." Here vanity is no longer mere emptiness, but more like what philosophers call "appearance"—the painted veil which we call life. Things, circumstance, action, suffering, thought, all the relations among which man moves are mere appearances. That implies reality somewhere : he never questions that God is and works : only, shall man ever profit of this hidden reality ?

Then indignation stirs him, righteous indignation and passionate sympathy :

> Then I returned and saw all the oppressions that are done under the sun : and behold, the tears of such as were oppressed, and they had no comforter ; and on the side of their oppressors there was power, but they had no comforter. Wherefore I praised the dead which are already dead more than the living which are yet alive ; yea, better than them both did I esteem him which hath not yet been, who hath not seen the evil work that is done under the sun. —4. 1–3.

He falls back into his melancholy, but he has said enough to show a strong generous emotion, such an emotion as breaks through into reality, though a man be not conscious that it so does. And this powerful earnestness is what forbids our acquiescence in attempts to vindicate for the Preacher himself those few bits of feebler morality which fit his onward battling debating soul so ill. If those were his he would not be the great soul which he surely is.

And evidence follows that he has been in touch with reality, or as he himself would assuredly express it, with God. He looks about at politics and governments with keen observation. And he takes a side, the side of right. To be sure he keeps dropping back upon his melancholy formula, but you cannot help feeling he is not in fact so melancholy as he was. There is duty, and there is joy. Sheol may bring even good work into the scheme of vanity, yet work may be good. And there is something in courage, and the taking of chances. And (as the Jewish genius always tended) he cares for liberality :

> Cast thy bread upon the waters · for thou shalt find it after many days. Give a portion to seven, yea, even unto eight; for thou knowest not what evil shall be upon the earth. . . . He that observeth the wind shall not sow; and he that regardeth the clouds shall not reap. . . . In the morning sow thy seed, and in the evening withhold not thy hand . for thou knowest not which shall prosper, this or that, or whether they both shall be alike good. Truly the light is sweet, and a pleasant thing it is for the eyes to behold the sun —11. 1–7.

And then youth : the sight of youth invigorates him, as it must a man who has a sensitive touch on life. " Rejoice, O young man, in thy youth " : how much more verve there is in his bidding to rejoice than in his perfunctory addition of warning. " Therefore remove sorrow from thy heart, and put away evil from thy flesh : for youth and the prime of life are vanity " : a nonsensical or malicious collocation indeed, if vanity means no more here than it did in the first chapter.

But it does mean more. The transition moves naturally to the description of failing strength, old age, and quiet death in chapter 12. That the Preacher enjoyed making that poetic description, who can doubt? But if it is but art for art's sake, how poor a thing it is. And the responsive soul of generations insists that it is no poor thing. He rises into poetry—the Hebrew way

—as the tangle of thought gets clear and the oppression lifts and conscience of God fills all. And so at last death, that central mystery of vanity, solves all that matters. The old faith suffices; it can expand to the needs of newest experience: the old phrase of Genesis is enough for a satisfying formula. The dust returns to the earth as it was; the spirit returns unto God Who gave it.

> We children of Beneficence
> Are in its being sharers;
> And Whither vainer sounds than Whence,
> For word with such wayfarers.[1]

It is still contested whether Ecclesiastes represents the hardest victory of Hebrew faith or its ignominious failure. Some who hold by failure may think that our conclusion has been reached by allowing too much to the Preacher's credit which is really due to his editor. Some will raise another kind of objection. Allowing him a fine faith they will say that it conflicts with the faith of the Gospel: for the Gospel was the assurance of God's power to create a new thing, new life: so too Isaiah, but not so the Preacher who declares that there is nothing ever new under the sun. But he said that in the first chapter, and he travels afterwards. His own book is in fact itself a new thing. He first faces the difficulties of a new age, and at last finds the old faith capable of new application. He does this with pain and labour, not exultantly. You almost doubt whether he has done it. But new life may be quiet life: creation sometimes issues from a process which seems on the surface to be stagnation.

[1] George Meredith: "The Question Whither" in *A Reading of Earth*.

CHAPTER 31

ALEXANDRIA

AT the battle of Issus, 333 B.C., Alexander the Macedonian defeated Darius the Persian. Thus ended the Persian period in Jewish history and the Greek began. In 323 B.C. Alexander died and his wide empire was broken up among his generals. Syria, as we have already seen, fell to the Seleucids; Egypt to the Ptolemies. And in Egypt Alexander had founded Alexandria which did more than all his battles to hellenize the world. It was a city of Greek beauty and Greek learning. It had a university where the classics of Hellas were studied, a new poetry all but classic was written, and students coming and going carried the flame of knowledge throughout the earth.

Thither came many Jews, not altogether strangers: for Jews had already traded in Egypt, served as soldiers, settled there. At Assuan or Syene, far up the Nile, was a colony of Jews in the sixth century B.C. We know much of this colony's life business religion. For not long ago many documents were discovered, written by them on the "paper" used in Egypt, made from the water-plant of the Nile, the papyrus. These documents are in Aramaic, a cousin language to the Hebrew, spoken with variety of dialect by many people from Babylonia to the Mediterranean Sea. By degrees the western Aramaic made inroad upon, and at last ousted Hebrew in Palestine; so that by Gospel times Hebrew was like

Latin to-day in Italy, the language of worship while Aramaic was the language of common life : when our Lord said Talitha cumi, when He spoke on the cross a verse from the twenty-second psalm—Eloi, Eloi, lama sabachthani—He used Aramaic. He had heard that Aramaic version of the psalm in the synagogue ; for interpretations, called targums, were interspersed in worship. And so it must have been at an earlier date in Alexandria. The Jews there spoke Greek, as in Palestine they spoke Aramaic. The sacred Hebrew needed translation in their services. Hence was formed the Greek Bible, the Alexandrine version, the Septuagint, or version of the seventy, as it is commonly called.

A story was told of its origin which accounts for that title. It is preserved in The letter of Aristeas [1] which tells how Ptolemy Philadelphus, 285–247 B.C., brought seventy elders from Jerusalem to make a translation of the Law into Greek for his library : they made the translation and it was received with joy by the Jewish people in Alexandria. These may be facts, but they are surrounded by so much pomp and ceremony in the letter that we cannot but wonder as we read. And the abundant discovery of papyri of late in Egypt compels more doubt. These papyri show what the vulgar tongue was in Alexandria at that time. It was a very different tongue from what kings courtiers and librarians cared for. It was what we find in the Septuagint, and what the Jews would want in their worship : this Greek version of the Old Testament is much more likely to

---

[1] The letter of Aristeas may be read in Dr. Swete's *Introduction to the Old Testament in Greek*, Cambridge University Press, 1900 ; new edition revised and enlarged by Mr. Ottley. S P.C.K. has published a translation.

PAGE OF AN ELEVENTH-CENTURY MS. OF THE SEPTUAGINT

have sprung from the synagogue than from a royal command.

Thus it would begin and grow naturally, spontaneously; and the spontaneity of the Septuagint is its great charm. A really vernacular version of Holy Scripture is hard to come by. Even those that are made to-day in the mission field are the work of European scholars who mingle scholarship with the spoken language. S. Jerome's Latin Vulgate and our English versions are the outcome of a series of translations from translations and revisions of earlier forms: their language is peculiarly fit for their purpose, it is better than the vernacular: but it is not the vernacular, it is a treasure apart. Of course some art must affect all written books: the diffuse disjointed speech of even good conversation would be intolerable to read. But when the art of composition goes no further than is just necessary, when you seem to be hearing everyday speech as the book is read, you have uncommon pleasure. The Jews of Alexandria had that pleasure, Greek scholars to-day may at least fancy they have that pleasure when they read the Septuagint. That does not mean that the Septuagint is in so unsophisticated a style throughout. There is no reason to doubt that the Law was translated in the reign of Ptolemy Philadelphus. It wins credit for Aristeas that he tells his story only of the Law. The Law was done first and most simply. Books in frequent use like Isaiah and the Psalms would be treated in the same way a little later. Others were dealt with later and by degrees. A Greek Bible began to be formed, and books were added to it from private pens of varying skill. Not at one stroke or in one manner was the Septuagint created. Nearer to the real speech of daily life on the whole, and more spontaneously than any other version, it reached maturity by natural growth.

The Palestinian targums are strange affairs. They are free paraphrases, embroidered with story legend fancy, often very trivial. That was too late or too eastern for Alexandria. And the targums never became a Bible ; the Septuagint did and was purged in the process. But it has its additions. Esther and Daniel are filled out. The Song of the Three Holy Children, our Benedicite, is from the Alexandrine Daniel ; so is the offertory prayer in the Roman mass : " In a contrite heart and in a humble spirit let us be accepted, and so let our sacrifice be in Thy sight this day, after Thy kindness and according to the multitude of Thy mercy." But chiefly, it includes whole books which are not in the Hebrew. These books, 1 Esdras, Tobit, Judith, Wisdom of Solomon, Ecclesiasticus, Baruch, 1 and 2 Maccabees, make up nearly the whole of our Apocrypha. The Greek Bible was the Bible of most of the New Testament writers and of the early Church, and some of these books were most acceptable Scripture then. But a margin of inspiration was allowed then, and when the limits of the canon began to be distinctly drawn a difference was made ; though the Wisdom of Solomon was nearly always revered. S. Jerome, who had learned theology in Palestine, strove hard to exclude these marginal books : his is the sentence in our Sixth Article of Religion : " The other books the Church doth read for example of life and instruction of manners."

The Septuagint is of value as an aid to recovering the text of the Hebrew Bible where it has come to us in a corrupted shape. It cannot be disputed that this is sometimes, if not frequently the case. An obvious instance may be seen in 1 Samuel 13. 1, where the Hebrew has "Saul was a year old." But, as the note in R.V. margin indicates, the Septuagint gives little help there. In the Psalm of Habakkuk we have an example of its yielding very real help. "The oaths to the tribes were a sure word" (*Hab.* 3. 9). What can that mean? Mr. St. John Thackeray, following the Septuagintal clue, shows that this is no part of the psalm, but a rubric. "Weeks (not "Oaths" which is a very similar word in Hebrew), Rods, Word (or Promise)": that is the whole line in the original. Each word is a catchword, referring to passages in the Torah which were to be read with this psalm on proper occasions. And, handling his Septuagint with skill, Mr. Thackeray has restored much more of this grand poem to simplicity and force; as may be partly recognized in Canon Dalton's version in our chapter on Habakkuk, pp. 141–2, above.[1]

The Septuagint is almost the only aid we have for such restoration. There are no very ancient manuscripts of the Hebrew Bible, as there are of the Greek New Testament. Worse than that, all the manuscripts we have are in a bond to tell one tale. The received or masoretic Hebrew text must have been officially settled, probably in the second century after Christ, and measures must have been taken to abolish all traces of variant texts. But the Septuagint was evidently made while variant texts existed, and it serves as record of earlier varying Hebrew manuscripts. It adds to the interest of our Prayer Book version of the Psalter

[1] See also *The Septuagint and Jewish Worship, a Study in Origins*, by H. St John Thackeray. The Schweich Lectures for 1920. Published for the British Academy by Humphrey Milford, 1921.

that its pedigree goes back to the Septuagint. Coverdale was largely dependent on the Latin Vulgate. The Vulgate of the Septuagint was Jerome's revision of the Old Latin, not as in the rest of the Old Testament, his direct translation from the Hebrew. The Old Latin was translated from the Septuagint. Thus our Prayer Book Psalter may in some few places help those who do not read Greek to appreciate this usefulness of the Septuagint as witnessing to early lost Hebrew varieties of reading.

And sometimes the Septuagint is spoken of as though it had no other than this textual interest. Let those who can read Greek read it and consider whether it be not a very delightful Bible in its own right. Mr. J. H. A. Hart (whom we shall meet in our next chapter) said prettily to a Greek Bishop who told him that the Septuagint is still the Bible of the Greek Church, " May your church then last for ever."

CHAPTER 32

SIRACH AND SOLOMON

MR. HART wrote a book on Ecclesiasticus [1] which ought to be well known. The main body of it is indeed a textual commentary which will not much interest Everyman : but the very original introduction will. Ecclesiasticus is The Wisdom of Jesus, son of Sirach, or Sirach as he is more shortly and conveniently styled. This learned and genial Jew wrote a Hebrew book, gleaning, as he describes it, after the grape gatherers, in Palestine. His grandson carried it to Egypt and translated it into Greek. So for centuries it has been known, and so our English Authorized and Revised Versions were made from the Greek. Of late the greater part of the original Hebrew has been recovered, and an English translation made from it may be read in the S.P.C.K. series already mentioned above (p. 223) or in the large collection edited by Dr. Charles.[2] The grandson tells us in a preface when he came to Egypt ; it was in the eight and thirtieth year of Euergetes the king. But there were two Euergetes. It is generally agreed that Euergetes II is meant ; if so the translation was made about 130 B.C. and Sirach wrote his Hebrew about 180 B.C. But Mr. Hart argues for

[1] *Ecclesiasticus, the Greek Text of Codex* 248 *with Commentary and Prolegomena.* Cambridge University Press, 1909.
[2] *Apocrypha and Pseudepigrapha of the Old Testament.* 2 vols. Oxford University Press, 1913

A Synagogue in Jerusalem, showing Holy Place and Reader's Platform.

247 B.C. as the date of the translation, the thirty-eighth year of Ptolemy Philadelphus and the first of Euergetes I. The peculiar turn of the Greek phrase exactly suits that, and it is at least possible that the earlier date should be preferred. The question need not be laboured here: Sirach will instruct and please whatever be his date.

"Example of life and instruction of manners": S. Jerome's phrase just suits him. We call his Wisdom Ecclesiasticus the Church book, as though of all the Apocrypha it were especially suitable for reading in church. And so it is. One glory of the book all churchmen know : " Let us now praise famous men, and our fathers that begat us." But the quiet tenor of the whole is quite as good. Kindly sensible, robust and cheerful in its piety ; broadminded reverent, founded on the old faith yet on the whole friendly to new ideas ; experienced and charitable, generous and liberal, setting value on all the activities of men but setting Wisdom or devotion to truth first of all—"Strive for the truth unto death, and the Lord God shall fight for thee" (4. 28)—there is the mind of Sirach : those who hear him for the first time are astonished by his excellence, to his constant readers he becomes a living friend.

He is rich in good sayings about friendship :

If thou hast drawn a sword against a friend, despair not ,
For there may be a returning.
If thou hast opened thy mouth against a friend, fear not ,
For there may be a reconciling ;
Except it be for upbraiding, and arrogance, and disclosing of a secret, and a treacherous blow :
For these things every friend will flee.—22. 21 f.

That shows understanding, as always in Sirach. All the

A Synagogue.

Wisdom writers are generous to the poor, but Sirach understands and gives the poor man his best breeding :

> My son, deprive not the poor of his living,
> And make not the needy eyes to wait long.
> Make not a hungry soul sorrowful ;
> Neither provoke a man in his distress.
> To a heart that is provoked add not more trouble ;
> And defer not to give to him that is in need.—4. 1 ff.

> My son, to thy good deeds add no blemish ;
> And no grief of words in any of thy giving.
> Shall not the dew assuage the scorching heat ?
> So is a word better than a gift.
> Lo, is not a word better than a gift ?
> And both are with a gracious man.—18. 15 ff.

He understands forgiveness :

> Reproach not a man when he turneth from sin :
> Remember that we are all worthy of punishment.—8. 5.

> They that fear the Lord will prepare their hearts,
> And will humble their souls in His sight ;
> We will fall into the hands of the Lord,
> And not into the hands of men :
> For as His majesty is,
> So also is His mercy.—2. 17.

> The mercy of a man is upon his neighbour ;
> But the mercy of the Lord is upon all flesh ;
> Reproving, and chastening, and teaching,
> And bringing again as a shepherd doth his flock.—18. 13.

And he has something more to say :

> O death, how bitter is the remembrance of thee to a man that is at peace in his possessions,
> Unto the man that hath nothing to distract him, and hath prosperity in all things,
> And that still hath strength to receive meat.

> O death, acceptable is thy sentence unto a man that is needy, and that faileth in strength,
> That is in extreme old age, and is distracted about all things,
> And is perverse, and hath lost patience.
> Fear not the sentence of death ;
> Remember them that have been before thee, and that come after
> This is the sentence from the Lord over all flesh.
> And why dost thou refuse, when it is the good pleasure of the Most High ?
> Whether it be ten, or a hundred, or a thousand years,
> There is no inquisition of life in the grave.—41 1 ff.

Sirach is stern enough about sin. Sin brings woe: death itself may be the penalty. But with death the account is closed : there is no inquisition of life in the grave. Startling though that sounds in the Bible, S. Paul says almost the same in Romans 6. 7, " He that hath died is justified from sin "—where A.V. is not quite honest. S. Paul in this one place reflects the old-fashioned Jewish orthodoxy, older than his Christian, older than his Pharisaic faith, the old orthodoxy of Sirach and the patriarchs—in death we go to God and that is enough. So Sirach firmly held. In his day the Pharisaic doctrine of resurrection and judgement after death was coming in : and of that new doctrine he would have none. There was a strange irony of fate in store for him. Mr. Hart calls attention in his introduction to the many places where R.V. omits a verse or a line which is found in the A.V. of Ecclesiasticus. He explains that R.V. is following the great fourth-century manuscripts, A.V. the mass of later ones. He examines these interpolated verses, and comparing them with S. Paul and other Pharisaic literature, he shows that they are all distinguished by Pharisaic terms, words, ideas. In some places these ideas are of life beyond

HEBREW SYNAGOGUE ROLL
(Fourteenth Century Original height, excluding rollers, 17 ins)

the grave. It happened to Sirach as it happened to Ecclesiastes. A popular book had a new ecclesiastical edition. Where it fell short of the stricter orthodoxy it was touched into line. What would Sirach and the Preacher have said to this? However :—

> Their glory shall not be blotted out.
> Their bodies were buried in peace,
> And their name liveth to all generations.
> People will declare their wisdom,
> And the congregation telleth out their praise

No one knows the date of the Wisdom of Solomon : widely different guesses have been made. It is pretty safe to say that it was composed later than Sirach, earlier than Philo the Alexandrine Jewish philosopher, and therefore earlier than the birth of our Lord. At what sort of time it was composed we can tell by reading the book itself. The righteous, and that is the righteous Jews, were being persecuted by heathen neighbours or heathenizing compatriots.

> For they said within themselves, reasoning not aright,
> Short and sorrowful is our life ;
> And there is no healing when a man cometh to his end.
> Come therefore and let us enjoy the good things that now are ;
> And let us use the creation with all our soul as youth's possession.
> Let us fill ourselves with costly wine and perfumes ;
> And let no flower of spring pass us by :
> Let us crown ourselves with rosebuds, before they be withered :
> Let none of us go without his share in our proud revelry.
> But let us lie in wait for the righteous man,
> Because he is of disservice to us,
> And is contrary to our works,
> And upbraideth us with sins against the law,
> And layeth to our charge sins against our discipline.
> He professeth to have knowledge of God
> And nameth himself servant of the Lord.

> He became to us a reproof of our thoughts.
> He is grievous to us even to behold,
> Because his life is unlike other men's
> And his paths are of strange fashion.
> Let us see if his words be true,
> And let us try what will befall in the ending of his life.
> For if the righteous man is God's son, He will uphold him,
> And He will deliver him out of the hand of his adversaries
> With outrage and torture let us put him to the test,
> That we may learn his gentleness,
> And may prove his patience under wrong.
> Let us condemn him to a shameful death ;
> For he shall be visited according to his words.—2.

His gentleness and his patience : that is just what they would learn from this book. The author sought consolation. He had his faith as a Jewish churchman in the Spirit of the LORD. That faith had expanded and deepened by the later doctrine of the Wisdom of God. There was a philosophic teaching about the divine Spirit, half Platonic, half Stoic in the schools of Alexandria, which was permeating the pagan world. Virgil sketches it in his fourth Georgic :

> There is in bees a portion of the divine mind and an aery origin. For God proceeds through all the lands and tracts of sea and the depth of heaven. From that mind flocks and herds and all the wild creatures claim at birth their own spiritual life. And then, you know, all that is must thither be returned ; resolved into its elements it is drawn back thither. And so there is no death, but in continuous life all seeks the height of heaven.

Virgil sketches it as a poet. The author of Wisdom learned it in the streets, or as he sat and talked by the seashore at Alexandria. It received interpretation from his Jewish faith, and fusing with his Jewish faith illuminated the dark days. The Spirit of Wisdom, the

THE SAMARITAN PENTATEUCH ROLL
(Original height, excluding rollers, about 15 ins.).

Spirit of God : that Spirit is the earnest of immortality and the martyr need not fear to die : that Spirit fills all, and may turn the heart of our enemies persecutors and slanderers till they with us love God.

And so he sings his happy creed :

The souls of the righteous are in the hand of God,
And no torment shall touch them.
In the eyes of the foolish they seemed to have died ;
And their departure was accounted to be their hurt,
And their journeying away from us to be their ruin
But they are in peace : their hope is full of immortality —3 1 ff.

For there is a Spirit quick of understanding, holy,
Only-begotten, manifold,
Subtil, freely moving,
Clear in utterance, unpolluted,
Distinct, unharmed.
Loving what is good, keen, unhindered,
Beneficent, loving toward man,
Stedfast, sure, free from care,
All-powerful, all-surveying,
And penetrating through all spirits
That are quick of understanding, pure, most subtil.
For wisdom is a breath of the power of God,
And a clear effluence of the glory of the Almighty,
An effulgence from everlasting light,
And an unspotted mirror of the working of God,
And an image of His goodness
To the light of day succeedeth night,
But against wisdom evil doth not prevail
But she reacheth from one end of the world to the other with full strength,
And ordereth all things graciously.—7. 22 ff.

Through this all-pervading, divinely loving and conquering Spirit hope springs for all men. The punishment of the wicked is God's loving correction, "that they might learn." He might have destroyed them by a single breath if justice were all His thought. But

> Thou hast mercy upon all men, because Thou hast power to do all things,
> And Thou overlookest the sins of men to the end that they may repent
> For Thou lovest all things that are,
> And abhorrest none of the things which Thou didst make.
> And how would anything have endured, except Thou hadst willed it?
> Or that which was not called by Thee, how would it have been preserved?
> But Thou sparest all things, because they are Thine,
> O Sovereign Lord, Thou lover of souls;
> For Thine incorruptible Spirit is in all things
> Wherefore Thou convictest by little and little them that fall from the right way,
> And putting them in remembrance by the very things wherein they sin, dost Thou admonish them,
> That escaping from their wickedness they may believe on Thee, O Lord.—11 23–12. 3

Thus ends one of the most tender and true books ever written. The last three verses clearly show, as indeed does the whole context, what is meant by 11. 16, "that they might learn, that by what things a man sinneth, by these he is punished." But 12. 2 is followed by a long illustration of that maxim, taken in quite another sense; how the enemies of Israel suffered vengeance which corresponded with their wickedness. The awful vengeance, not the saving purpose becomes the theme. Style and language changes at the same point. From 1 to 12. 2 we read noble thought expressed nobly but in somewhat awkward language, such as one might use who is writing in a half-acquired foreign tongue. From 12. 3 the language is pretentious yet ineffective, the language of one who would use no tongue well. The last chapter must be separated from the former by any one who would enjoy the book of Wisdom, whatever critical reason he may prefer for the separation.

CHAPTER 33

THRONED ON THE PRAISES OF ISRAEL

"YET still Thou art the holy One: and rightly throned on Israel's songs of praise." So Canon Dalton renders psalm 22. 3 in the fine version which he made for his edition of the Book of Common Prayer, mentioned above (p. 140). And in like manner Dr. Cheyne in his fine version,[1] first published in the best commentary ever written upon the Psalter,—affluent scholarship, terse handling, aflame with heart-religion. "Throned on the praises of Israel" is a spiritualizing of "throned upon the cherubim," typical of the Psalter.

Richard Hooker (*Ecclesiastical Polity*, V. xxxvii. 2) puts one in a right frame for studying the Psalter:

> The choice and flower of all things profitable in other books the Psalms do both more briefly contain, and more movingly also express, by reason of that poetical form wherewith they are written. The ancient when they speak of the Book of Psalms used to fall into large discourses, showing how this part above the rest doth of purpose set forth and celebrate all the considerations and operations which belong to God; it magnifieth the holy meditations and actions of divine men; it is of things heavenly an universal declaration, working in them whose hearts God inspireth with due consideration thereof, an habit or disposition of mind whereby they are made fit vessels both for receipt and for delivery of whatsoever spiritual

---

[1] *The Book of Psalms*: Kegan Paul & Trench, 1888; out of print now, but the version has been published separately, and can be still bought at a small price

A second edition of the commentary, in two volumes, was a daring experiment in textual criticism, not of general interest

perfection. What is there necessary for man to know which the Psalms are not able to teach? They are to beginners an easy and familiar introduction, a mighty augmentation of all virtue and knowledge in such as are entered before, a strong confirmation to the most perfect among others. Heroical magnanimity, exquisite justice, grave moderation, exact wisdom, repentance unfeigned, unwearied patience, the mysteries of God, the sufferings of Christ, the terrors of wrath, the comforts of grace, the works of Providence over this world, and the promised joys of that world which is to come, all good necessarily to be either known or done or had, this one celestial fountain yieldeth. Let there be any grief or disease incident into the soul of man, any wound or sickness named, for which there is not in this treasure-house a present comfortable remedy at all times ready to be found. Hereof it is that we covet to make the Psalms especially familiar unto all This is the very cause why we iterate the Psalms oftener than any other part of Scripture besides ; the cause wherefore we inure the people together with their minister, and not the minister alone to read them as other parts of Scripture he doth.

The richness, the universal fullness of the Psalter impressed Hooker. That side of its inspiration had a natural cause. The Psalter was the Hymns ancient and modern of the Jewish Church. It had sources far back and tributaries all along the stream of history. All sorts of occasions and many kinds of mind contributed psalms. It is easy to discern five earlier collections which have been gathered into the one final Psalter. Its Book I (1–41) has "of" or "to David" at the head of nearly all its psalms : this is the oldest Davidic psalter. Books II and III (42–89) are made up from a second Davidic collection and two Levitical (sons or choir of Korah, Asaph, etc.). Books IV and V are generally anonymous and contain the psalms which were gathered in later years when the one complete Psalter was being formed. If we look at psalm 14 in the earliest collection we see what seems prayer from the exile at the end of it. Hence we infer that none of these collections were earlier than the exile, and the completed Psalter comes from the period of the second temple. Of course that does not prevent its including psalms which severally came from far earlier times. Psalm 19 with its almost mythologic flavour, the sun a sky-roaming giant, may have been

A PAGE FROM A MODERN HEBREW PSALTER

originally a very antique song, earlier than David. But if so it has been altered, as hymns have been altered in our hymn books, from its primitive form. A meditation on the Law has been added, and the primitive myth transformed: no one thinks of the sun now as a real giant in Psalm 19, any more than we suppose the "all gods" in psalm 95 to mean that there are real gods beside the One. The pure faith of the Jewish Church has assimilated these imperfect fancies and composed a treasury of sacred lyrics worthy of Hooker's praise.

Some of these lyrics may have been made by David: psalm 18 is included in the appendix to the book of Samuel and is there ascribed to David. In the Psalter nothing is ascribed to him in that way. The preposition translated "of" in the titles a "Psalm of David" is quite vague. One psalm, 72, has "of Solomon" at the head of it, and at the end "The prayers of David the son of Jesse are ended." "Of Asaph," "of Korah," in the Levitical psalters, point to the interpretation of the Davidic titles. Prosaic rabbinism really believed David to be the author of all the psalms, but the worshipping church treated them more fervently. The Psalter was not written by David, but was about David, full of David, Israel's dream of David the good king after God's own heart, who had reigned in a golden age on which imagination played, for the romance and the greatness of which they gave God thanks: who—and this meant more to them— would come again in the person of a divine successor to reign at the last days in the holy kingdom of God. To the worshipping Jewish Church psalm 2 and psalm 110 were really Messianic. That David should have written those psalms, describing a royal birthday or a royal battle of the dim past, would be but little: that the Holy Spirit was in those psalms inspiring a dream of a perfect David, a dream which would come true, was everything.

A dream: is the term an impropriety? It means what S. Paul meant when he wrote to the Corinthians, "The Lord is the Spirit . . . wherefore we henceforth know no man after the flesh: even though we have known Christ after the flesh, yet now we know Him so no more." Yet dream seems right. It suits the poetic character of the psalms. "More movingly express by reason of that poetic form wherewith they are written": Hooker reminds us how ill we shall understand the Psalter if we forget its poetic form. There is actual form for poetry in Hebrew. It may be hard to define precisely. It would be tedious to select from the endless discussions about accent metre strophes and so on. But one thing is clear. The very nerve of Hebrew poetry is its parallelism, its answering lines, the thought repeated with a fulfilling difference:

> O come let us sing unto the LORD:
> Let us heartily rejoice in the strength of our salvation

Robert Lowth, catching a hint from an Arabic author, pointed this out in his Oxford Lectures on The sacred poetry of the Hebrews.[1] He did it in his quiet way, scarce more than a remark in passing; but he made psalms canticles and prophecies live with a new life for all who read them since. For this poetic form is of a natural simplicity, the waving of wings,

[1] *De sacra poesi Hebraeorum*, Oxonii 1763

274 THRONED ON THE PRAISES OF ISRAEL

Bishop Lowth, †1787.

the coming and going of the wind, an outdoor freedom, a nerve rather than a limiting form, "something understood." Add that the lines are measured by accented syllables, generally three but here too variety is ever intervening, while there may be any number of unaccented syllables that the structure of Hebrew words renders possible, and you feel how liquidly the brook or the torrent of Hebrew poems may flow : the effect is fairly reproduced in the Prayer Book version of psalm 80, " Hear, O Thou Shepherd of Israel. . . ."

Poetry is always near to nature, and the psalms are full of earth and sky and sea ; in this last, sea, going beyond the rest of the Old Testament. Dean Stanley in *Sinai and Palestine* [1] (p. 137) says, "Those who describe Palestine as beautiful must have either a very inaccurate notion of what constitutes beauty of scenery, or must have viewed the country through a highly-coloured medium. As a general rule, not only is it without the two main elements of beauty—variety of

[1] *Sinai and Palestine in connection with their history*, by Arthur Penrhyn Stanley. Murray. Fourth edition, 1857.

outline and variety of colour—but the features rarely so group together as to form any distinct or impressive combination. The tangled and featureless hills of the lowlands of Scotland and North Wales are perhaps the nearest likeness accessible to Englishmen, of the general landscape of Palestine south of the plain of Esdraelon." He allows beauty in Esdraelon and grandeur among the northern mountains. Who indeed could climb to Hermon and not be enraptured by that incomparable four-faced view? Nor will those who know the Pentlands or Wales be too much depressed by this wholesome warning against exaggeration. But the Hebrew prophets and poets rejoiced in their "glorious" their "delightsome" land and pined for its hills brooks forests as exiles from *Italia superba* did for theirs. Think of that poem which we call Canticles, Cantica, the Song of Solomon. Is it a story of Solomon, an allegory of the church? Is it not at any rate a spring song most welcome in our Easter services, as from of old in the Passover services?—when

> Lo, the winter is past,
> The rain is over and gone;
> The flowers appear on the earth;
> The time of the singing of birds is come,
> And the voice of the turtle is heard in our land;
> The fig tree ripeneth her green figs,
> And the vines are in blossom,
> And give forth their fragrance
> Arise, my love, my fair one, and come away.

Allegory is precious. The A.V. headings to Canticles are sweet with grace—The love of the church to Christ. The vehemency of love. The calling of the Gentiles. The church prayeth for Christ's coming—but great art works more directly, and Hebrew poetry is great art. The very picture of the daedal world in psalm 104 exalts the soul : " He toucheth the mountains, and they smoke " needs no allegorizing. It is directly sacramental. The artist creates his phrase, touches true, and God is indeed in the storm : you spoil it by explaining how.

> Hark: the voice of the LORD is upon the waters of the storm clouds : the God of glory thundereth, even the LORD, that ruleth the sea
> The voice of the LORD is mighty in operation the voice of the LORD is full of majesty.
> The voice of the LORD breaketh the cedar-trees . yea, the LORD breaketh in pieces the cedars of Lebanon.
> He maketh them also to skip like a calf · Lebanon also, and Sirion, like a young wild ox
> The voice of the LORD heweth the rocks, yea, heweth them with flames of fire the voice of the LORD shaketh the wilderness, yea, the LORD shaketh the wilderness of Kadesh.
> The voice of the LORD maketh the hinds to bring forth young, and strippeth bare the forests while in His temple on high doth every thing tell forth and echo His glory.
> The LORD sitteth throned above the storm-flood : yea, the LORD is enthroned as King for ever
> The LORD doth give strength unto His people : the LORD will refresh His people with the blessing of peace.
>
> *Ps.* 29.   Canon Dalton's version

That is what a psalmist can do with, not teach from, " the sevenfold thunder peal."

There are glooms in the Psalter. Look again at psalm 88, already referred to above (p. 228).

> My life draweth nigh unto hell.
> I am counted as one of them that go down to corruption . and I am become the very ghost of a man, even as one of the feeble shades of the dead ;
> Whom Thou rememberest no more, seeing they are cut off from Thy help and protection.

THE PSALTER

Mine eye wasteth away for very trouble : O LORD, I have called daily upon Thee, I have spread forth my hands unto Thee, and there is no reply.

Wilt Thou show wonders among the dead . or shall the shades rise up again, and give Thee thanks ?

Shall they tell of Thy loving-kindness in the grave : or of Thy faithfulness in the land of Perdition ?

Shall Thy wondrous works be known in the Dark and Thy righteousness in the land where all things are forgotten ?

The language is pagan, frankly mythological ; as Canon Dalton indicates by the capital letters. Possibly this psalm was once a dirge of the popular superstition of Israel. But it is evidently not so used here. The antique terms are retouched not naively repeated ; and some deep application is being made. "As a leper in utter desolation and despondency" is Canon Dalton's heading. We think of Isaiah 53. The Servant of the LORD, or afflicted Israel, is crying. This is a premonition of Eloi Eloi lama sabachthani. And a commoner application can be allowed. Souls, Jewish and Christian, are daily overwhelmed with grief.

HARPER AND CHOIR, 3000 B.C.

In the hour of the blow many cannot call their faith to aid. The broken heart can only bear sympathy. And in this psalm sympathy is offered. But the hour passes, the pagan misery wanes, faith wakes again. So psalm 88 is followed by 89 " My song shall be always of the loving-kindnesses of the LORD," a psalm with sorrow in it too, but steadfast in faith. Such purposeful juxtaposition is frequent in the Psalter: often it increases grace: sometimes it softens what is hard.

Are there no stains upon the Psalter, worse than glooms? That can scarcely be denied. Of psalms 69 and 109 the best that can be said is that those who are so awfully cursed have persecuted the poor helpless man: him that was cowed in heart would they do to death: they persecute him whom God has smitten: and they add to the pain of them whom He has wounded. In psalm 137 a melancholy addition has been made. The first five verses are a genuine lament of the very days of exile, an exquisite broken cry: " If I forget thee O Jerusalem: let my right hand forget." With an artist's instinct Dvorak finishes his musical setting there. For the next verse is a prosaic variation of the true close. At this point the good Hebrew degenerates into poor late stuff. Hatred becomes venomous against Edom and Babylon. The best here that can be said is that such spite became in time conventional, when the fall of Jerusalem was one of the " old unhappy far-off things and battles long ago."

Let us not reason about these flecks, but regard and pass. For after all they are few. The bitterness, even the severity of the Psalter is to its love and forgivingness as one to a thousand.

> Nevertheless when He saw their adversity: and when He heard their bitter cry for help,

He remembered His covenant, and relented, according to the abundance of His loving-kindness.

O Israel, hope in the LORD, for with the LORD there is loving-kindness : and with Him is plenteous redemption.

And He—even He will redeem Israel from all his sins.

He will not alway be chiding : neither keepeth He His anger for ever.

Not according to our sins hath He dealt with us : nor according to our wickednesses hath He requited us

For look how high the heaven is in comparison of the earth so great is His loving-kindness over them that fear Him

Look how wide also the east is from the west so far hath He set our sins from us

Yea, like as a father hath compassion upon his own children . even so hath the LORD compassion upon them that fear Him.

For He—He knoweth whereof we be made . He remembereth that we are but dust,

That the days of frail man are as grass as a flower of the field so he flourisheth.

For as soon as the hot wind passeth over it, it is gone : and the place thereof doth know it no more

But the loving-kindness of the LORD is from everlasting to everlasting

That is the staple of the Psalter, as it is of the whole Old Testament and New. "I believe in the forgiveness of sins," "Forgive us our debts, as we also have forgiven our debtors," "Have patience with me, Lord, and I will pay thee all," "God is greater than our heart, and knoweth all things."

And more than that. What is the end of all religion ? What is the purpose of God ? What but happiness ? It is a bold epithet in the Pastoral epistles, *makarios*, "the happy God"; bold, but noble theology. The Gospels are four tragedies, but the happiest books in all the world. Happy—*makarioi*—are the poor in spirit; so the Gospel law begins, as in Deuteronomy the old law ended.

And to Gospel and Law the Psalter brings a happy chorus. Only it is not vulgar happiness, but the ascetic, nomad, Messianic treasure in heaven. Sons like saplings, daughters like pillars of a palace, garners full and plenteous with all manner of store, no breach in wall, no captivity, no mourning ;

> Happy is the people that are in such a case :
> Nay rather happy is the people who have the LORD for their God.

So the Septuagint in psalm 144, in consonance with all the well-tuned music of the Psalter.[1]

---

[1] cf pp 2 and 140 above.

CHAPTER 34

THE SERVANT OF THE LORD

AND now let us look back at the Comfort ye prophecy. And let us look around at the Writings of the Jewish Church and collect our memories of the problem of suffering, the desire of nations, persecution and aspiring faith in eternal life, forgiveness and the breadth of the divine loving-kindness. It is the dream of the Christ emerging from the night watches, making ready to come true. Let us lastly look at the Servant Song in Isaiah 52–53, and see how all this is gathered up and brought to height there.

The title Servant of the LORD, My servant, runs through the Comfort ye prophecy. It seems a name for Israel. But in four passages it has a meaning more concentrated far-reaching and profound. These passages are 42. 1–7, 49. 1–6, 50. 4–9, 52. 13–53. They have been called Songs, and they do stand out from the context with a marked singing rythm of their own. They are complete in themselves and make a series. They distribute the prophecy somewhat as the inserted songs in Tennyson's *Princess*.

In the first the LORD commissions the Servant: "I have put My spirit upon Him; He shall bring forth judgement to the Gentiles. He shall not cry, nor lift up, nor cause His voice to be heard in the street. A bruised reed shall He not break, and the smoking flax shall He not quench ... to open the blind eyes, to bring the prisoners from the dungeon, and them that sit in darkness out of the prison house."

Such is the quiet and world-wide gospel of the Servant; "a light to lighten the Gentiles and the glory of My people Israel."

In the second the Servant confesses failure, and the LORD answers that He has not taken His commission largely enough: "It is too light a thing that thou shouldest be My servant to raise up the tribes of Jacob, and to restore the preserved of Israel: I will also give Thee for a light to the Gentiles, that Thou mayest be My salvation unto the ends of the earth."

In the third the Servant tells of His happiness in communion with the LORD: "The Lord GOD hath given Me the disciple's tongue, that I should know how to sustain with words him that is weary: He wakeneth morning by morning, He wakeneth Mine ear to hear as they that are taught." He has met with persecution: "I gave My back to the smiters, I hid not My face from shame and spitting." But He enters the more intimately into the refuge of the heart of His Master, is thereby refreshed and confident.

Then in the last song the LORD proclaims His Servant's faithfulness and its great effect. But other voices break in. The nations and the kings to whom the Servant went have murdered Him. They confess it, but they tell how His humiliation and solitary death have moved them to admiration, penitence, love, yearning: what shall they do to be saved? With majestic grace the LORD answers:

> It pleased the LORD to bruise Him   He hath put Him to grief: when thou shalt make His soul an offering for sin, He shall see His

ISAIAH 53   283

seed, He shall prolong His days, and the pleasure of the Lord shall prosper in His hand   He shall see of the travail of His soul, and shall be satisfied   by His knowledge shall My righteous servant justify many . and He shall bear their iniquities   Therefore will I divide Him a portion with the great, and He shall divide the spoil with the strong   because He poured out His soul unto death, and was numbered with the transgressors . yet He bare the sin of many, and made intercession for the transgressors.

The problem of suffering, of eternal life : how far these are carried here beyond all that we have found hitherto in our study. For here the solution is in sacrifice. Again, how far the meaning of sacrifice is deepened beyond all that we have found in Ezekiel or Leviticus.

That holds though there be dispute about particular words : the essential meaning is unmistakable. The alternative renderings in R.V. margin show that there are many difficulties in the Hebrew of this passage. Some think this due to corruption in the text : we have not the original as it came from the author. It seems as likely that the author wrote when Hebrew was losing its earlier simplicity and precision. It had fallen off from that in the same degree that the English of the twentieth century has fallen off from the English of the sixteenth and seventeenth centuries. But this later English can express very much which could not have been expressed in the earlier. Grandeur, directness, grace have gone, but instead of these we have the power of talking and writing about discovered facts, elaborated ideas, which our forefathers could have framed no sentences to deal with. We do it awkwardly : our books will be harder for a new age to interpret than the Elizabethan will be. Yet awkwardly or not, we do it with wonderful skill. We can express the recondite, essential thing.

THE SEA OF GALILEE.

Now consider the idea of atonement. Compare the artless rubrics of Leviticus, the vague though vividly picturesque metaphors in Ezekiel or this Comfort ye prophecy, with the profundity of this last Servant song. Surely it comes later in time, maturing noblest thought, the consummation of the faith of the Old Testament. The other three songs are not like it in this respect. They may well be part of the rest of the prophecy. This song of martyrdom (which cuts an exultant Te Deum into two pieces) has been most happily added to conclude them.

So Dr. Kennett thinks,[1] though not quite for the reasons just advanced. He assigns the passage to the period of the Maccabees, and it is well to get exact dates when possible. And yet—are not exact dates apt to become the scandal of criticism? About this passage criticism will not cry in the street at all. If any prefer to ascribe it to Isaiah himself, let them do so with charity and give God thanks. The point is that in the development of the faith of the Old Testament it comes as crown, at last. It shows the meaning of the whole and explains our Seventh Article of religion:

> The Old Testament is not contrary to the New. for both in the Old and New Testament everlasting life is offered to mankind by Christ, Who is the only Mediator between God and Man, being both God and Man Wherefore they are not to be heard, which feign that the old Fathers did look only for transitory promises.

The only Mediator : kings prophets priests, who were the LORD's Christs ; the divine Wisdom in Proverbs ;

---

[1] See his Schweich Lectures, *The composition of the Book of Isaiah in the light of archaeology and history*. Published for the British Academy by Humphrey Milford, Oxford University Press, 1909 ; and his smaller book *The Servant of the Lord*.

the all-pervading Spirit in the Wisdom of Solomon ; the dream of David in the Psalter ; through all these this Mediator was taking form. But here He is in very truth. Here is a Gospel before the Gospels. Cool criticism, comparison of religions, analysis and tracing the history of faith ; we are almost scared to remember such occupations of our leisure when we turn from them to the Old Testament itself and become again readers of the Bible. For there God is ; all-holy, all-ruling.

Yet the Servant Song forbids our staying thus. Adoration is more intimate than that, more like freedom.

Elohim means God as He is worshipped under vast sky in plain and fen, " one living and true God, everlasting, without body, parts, or passions ; of infinite power, wisdom, and goodness."

Jahveh means God Who dwelt on Sinai, afterwards at Jerusalem ; Who gives His Law ; is known in battle and in sacrament ; Who has a royal name like kings on earth.

But the Servant is the Child of God. In the Greek Bible, Old and New Testament alike, one word is used : it comes in Acts 3 and 4 "Thy holy Child Jesus." Here is the only Mediator, here is Our Father in heaven.

> I struck the board, and cry'd No more ;
> I will abroad,
> What shall I ever sigh and pine ?
> My lines and life are free ; free as the road,
> Loose as the winde, as large as store.
> Shall I be still in suit ?
> Have I no harvest but a thorn
> To let me bloud, and not restore
> What I have lost with cordiall fruit ?
> Sure there was wine,
> Before my sighs did drie it : there was corn,
> Before my tears did drown it

ISAIAH 53

      Is the yeare onely lost to me?
         Have I no bayes to crown it?
No flowers, no garlands gay? all blasted?
           All wasted?
    Not so, my heart. but there is fruit,
        And thou hast hands.
     Recover all thy sigh-blown age
On double pleasures leave thy cold dispute
Of what is fit, and not forsake thy cage,
        Thy rope of sands,
Which pettie thoughts have made, and made to thee
    Good cable, to enforce and draw,
          And be thy law,
   While thou didst wink and wouldst not see.
       Away   take heed ·
       I will abroad.
Call in thy deaths head there tie up thy fears,
       He that forbears
        To suit and serve his need,
         Deserves his load.
But as I rav'd and grew more fierce and wilde,
        At every word,
    Methought I heard one calling, Childe.
     And I reply'd, My Lord

                George Herbert ✠ 1632.

EPILOGUE

THIS book is not meant to teach so much as to invite; not to answer old questions so much as to get new questions asked. It might be taken as one side of a conversation in which the reader will supply the other, agreeing objecting following up what is here started. Thus it would be an invitation to the reader to study the Old Testament again for himself, with fresh thought enjoyment and awe. It is the story of the Old Testament, the story of the people to whom it first belonged, of their experience politics faith. The making and collecting of the books which compose it was part of this people's activity: so this is also a story of the writings. It is a proper story which continuously moves onward, and the further we follow it the clearer we see that its main interest is in the purifying and deepening of conscience. Conscience of God S. Peter calls conscience, and thus it is the story of the growth of faith manifesting itself in godly life; a progressive revelation of God through the Spirit of God in men.

The story itself fills the whole of a book of this size. No room was left for discussing critical problems, and it is little use to formulate the results of criticism without discussion. And such discussion was beside the purpose of this book. One of the quips in *Fors clavigera* is to the effect that people should understand how different are the Latin roots of edit and edify, and I have been so presumptuous as to pass very lightly over the processes of its editing in the hope of showing how edifying the Old Testament is. If any readers I may be fortunate enough to get wish to learn about the editing, let them go to Robertson Smith's *Old Testament in the Jewish Church*,[1] Driver's *Introduction to the Literature of the Old Testament*,[2] Box's *Short Introduction to the Literature of the Old Testament*,[3] or Mr. Chapman's *Introduction to the Pentateuch* in the Cambridge Bible for School .

But the labour of critical scholars has enriched the faith, and this *Story of the Old Testament* has been shaped by them on every page. To the latest school of all it owes the most. More than a century ago critical difficulties were felt and solutions sought. Discrepancies in the Pentateuch

A. P. STANLEY, D.D.,
Dean of Westminster.

showed that it could not have been written throughout by Moses. Deuteronomy was very different from Genesis Exodus and Numbers, and in those three books the history seemed to break up into fragments. A clue was presently found in the distribution of the divine names, Jahveh and Elohim. The continuous history

[1] A. & C. Black, 1881.   [2] T. & T. Clark: ninth ed., 1913.
[3] Rivingtons, 1909.

which we read in the Bible was derived, so it seemed, from two earlier written books. And still there was an element to be accounted for, the legal antiquarian framework of the whole. Ewald called this The book of origins, and he called the bright narrative The prophetic history. The relationship of these parts was as yet far from clear; but Dean Stanley, adapting Ewald for English readers in his immortal *Lectures on the Jewish Church*, showed what delightful aid criticism could already bring to students of the Old Testament. Then Wellhausen set the Pentateuch, the Torah of the Jewish Church, with its narrative poetry sermons laws, in the full stream of the national story as the story was told or illustrated by the whole of the Old Testament. The three main stages were displayed: the early code of Exodus ruling through the period of the early prophets; the law and theology of Deuteronomy coming in with Jeremiah and Josiah's reformation; the complete Levitical law entering effectively into Israel's life when Ezra visited the restored community in Jerusalem. As Ewald was made known to England by Stanley, so Robertson Smith brought light from

ROBERTSON SMITH.

Wellhausen. Those are growing old now who remember the exhilaration, almost the conversion, wrought in them by their first reading of *The Prophets of Israel*.[1] The Old Testament had become a dull book, so far it seemed from actual life. Now Isaiah and the kings and people sprang into life. Israel's wars and politics were real, like our own ; and God in the Old Testament was real, the living God Who made Himself felt in history. All this was first told in Scotland, and Scotland received it with admiration and indignation. In England it scarcely spread beyond a little circle. Driver brought it home to the people. His *Introduction* was a student's book.

S. R. DRIVER, D.D.,
Regius Professor of Hebrew, Oxford.

But his *Commentary on Genesis*[2] answered questions which were causing a good deal of uneasiness. It was widely read, and the new criticism was adopted in schools. It won victory. By degrees opposition died away. Dr. Driver was quiet and reasonable. He

[1] A. & C. Black, 1882.
[2] Methuen : Westminster Commentaries, 1904.

understood how people felt about these difficulties. He wrote with patient clearness, trying above all else to be useful. His was a saintly scholarship and it brought peace and hope. Yet disappointment followed.

For the victory was in a manner too complete. The new criticism became a new convention. The stream of discovery froze. Dr. Driver's guidance was petrified into dogma, simplified into formula. Indeed there was a double loss. First the study of the Old Testament became, even for scholars, an exercise in analysis of documents. Secondly the historic sense which had been awaked was even too reasonable. The Child, divine and wonderful, of Isaiah 9 was accounted for as but a prince of promise born to a contemporary king of Judah; and this was typical of the whole exegesis. *E pur sì muove*, said old-fashioned people to themselves; it was indubitable that the tremendous verses had meant from the first more than that.

And others who were not old-fashioned said so too. Dr. Cheyne was a brother professor with Dr. Driver at Oxford. Dr. Cheyne was learned, bold, eccentric. He was a poet and intense in religious faith: he might be called a fiery rationalist. His early commentary on Isaiah [1] is happily still reprinted. It anticipates much that was hardly dreamed of when it was first published, though it also includes much which he passed far away from and beyond in later years. But it had something which, late or early, he never changed, spiritual insight and the faculty of wonder. For Dr. Cheyne Isaiah could never be sufficiently explained as a sober reasonable statesman who trusted God. And the something more

[1] *The Prophecies of Isaiah*, *a new translation with commentary and appendices* Kegan Paul & Trench, 1880

EPILOGUE

than that, the wonderful element, the daring inspiration, Dr. Cheyne set himself to prove : he proved it by a wider and deeper search into the ideas of Old Testament time and place. He wrote another commentary, on the Psalter,[1] spiritual and poetic, original and learned. And he wrote Bampton Lectures on the Psalter.[2] In these lectures all kinds of novel scholarship cropped up in unexpected places. In particular it appeared that he had wearied of analysis of documents and was approaching the Old Testament from the other end. How did the post-exilic Jewish Church compose their Bible ?

T. K. CHEYNE, D.D.,
Oriel Professor of the Interpretation of Holy Scripture, Oxford.

What was the faith of the post-exilic Jewish Church ? What did these books, completed and arranged by the church, mean to Jewish churchmen, and therefore to us ? What is their significance as considered theologically ? In a small volume of lectures given in America, *Jewish religious life after the exile*,[3] he

---

[1] *The Book of Psalms or the Praises of Israel.* Kegan Paul & Trench, 1888.
[2] *The origin and religious contents of the Psalter.* Kegan Paul & Trench, 1891.
[3] Putnam, 1898.

brings these questions together and answers them in part; provocatively rather than finally, as was his delightful habit. And already other scholars were working from a like point of view. Two commentaries on Isaiah may be referred to as examples, Dr. Buchanan Gray's [1] and Dr. Box's [2] : also the *Ezra Studies* [3] of the American professor Dr. C. Torrey.

This, the later criticism, is even now too little known. It recognizes the importance of the four centuries before the birth of our Lord. It shows how our Lord did come, as S. Paul said, in the fullness of time not in the deadness of Jewish faith. It is a theological criticism, not merely literary or historical : and it is surely an advance in truth. And a testimony to its truth is this : it restores authority and splendour to the Old Testament.

For the mischief of making criticism popular is that it engenders a cool detached temper. This comes very much from our reading books about the Old Testament instead of the Old Testament itself. Read the prophets historians and psalmists themselves, and you cannot but be awestruck and enkindled by the presence of God. They have no doubt about the reality power wisdom holiness of the living God Who is the theme of all their writing, before Whom they bow their heart. Here is the difference between the Old Testament and all other books of the ancient world. Now and then a Babylonian or Egyptian rises towards this height, as Akhnaton in his hymn to the sun. But he falls short ; and to us there must be a lack of reality in the noblest hymn to the sun. In Plato there is true theology, but this bowing of the

---

[1] T. & T. Clark, 1912.   [2] Pitman, 1908.
[3] University of Chicago Press, 1910.

heart before the LORD was not in him. We can see, as we read the Old Testament, that the earlier Israelites in the mass were far enough from it also; and if we could recover the earlier documents which were used for the making of the Old Testament it is likely that this impression of majesty and holiness would not be made by them. But the Old Testament itself, the Bible of the Jewish Church, is superior to the primitive or the popular religion of Israel. The thorough scholars are aware of that, and while they dig up the primitive and popular superstition they feel the great theology all the more. But when we classify the results of their excavation, and formulate the stages in the religious education of the people, without constant refreshment from the great finished book itself, we may be interested but our soul is not converted. The law of the one sanctuary? the priestly code?—"And God said, Let there be light: and there was light. . . . The LORD is my Shepherd; He leadeth me beside the still waters; Yea, though I walk through the valley of the shadow of death. . . . Against Thee, Thee only have I sinned; Create in me a clean heart, O God, and renew a right spirit within me. . . . Whom hast thou reproached and blasphemed? and against whom hast thou exalted thy voice and lifted up thine eyes on high? even against the Holy One of Israel. . . . The LORD is in His holy temple: be silent before Him, all the earth."

This is the authority of which Dr. Hamilton spoke in *The People of God*.[1] He says that to our Lord and His Apostles the Old Testament was authoritative, whereas to us it is no longer authoritative, whatever else it may be. But the authority which is felt in the quota-

[1] Clarendon Press, 1912

tions just made is an authority of thought and conscience. It is inward, reasonable : to use a pregnant Biblical word, it is an authority of goodwill. And those who read the Old Testament as a story right through (much helped in so doing by historical criticism) know how externals fall away as the story goes on, and the inward sway thereby gathers power : even the Old Testament is the story of the growth of love. And such authority still lasts and deepens. If the Old Testament were really known it would be more authoritative to-day than it was in the days of the Apostles.

In their day the opening of the Gentile world was a shock to the authority of the Jewish Bible. In our day the widening of our knowledge of man and mind and nature is the difficulty. The mere addition of items of knowledge goes on for a long while without causing offence. The offence comes in those seasons when the gathered knowledge springs into creative force ; when men suddenly know themselves in a new way, are freshly conscious of the divinity of the Spirit within themselves. Then there seems no room for a God without. The authority of popular religion is sapped. Even time-honoured philosophies are discredited, for they have hardened into systems instead of being visions of reality. Such a season came to Athens when both sophists and Socrates turned against accepted truth, and presently Plato showed that what had happened was no loss but a fuller grasping of real truth. At such a season Milton wrote *Paradise Lost* and *Paradise Regained*, in which his poetry conveys an inward doctrine of man's fall and redemption : for more and more Milton's Christ becomes the Spirit within man ; as long ago S. Paul had said " The Lord is the Spirit." And just such a season is recurring now, when philosophers are finding reality in history, in the event or experience itself, not in a creative ground beyond ; and theologians appeal from the disputed record of Christ's deeds of long ago to His present and eternal action as the indwelling Word. In all of which there is the onesidedness of reaction : we wait for the Christian Plato to sift and reconcile and bring what is really new and true into clearness. But divine authority such as the authority which the Old Testament indeed possesses, is not superseded. It is an authority of reason and conscience, of reverence and love, and as the Spirit in man answers more directly to the Spirit Who spoke by the prophets, this authority comes the more by its own.

It might be objected that though this inward authority may be discovered in the Old Testament, it is not wholly characteristic therein. At least it is far more characteristic of the New Testament ; and if so, why go back to the Old and its imperfect truth, when we have the full perfection in the New Testament ? But is that a complete account of the New Testament ? It is promised therein that the Spirit shall still guide us into all the truth. In the New Testament a very perfect word is given us, and given once for all. But its perfection is revealed by its never wearing out. It answers to all generations. Its inspiration becomes clearer and more useful as knowledge grows, and man's hopes trials responsibilities increase. It has been perfectly given but our interpretation of it is still to be improved. As the first disciples, so we have still to understand what our Lord meant by what He said and did and suffered. We shall not understand if we cease to study the Bible which was authoritative to Him ; and revealed the Father to

Him; and helped His first disciples to receive His revelation of the Father and of Himself the eternal Son. All history and all great ancient books contribute to the understanding of the New Testament, but the Old Testament stands in an unique relation to it, and is happily within reach of the simplest people.

But the argument, I have the New Testament : why then need I read the Old ? is a very miserly one. If a utilitarian theology could possibly exist there might be something in it, but utilitarian theology is impossible. Our pure enjoyment of the Old Testament is to its theology what music is to the meaning of music. And how much there is to enjoy in the Old Testament which is not to be found in the New. Think of its narratives. These do not rival the Gospel narrative, but they have a different charm, very rich and very various. There is nothing in the New Testament like Elijah on Carmel, or Jacob at Peniel, or the four lepers in the deserted Syrian camp. Nor is there anything like Job, or like the rhetoric of the prophets : it would be a dull world in which Isaiah was forgotten, and it would be a world which had lost part of its true knowledge of God. The revelation of God received by Isaiah was imperfect : in our Lord Jesus Christ we may see the Father. But is that vision always clear ? Isaiah helps to clear it. Imperfect though he be, he knew something and he tells us something which is told nowhere else. And his own imperfect imaginative style of telling it is necessary for our receiving just this particular element of the truth : the very words, the special styles of these Old Testament writers, are integral with their messages. If we did not read them we should lose something which could be replaced by nothing else.

It is well indeed that it should be so. For thus the simplest unlettered persons may go to church, and (if the lessons are read as they should be) get at least half of what the Old Testament has to give. But there is another half, a very precious addition which can only come by thought and study. " The Bible is itself a literature and it leads us into many various literatures and into the society of scholars." That is the kind of study the Old Testament promotes, large sociable joyous continuous. It introduces us to many other literatures. Literatures are approached by languages, and languages themselves are education. It is much in reading the Old Testament to know even a little of its own Hebrew language. When you know how picturesque and dramatic Hebrew is, the theology of the Old Testament becomes a different thing, not dogmatic, matter of fact. Hebrew seldom describes thinking, the working of conscience and so on, except by speech and dialogue : Balaam and the ass is not a problem or a jest to a Hebraist. And it is an easy matter to learn enough Hebrew to translate the narratives of Genesis or parts of Kings. The painful discipline of grammar is not thoroughly required, nor is that discipline the only way of forming a scholarly taste.

There are many lines of study, and in these days each may train himself in the line that he is apt for. Translations abound and are a good substitute for originals, if any one is not fond of languages. And a scholarly use of translations allows that widening of the field which is so desirable. Even the accomplished Hebraist is not equipped for the Old Testament if Hebrew is his only interest. Something must be known of Babylonian and Arabic literature ; of Egypt too ; and certainly of Rome and Athens and Alexandria. And much may be known even by quite busy persons if they will read translations. At least this much is necessary: the spirit of the east must be caught. That spirit is awakening anew to-day. Many know the poems and lectures of Rabindranath Tagore. These are more serious than appeared in their first, aesthetic popularity. They tell now of the renunciation the inwardness the sense of unity of men with men and with God, which the east is recovering and offering to the scientific business-like west; which the east is aspiring to win freedom for again, even by revolt. This eastern spirit is the spirit of the Old Testament. India and the Old Testament, with great differences indeed also, explain one another; and the student of the Old Testament should understand how.

Then there is the field of archaeology ; which the great linguists themselves dare not neglect. And here too ordinary persons may enjoy a great deal at good second-hand: Londoners who care about the Old Testament should be often in the British Museum. Neither scholars nor travellers labour in vain. The commonalty enter into their labours. And this popularizing, this community in knowledge is the opportunity for our modern renascence. Accumulated knowledge threatens to destroy divine authority. Disseminated, shared knowledge deepens our perception of the authority which is truly divine, the authority of reason and conscience, the authority of the Bible.

This popularizing must not be abused. Vulgar superficial minds will never make much of the Old Testament. The Old Testament is literature, and its readers need the breadth and geniality of humane letters. An Englishman gets this most naturally by knowing good books in his own language, perhaps especially poetry; by hearing good lectures, by interchanging good talk. For all which the way lies open to-day as it never has before.

Yet if after all it lie not open. If lack of time, the accidents of place and fortune, shut any one out from all this; then reverse the picture. The Old Testament itself in the noble English Version, A.V. if you like, R.V. for lovers of truth still better, is itself an epitome of all. But read it in large continuous draughts. Treat it not as a store of mechanic piety but as sacred literature, the eloquence of the Spirit of God.

However, prepared as best we may, and still preparing, let us launch into the stream of revelation. It runs through the whole of life. When those seasons of renascence come, and man seems to be putting his own mind in the place of God, that pride will have a fall. But it is not altogether pride. " 'Tis revelation what thou thinkst discourse." This turning inward upon reason proves to be recognition of God more and more as Spirit, less as a fanciful reflected picture of human kings and judges.

. S. Paul says Christ is that Spirit, the Spirit in and around men, in either mode divine. That is implied in our seventh Article of Religion: " The Old Testament is not contrary to the New : for both in the Old and the New Testament everlasting life is offered to mankind in Christ, Who is the only Mediator between God and man, being both God and man." Christ is not only the historical person Jesus of Nazareth. He is the eternal

Word of God; the idea that works through the whole continuous life of man, in Israel and in Galilee, in Asia and Europe: the dream that is continuously coming true: the reconciliation of giving and receiving, sacrifice and redemption, transcendence and immanence, ideal and historical. Through this one Christ the seasons of renascence when manhood reasserts itself become the continuation not the contradiction of the mediaeval periods when manhood loyally denies itself: all for Christ's sake; not only to put our trust in Him but also to suffer for Him; as S. Paul wrote to the Philippians, S. Paul that mediaevalist reborn.

This process, alternating and expanding, becomes more complicated as the relationships of men and nations grow more intricate. In each man's immediate time and place there seems to him more confusion than ever was before. But that is the way by which alone true simplicity is won. When we look back we can distinguish cycles of thought and trace just that development within them. There is such a cycle in the Greek drama: and in the New Testament. And one main attraction of the Old Testament also is the view it gives of such a cycle of revelation sweeping on, and round upon itself, and deeper, in the growing mind and conscience of the children of Israel. This is the theological interest of JEDP. The symbols JE represent the early prophetic narrative in two stages, the Jahvist and the Elohist. These represent more widely two schools, two periods of thought. In J there are grand theophanies and God is frankly reverenced in the imagery of manhood. In E the mystery of deity is felt more awefully and tenderly, idolatry is hateful, even the imagery of language is restrained. In D, the

Deuteronomic school, this restraint is carried further, but is transformed into a new freedom of the heart ; love grows between God and man, and the old religious phrase, the fear of God, gets a more beautiful meaning. Then the fall of Jerusalem and the captivity shake the ancient frame of things to pieces, and in the restoration many traditions and ideas jostle together. The old popular religion of the people, sacrifices and superstitions, reassert themselves, and are set in holier order on a higher plane by Ezekiel and Ezra. The idealism of the prophets rises to its climax in the Comfort ye chapters of Isaiah. Presently it breaks into lurid sublimity in the apocalypses. The Jews of the dispersion foster liberal association with foreign nations. Some sit lightly to the law and the sacrifices. Others, partly admiring partly compassionate to Gentile seekers after God, promote missionary enterprize in various manner. Some too protest and criticize : old dogmas begin to wear out and give offence. In Job the spirit within man revives ; the external God seems cruel or impotent, but the very God is all in all within. What conflict, what confusion, how vague the boundaries of faith. But turn to the Psalter. Join in the worship of saint and sinner, simple and scholar, enthusiast and quietist, in the one Jewish Church : there is the ultimate simplicity, found unconsciously, given not devised :—" Why should any cogitation possess the mind of a faithful communicant but this, O my God Thou art true, O my soul thou art happy ! "

This paragraph will seem but dull to true lovers of the Old Testament. They will perhaps allow its correctness, but the Old Testament is much better than correct. The fair theology we cull from it comes all marred with antique superstitions and vestiges of human gloom. It comes too all glowing with light and warmth. For it comes as a story, a vivid story of men's hope and trust, and doing and suffering, and goodness and badness, error and loyalty and affection and passion. Every several character in the drama touches our heart. The generations move onward to a goal of which they are only in part conscious; their life itself is their appointed business. This is Israel's story, an entrancing story which he may read who runs.

It is a moving story in both senses, transitive and intransitive. It moves us and converts the soul as we read. There is awe and joy and grandeur in the story and in the telling of it. It is a theophany of God to be adored, importunate for love. The Old Testament, the Bible of the Jewish Church, was made for the Church's worship.

A good scholar does not only read and write. He muses. Retrospect is happiness to him. Some find a diary of the day's work helps them. But it needs a peculiar genius to keep a diary. Yet there is a kind of scholar's diary which might be very generally used. At the close of day, or end of week, or finishing of subject, think back, and let your musing run out into prayer or praise. Sift, select, prune. Then write down, with date, in tersest sentence, a collect which represents the lesson learned. Models for such collects may be found in the *Mozarabic Psalter*, edited by Mr. Gilson for the Henry Bradshaw Society: each psalm is there summed up in a collect, pointed and uncommon, with just that touch of freedom and flourish which the Spaniard dares.

EPILOGUE

Story telling, thinking, worshipping : that is theology, a sweeter term surely than religion. No one can study the Old Testament without entering, will he nill he, into the garden of theology. There is no better guide book for this domain than Dr. A. B. Davidson's *Theology of the Old Testament*.[1] There is nothing cut and dried in this book. Dr. Davidson died before he had put the finishing touches; and it might be supposed that the singular freedom and rich irregularity of the treatment were accidental : inconsistencies would have been smoothed away, problems more neatly solved.

A. B. DAVIDSON, D.D.

There is no likelihood in the supposition. Dr. Davidson was too good a philosopher, too knowing in actualities to trust that kind of completeness. He gave us many a good gift ; none so mature as this.

And now I bid Every Man farewell, fain to hope that the writing and reading of these pages may have made us friends. If the little book might but afford a few

[1] T. & T. Clark, 1904.

hours' innocent entertainment I would be nearly satisfied. Yet I cherish a larger ambition. I should rejoice if it contributed in however small a measure to the coming of the day when indeed every man in our kindly islands who speaks with Saxon or with Celtic tongue shall enjoy great literature and believe in God.

A TABLE OF DATES

THE dates often printed in the margin of the English Bible are no part of the Bible itself but a kind of commentary added by Archbishop Usher in 1650. The figures in the Old Testament on which Usher relied are too vague for such precise deduction. Some are round numbers : for some the text is uncertain: some are inconsistent with other figures in the Old Testament itself. We can check the date Usher gave for the creation by facts ascertained through science ; and there can be no doubt that the earth is very much older than he supposed. This checking of Old Testament dates from outside is always necessary for it was long before the Old Testament writers aimed at exactness in such matters. Assyrian and Babylonian writers did, and their records help us toward a trustworthy chronology.

Hammurabi, who was king of Babylon at about 2100 B.C. and author of a famous code of law, is perhaps the same as Amraphel in Genesis 14. If so, a date is indicated for Abraham.

It is generally said that Rameses II (died 1225) was the Pharaoh of the oppression and Merenptah or Merneptah II (1225–1215) the Pharaoh of the Exodus. That does not easily fit in with 1 Kings 6. 1, whether we read 480 years with the Hebrew or 440 with the Septuagint. For 1 Kings 11. 40 makes Solomon contemporary with Shishak who was king of Egypt in the latter half of the tenth century B.C. But Hebrew Septuagint and Josephus differ about the figures in

1 Kings 6. 1, and little stress need be laid upon them. Solomon's reign may be dated about 980–940 ; and that will give us 1000 B.C. as a convenient central date for David.

From this point onwards we have more certainty. The following table is based upon Dr. W. E. Barnes' chapter (xv) in the Cambridge *Companion to Biblical Studies*.[1] Dr. Driver's commentary on Genesis,[2] Introduction §2, should also be read, and Hallam's *Introduction to the literature of Europe in the fifteenth, sixteenth, and seventeenth centuries*,[3] vol. iv, pp. 14 f.

A TABLE OF DATES

854	AHAB of Israel under the hegemony of Syria fights against Shalmaneser II at the battle of Karkar	Elijah.
842	JEHU of Israel pays tribute to Shalmaneser II.	
745–727	Reign of TIGLATH-PILESER of Assyria, called 'Pul' in 2 Kings 15. 19	
738	MENAHEM of Israel pays tribute to Tiglath-Pileser	
733	Rezin, the ally of Pekah, king of Israel, besieged in Damascus by Tiglath-Pileser.	

[1] *A Companion to Biblical Studies*, being a revised and re-written edition of The Cambridge Companion to the Bible, edited by W. Emery Barnes, D.D., Hulsean Professor of Divinity.   Cambridge at the University Press, 1916.

[2] *The Book of Genesis with Introduction and Notes*, by S. R. Driver, D.D. (Westminster Commentaries)   Methuen, 1904

[3] Murray, ed 1872.

A TABLE OF DATES

727–722	Reign of Shalmaneser IV of Assyria.	Amos
722	Samaria taken by the Assyrians (after the death of Shalmaneser). Hoshea the last king of Israel.	and Hosea.
722–705	Reign of SARGON, king of Assyria.	
705–681	Reign of SENNACHERIB of Assyria.	Isaiah and
701	Philistines and their Egyptian allies defeated by the Assyrians at the battle of Altaku. HEZEKIAH compelled to pay tribute to Sennacherib.	Micah.
681–668	Reign of ESAR-HADDON, son of Sennacherib. To him MANASSEH of Judah paid tribute.	
668–626	Reign of ASSHUR-BANIPAL To him also Manasseh paid tribute.	Jeremiah. Zephaniah.
608	Pharaoh-necoh's expedition into Syria Death of JOSIAH, king of Judah.	
606	Destruction of Nineveh.	Nahum. Habbakuk.
597	JEHOIACHIN surrenders to Nebuchadrezzar.	Ezekiel.
586	Jerusalem captured and the Temple destroyed by the Chaldeans	
561	Evil-merodach, king of Babylon Jehoiachin's captivity relaxed	
559	Neriglissar (Nergal-sharezer), king of Babylon.	

555	Nabonidus (Nabu-naid), king of Babylon.	Isaiah 40 ff.
538	Fall of Babylon.	
537	Decree of CYRUS for the return of the Jews.	Rebuilding of the Temple.
529	Cambyses, king of Persia.	
521	DARIUS Hystaspis, king of Persia.	
520	The hindered temple-building resumed.	Haggai and Zechariah.
486	XERXES (Ahasuerus), king of Persia.	
465	ARTAXERXES Longimanus, king of Persia	
458	Commission of EZRA.	
444	NEHEMIAH appointed governor of Judaea	Malachi.
432	Nehemiah's second mission to Jerusalem.	
336	Darius III Codomannus, king of Persia Philip, king of Macedon, slain.	
333	ALEXANDER of Macedon defeats Darius at the battle of the Issus.	
323	Death of Alexander and dismemberment of his empire. Ptolemy Lagides obtains Egypt.	
312	Seleucus Nicator, king of Syria	
285	Ptolemy Philadelphus, king of Egypt. Antiochus Soter, king of Syria.	The Septuagint translation of the Law.
246	Ptolemy Euergetes I, king of Egypt.	

A TABLE OF DATES

217	Egyptian victory at Raphia over Antiochus. Palestine secured to Egypt
198	Victory of Antiochus at Paneas. Judaea falls to Syria.
175	ANTIOCHUS Epiphanes, king of Syria
170	Antiochus invades Egypt and attacks Jerusalem on his return and pollutes the Temple
168	Daily sacrifice interrupted
166–5	Victory of JUDAS MACCABAEUS at Emmaus.
165	Cleansing of the Temple and Dedication of a fresh altar by Judas.
161	Death of Judas Maccabaeus at Elasa

INDEX

Abijah, 208.
Abimelech, 39
Abraham, 1, 2, 4, 14, 307.
Absalom, 48, 49, 54-5
Achan, 30
Adam, 12-13.
Agur, 237.
Ahab, 77, 82, 83, 86, 88-9, 308
Ahasuerus, 229-32.
Ahaz, 117, 118, 129, 133.
Ahaziah, 89.
Ahijah, 73.
Ai, 29-30
Ajalon, 31
Alexander, 198, 214, 221, 249, 310.
Alexandria, Jewish Church at, 10, 158, 183, 211, 249; Septuagint formed at, 250-2, Wisdom teaching at, 264
Amon, 137, 145.
Amos, his life and teaching, 96-104, 105-7, 109-10; also mentioned, 111, 116, 123, 163, 309.
Amraphel, 307.
Antiochus Epiphanes, 214-16, 221, 222, 223, 311.
Apocalyptic writings, 118, 128, 198, 203, 213, 223-26.
Apocrypha, 10, 193, 235, 243, 253, 258
Aramaic, 249-50.
Aramaeans, 74, 98
Artaxerxes, 185, 186, 189, 194.
Asa, 145.

Assyrians, the, 98-9, 102, 106, 108; take Samaria, 111, 309; their wars against Judah, 112 sqq, 133-4, 309; conquered by the Chaldaeans, 137-8.
Assyrian bulls, 110.

Baal, 82-5, 143, 146, 153, 176.
Babel, Tower of, 208.
Babylon, wars of against Judah, 157-8, 308-9; Jewish exile in, 8, 102, 162, 174-5, 184, 194, 207, 221; captured by Chaldaeans, 115, 138; captured by Cyrus, 8, 174, 182, 310; also mentioned, 15, 74, 278, 307.
Bagoses, 214
Balaam, 26-8, 210, 299.
Barak, 37, 38, 65
Barcochba, 10.
Baruch, 9, 156, 163; book of, 253.
Bible, the Hebrew, formation of, 9-13, 207-12; arrangement of, 111, 202-4; also mentioned, 7, 21, 159 n, 181, 193, 295.

Canaanites, religion of, 82, 86, 146-7.
Canticles, 111, 229, 275-6
Carchemish, battle of, 137
Carmel, 73-4, 83, 90, 100, 176, 298
Chaldaeans, the, 115, 138-9, 154, 184, 222.

312

INDEX

Cheyne, J. K., 156 n., 242, 269, 292–3.
Chronicles, Books of, 10, 55, 66, 75–9, 137, 193, 195, 207.
Comfort Ye, prophecy, 15, 69, 174–81, 303
Creation, Hymn of, 1, 12, 208.
Cushan-rishathaim, 37.
Cyrus, 8, 115, 139, 168, 174, 182, 183.

Dalton, J. N., 60, 140, 254, 269, 276–7.
Damascus, 98, 102, 117.
Daniel, Book of, its character, 118, 202–3, 213; contents and intention, 221–8; also mentioned, 10, 179, 211, 234, 253.
Darius, 183–5, 249, 310.
David, his life and character, 54–60, 64, 71; as psalmist, 54, 61–3, 270, 272, 286; materials for his history, 43, 46, 48, 49; also mentioned, 2, 8, 41, 52, 65, 208.
Davidson, A. B., 53, 242, 305
Deborah, 33, 37, 38, 40, 65
Deuteronomy, its character and position, 12, 19–20, 36–7, 125, 146–9, 279; also mentioned, 44, 80, 290.
Doughty, Charles, 5
Driver, S. R., 222, 242, 289, 291–2.

Ecclesiastes, 202, 203–4, 229, 243–8, 263–8.
Ecclesiasticus, 193, 237, 243, 253, 256–61.
Eden, Garden of, 12, 208

Edgehill, E. A., 96–8, 100–1.
Eglon, 37
Egypt, the redemption from, 14–19, 100, 109, 176; later relations with, 108, 137, 175; history of, 307–11; also mentioned, 6, 155, 178.
Ehud, 37
Elijah, 82–9, 90, 98, 100, 123, 144, 176, 199, 298.
Elisha, 86, 90, 98, 123.
Elohim, meaning of, 21–5, 286.
Enoch, Book of, 223, 224.
Esau, 4–5
Esdras, Books of, 193, 195, 253.
Esther, Book of, 229–35, 253.
Eve, 12–13.
Exodus, Book of, code of law in, 12, 66, 146, 290; other contents of, 15–20, 80, 92; also mentioned, 23, 26, 289.
Ezekiel, his life and work, 162–73, 303; his prophecies and theology, 12, 69, 70, 80, 159, 191, 206; also mentioned, 9, 21, 283, 285, 309.
Ezra, his life and work, 185, 186, 189, 193–5, 202, 290, 303; also mentioned, 9, 12, 179, 201, 210, 212, 214.

Frazer, Sir James, 82, 232, 233.

Genesis, 1–6, 10, 12, 23, 208–9, 210, 289.
Geshem, 186–7.
Gibeon, 30–1.
Gideon, 39.
Gilead, 74, 83.
Gilgal, 29.
Goliath, 49–50

INDEX

Habakkuk, 9, 138-42, 144, 254.
Haggai, his life and work, 183, 185, 195-6; also mentioned, 70, 179, 199, 200, 310
Haman, 230-3.
Hanamel, 157-9.
Hannah, 47.
Heliodorus, 219.
Hezekiah, his reign, 113-5, 118-22; also mentioned, 69, 125, 128, 133, 137, 145.
Hilkiah, 144, 145, 148, 150.
Hooker, Richard, 191, 269-70, 273.
Hosea, 105-10, 111, 123, 152, 158, 163.
Huldah, 145, 149.

Isaac, 4.
Isaiah, his life and work, 111-27, 132-5, 309; the Comfort Ye prophecy, 174-81, 303; authorship of the Book of, 211, 264, 285, work of scholarship on, 292-4; also mentioned, 12, 28, 137, 149, 152, 163, 196, 234, 252, 298.
Israel and Judah, kingdoms of, 8, 73-9, 98-101, 117, 120.
Ishmael, 4.

Jacob, 1, 4, 5, 6, 298.
Jael, 37-8.
Jahveh, meaning of, 21-5, 80, 126, 176-8, 286.
Jehoiakim, 156
Jehu, 98, 100, 308
Jephthah, 39-40.
Jeremiah, his life and work, 69, 125, 137, 150-61, 309; also mentioned, 9, 36, 145, 162, 163, 167, 175, 211, 290; *see also* Lamentations
Jericho, 29, 91
Jeroboam I, 71, 73, 77
Jeroboam II, 98, 113.
Jerusalem, siege of by Sennacherib, 114, 121, 137; siege and capture of by Nebuchadnezzar, 139, 157-8; the return to, 182-94, 290; prophecies concerning, 116, 131, 132-5, 143, 166-7; also mentioned, 65, 69, 115, 127, 152, 162.
Jesus the son of Sirach, 193, 237, 256-63.
Jew, meaning of, 7, 201.
Jewish Church, founded after the exile, 8, 168, 195; character of, 202, 209; history of, 214; and the Bible, 7, 16, 26, 31-2, 57, 96, 103, 155, 201, 212, 213, 270, 290, 293.
Jezebel, 22, 82, 85-8.
Joab, 55.
Job, 22, 202, 203-4, 233, 37-42, 298.
Jonah, 209-10.
Jonathan, 59.
Joseph, 1.
Josephus, 137.
Joshua, 28-32, 33, 91, 92, 190.
Josiah, his reign, 137, 144-51; also mentioned, 12, 36, 42, 69, 171, 190, 290, 309.
Judas Maccabaeus, *see* Maccabees.
Judah, *see* Israel.
Judges, Books of, 9, 33-41, 42, 111
Judith, 253

INDEX

Keturah, 4.
Kings, Books of, 9, 66, 75–9, 137, 144, 150, 195, 207.
Kishon, 37, 85, 176

Lamentations, 10–12, 229, 233; *see also* Jeremiah
Law, the, its stages, 9, 12, at Sinai, 18–20, *see also* Deuteronomy, Exodus, Leviticus.
Leviticus, 12, 18, 171, 283, 285, 290.
Lowth, Bishop, 273–4.

Maccabees, 179, 214–23, 234, 253, 285, 311.
Malachi, 70, 179, 196, 199–200, 202.
Manasseh, 137, 145.
Megiddo, battle of, 137
Merodach, 114.
Messianic prophecy, 47, 113, 117, 127–9, 197–8, 201, 203, 223–5, 272–3, 285–6
Micah, 132–6, 163
Micaiah, 88.
Midrash, 209
Miracles, 90–5.
Mordecai, 230–1, 234
Moses, his life, 14–16, 37, authorship, 10, 12, 36, 148; also mentioned, 24, 80, 171, 190

Naboth, 86, 100
Nahum, 138, 143
Nathan, 55, 57, 65
Nebuchadrezzar, 157
Nehemiah, 179, 185–95, 199, 202
Nineveh, 74, 138, 143.
Numbers, 28, 289

Omri, 82.
Onias, 161, 219.

Pentateuch, the, 9–12, 289–90
Philistines, the, 31, 48, 52, 75, 166, 191–2
Prophets, the books of the, 9–10, 75–6, 202, 211.
Proverbs, 63–4, 236–7, 285.
Psalms, the, 269–80; position of, in the Jewish Church, 62–3, 160, 202, 204; also mentioned, 155, 233, 252, 285.

Ramoth-Gilead, battle of, 88.
Rehoboam, 71, 73
Ruth, 10, 111, 191, 229.

Samaria, fall of, 105, 107, 108, 111, 113; also mentioned, 76, 82, 86, 102, 116.
Samaritan Schism, the, 192.
Samson, 34, 40, 41
Samuel, 41, 42–58, 111, 144, 149.
Sanballat, 186–7, 214.
Sargon, 111, 113, 309.
Saul, 31, 43–60, 64, 71, 254.
Sheol, 227–8
Septuagint, its origin and history, 250–5; also mentioned, 10, 16, 21, 66, 111, 140, 158, 193, 225, 280
Servant of the Lord, the, 127, 179, 234, 277, 281–6.
Shaphan, 145.
Sinai, 17, 19, 23, 92, 190.
Sisera, 37–9, 65.
Smith, Sir G. A., 28, 175, 199n.

Smith, Robertson, 290–1.
Solomon, 63–6, 71, 133, 208, 272; Wisdom of, 236–7, 243–8, 253, 286.
Song of Songs, *see* Canticles.
Song of the Three Children, 253.
Stanley, A. P., 31, 162–3, 274, 290.

Targums, 253
Temple, the, building and dedication of, 65–8; restoration of, 69–70, 185, 195–7; also mentioned, 122, 150, 169–70, 208.
Tobiah, 186–7.

Tobit, 253
Torah, 9, 19, 23, 26, 208, 254, 290.

Uzziah, 113, 116.

Vashti, 229–30.

Wisdom books, 64, 236–48
Writings, the, 10, 202, 211, 229.

Zechariah, 179, 183, 195, 197–9.
Zedekiah, 42, 157.
Zephaniah, 143–4, 149.
Zeresh, 231.
Zerubbabel, 183–5, 195–7, 199.
Zimri, 82.

THE three maps on the following pages illustrate the whole history of Israel as it is told in *Everyman's Story of the Old Testament*.

THE ANCIENT WORLD comes in at the beginning and the end. It shows the cradle of the Semitic nations in relation to the rest of the world : then it illustrates the history after the Captivity, the Persian Greek and Roman empires.

BABYLONIA ASSYRIA AND CANAAN explains the period of the great prophets from Amos to Jeremiah Ezekiel and the "Comfort ye" prophecy, when Assyrians first, then Chaldeans, were attacking or dominating Israel : and it also shows the advance of Cyrus " from the north " against Babylon.

THE KINGDOMS OF JUDAH AND ISRAEL illustrates the home-history during the whole period of the kingdom from Samuel Saul and David to Jeremiah and the fall of Jerusalem ; and will also be found useful for the earlier history from Joshua and the conquest of Canaan, and even for the movements of Abraham.

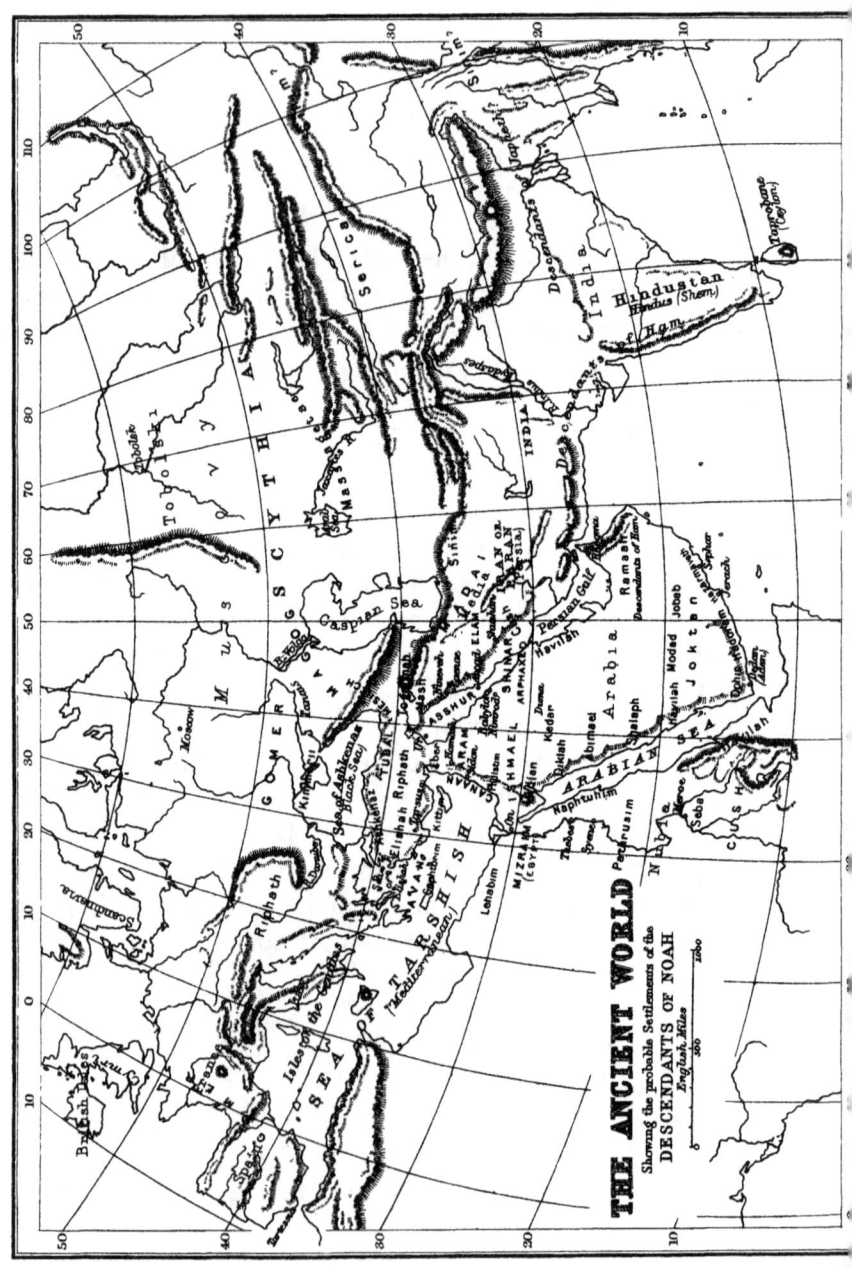

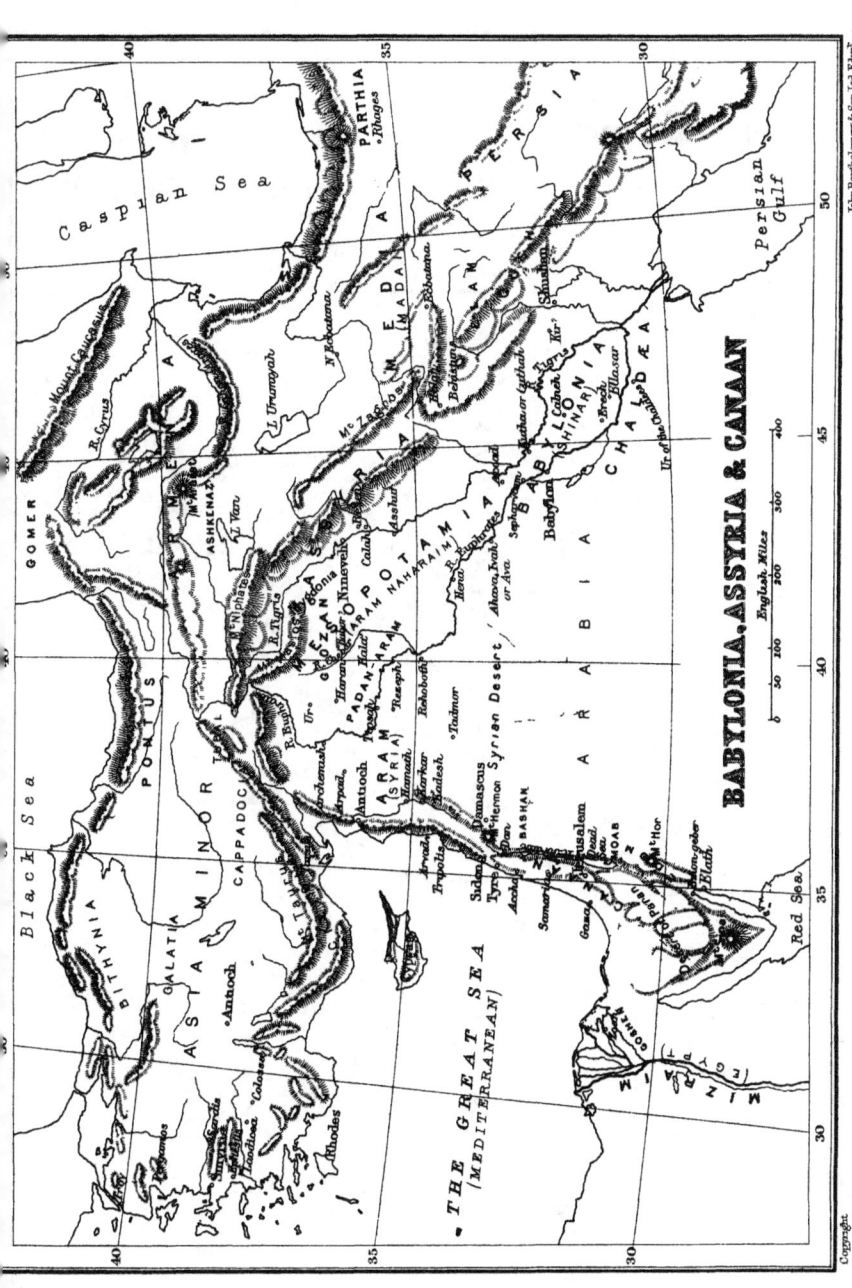

www.ingramcontent.com/pod-product-compliance
Lightning Source LLC
Chambersburg PA
CBHW050334230426
43663CB00010B/1853